CONFESSIONS
OF A QANTAS
FLIGHT ATTENDANT

CONFESSIONS *OF A* QANTAS FLIGHT ATTENDANT

OWEN BEDDALL
WITH LIBBY HARKNESS

EBURY
PRESS

An Ebury Press book
Published by Random House Australia Pty Ltd
Level 3, 100 Pacific Highway, North Sydney NSW 2060
www.randomhouse.com.au

First published by Ebury Press in 2014

Addresses for companies within the Random House Group can be found at www.randomhouse.com.au/offices

National Library of Australia
Cataloguing-in-Publication entry:

Beddall, Owen, author.

Confessions of a Qantas flight attendant: true tales and gossip from the galley/Owen Beddall.

ISBN 978 0 85798 219 3 (paperback)

Beddall, Owen – Anecdotes.
Flight attendants – Anecdotes.
Airlines – Anecdotes.

Other authors/contributers: Libby Harkness

387.742092

Cover design by Christabella Designs
Cover images: man © KieferPix/Shutterstock; button © Archiwiz/Shutterstock; plane symbol © Laralova/Shutterstock; newspaper format © Masksim Kabakou/Shutterstock
Typeset in 12/16 Sabon by Midland Typesetters, Australia
Printed in Australia by Griffin Press, an accredited ISO AS/NZS 14001:2004 Environmental Management System printer

Random House Australia uses papers that are natural, renewable and recyclable products and made from wood grown in sustainable forests. The logging and manufacturing processes are expected to conform to the environmental regulations of the country of origin.

This book is for all of the flight attendants the world over, answering those call bells and getting passengers home safely. Cabin crew, prepare for take-off!

CONTENTS

FOREWORD

I was asked to write this foreword by Owen as I've been a glamorous international air hostess for nineteen years; for one of those years, I had the pleasure of working with him.

I was both honoured and delighted to be asked, as it gives me the opportunity to 'spill a few beans' on the author himself, rather than it being targeted solely at us poor unsuspecting crew. After all, we are just doing our best to get through these bad-ass twelve-hour long-haul sectors without asphyxiating any annoying passengers, and landing looking as fresh-faced and smiley as when the darlings first boarded.

The first time I operated a flight with Owen, we were working on the upper-deck cabin of a Boeing 747. Owen liked working in this part of the aircraft as he could then avoid any of the onboard managers, whilst merrily making his way through the cheese trolley without prying eyes . . . ha! Owen felt at home up there.

My stint at Qantas was brief. For several years prior, I'd worked for another commercial airline; I had got into the private jet side of the industry but there was a delay while a private jet was being built, which is why I had stumbled

1

into working for Qantas. I needed to pay the bills . . . or so I thought!

During a break on this first flight with Owen, I opened my first Qantas pay-slip. The figure left me somewhat baffled, so I turned to my colleague, who had numerous QF years under his belt and asked, 'This is a weekly salary, right, Owen? This could barely keep one in hosiery.'

Laughing his head off, Owen replied, in his dulcet tones, 'No, darl! That's for the month! Welcome to Australia's finest.'

Owen's mirth at my horror was to be the start of a firm friendship that has spanned continents and years.

My year with Qantas was the most fun I've ever had flying. Some of the most notable misdemeanours include the infamous Mr Beddall.

At the end of a particularly heavy night in Hong Kong, Owen suggested we go for colonic irrigation. What on earth possessed me to do this, I have no idea. I could barely place one foot in front of the other, let alone have a highly intimate experience with a colonic pipe and a very jolly Hong Kong Chinese lady called Mandy. Going for colonics in Hong Kong was a real fad at that time; a lot of the crew did so as it was inexpensive and offered untold health benefits. Believing myself nothing if not game, I agreed and before I knew it we were making our way around the twisting, turning roads of the island.

Upon arrival at this uber-smart clinic, we were efficiently informed of our responsibilities and told what to expect for the next twenty minutes before being whisked off to adjacent cubicles. I'm not sure whether Owen was trying to do a solo of 'Waltzing Matilda' or whether it was the late-night carb fest we had indulged in to soak up the vodka jellies of Lan

Kwai Fong several hours earlier but those walls were thin and Owen wasn't holding back! All I know is that I could barely concentrate on the situation for laughing.

At the end of the ordeal, Owen and I sat together for the debrief; as part of it we had to swallow a horse-pill sized probiotic tablet. While I was shunned and told that I must try harder next time, Mandy informed Owen that he had done *very* well – teacher's pet!

I am sure that reading this book will be as entertaining and outrageous as the author himself! For my part, I shall be reading it from behind a cushion as many of the characters I will know personally. Perhaps one day I will give you all an insight into the world of what happens on private jets . . . until then, enjoy.

Samantha Hargreaves

PREPARING FOR TAKE-OFF

THE NEW GUY

The day I finished training as an international flight attend-ant, I went out and had a few drinks to celebrate. Officially, I was on a 4 am to 4 pm standby the next day but I'd been assured that there was absolutely no chance I'd be called out. The longest distance flights – to the USA, South America and Africa, which by the way was the least popular of the three – tended to leave Australia early in the morning; the European flights typically left in the afternoon to meet any curfew restrictions in Asia, where they stopped to refuel and to correspond with arriving early morning in London. Usually, only the most senior flight attendants worked on the longest international flights.

They were the dream gig: the passengers were generally easy and the overtime money on really long-haul flights was substantial. In those days, everyone got a fortnightly base salary, after which you earnt an hourly rate according to years of service. For a flight over twelve hours, a flight attendant was on double time, and anything over fourteen hours was long range and therefore a set exponential rate above and beyond double time applied. The minimum flight time to the US was about thirteen hours but generally those flights took fourteen or more hours. Because of the strict security and customs regulations, there were often delays while passengers were processed. Also the duty, or 'working time', allowed an extra hour and a half for signing on, getting the aircraft ready and half an hour post-flight to clear customs, immigration and so on. Ka-ching! What made the USA run especially coveted was that once you got there, the food was good, as were the hotels, and there was no language barrier.

Even though I was confident I wouldn't be called up, at 11 pm, I phoned Crewing to check. I was told there was nothing so I kept having fun.

At 3 am, I was in a pub in the city dancing around to a mega-mix and I thought, one hour to go and still no call. Keep on partying. At 4.01 am my mobile rang.

'Hi, Owen, it's Paul from Crewing. You have been given a duty today.'

'Pardon?' I was in shock at what I believed he was saying but I could hardly hear above the music blasting and people screaming to make themselves heard above it. I removed myself to the outdoor area where people congregated to smoke, get their jackets and the like.

'You are doing a five-day LA; you need to sign on at eight o'clock.'

Adrenaline and panic hit my mind and body at once. 'Shit, what am I going to do? I can't call in sick on my first duty and they will be watching me like hawks on my first flight.' It was 4 am and I was bloody well tanked. According to the rules, you couldn't drink within eight hours of a duty. Would I be done for DUI for flying intoxicated?!

Straightaway I grabbed a taxi home and tried to get a couple of hours' sleep. This proved impossible because I was too pissed and worried that if I went to sleep I wouldn't wake up in time. In the end I got up and showered and brushed my teeth, desperately trying to stay upright. It was impossible to say whether I was more nervous or more exhilarated: it was my first international flight and it was *to the United States*.

The only international crew I knew was the one I had trained with so I had no idea who I'd be flying with. Freshly minted, I turned up in the Cabin Crew Headquarters at the airport in my spanking new uniform, to be confronted with fourteen elderly flight attendants – well, I was twenty-seven and they had to be in their fifties and even sixties!

'Are you in the right briefing room?' asked one old drone, as if I was some low-life.

'Yes. Los Angeles.'

'How did you get this trip?' They appeared affronted and huddled to discuss this situation, muttering.

'Oh, Mara must have called in sick, that's why,' they decided.

There is a big divide between domestic and long-haul flight attendants – long-haul think they're way better than domestic. That's why almost everyone who wants to be a flight attend-ant tries to get into international and virtually no one wants to fly domestic. They quizzed me about my time on domestic. I told them I'd hated it (which I had) and that seemed to give me a couple of stars. They then asked me how I thought I'd go in long-haul.

'I'll be fine. It'll just be like Perth return.' (That's Sydney to Perth and back – about an eleven- to twelve-hour round trip.) They seemed highly amused by this.

It was not the workplace welcome I had been led to expect as part of the 'Qantas Family'. So much for that part of my training. Apparently there was a distinct unofficial hierarchy and I was about to get a lesson in it. Absolutely.

My new colleagues were very quick to assert their seniority even before we boarded the plane; I was told that Mara always did 'the assist'. I said okay, although I had no idea what 'the assist' was.

As I soon found out, the bloody 'assist' was a general dogsbody – no wonder Mara had called in sick. First I helped with the service in business class, after which I had to go upstairs to help do another service in business class. Then I had to see if anyone needed a hand in first; after that it was up the back to assist in economy. By the time I'd finished all that, I'd worked every cabin on the aircraft – the only upside was that I'd got to know all the other crew.

After service, the crew was allowed to eat; special meals were provided for crew, and I started to get one out. One of the others, Eddie, touched me on the shoulder and asked me if I had been taught the rules.

'What rules?'

'The rules about everything you learnt in training. See this compacting machine?' he asked, moving his hands in a square motion in the air.

'We take all of our rubbish – pick it up . . .' He held the imaginary box.

Standing there, confused, I followed his prompt and 'held up' a pile of nothing.

'Now blow on it,' Eddie commanded.

I blew.

'Harder.'

I blew harder on this empty space.

'Great. Now put it in the bin and compact it. Forget all that brainwashing nonsense they teach you in training.' He clapped his hands together once. 'This is how we do it in real life: grab a meal from first or business class – we don't eat the shitty stuff catering gives us. Then we go off to sleep. The company mandates you to have twenty minutes' rest every six hours; however, no one goes by that. I like to have five hours out straight then I'll come back to work and you can have five hours out straight.'

My head was spinning. Never having worked on a 747 before, I didn't even know there was such a thing as a horizontal 'crew rest', where crew could sleep. It was not something that was dwelt on during training. Sure enough, in the aft of the plane, up in the tail, there were eight bunk beds for crew. Who'd've thought?

Armed with all this inside information, I got stuck into the business-class cheese plate and mingled with the others who had congregated in the galley; they were discussing their mortgages and company politics and who was flying where over the next roster. Eddie, who was my working partner on the left side of the plane, and another one of the older gay guys, Brian, took me under their wing and took me through everything I needed to know about the company that I hadn't learnt in training, not to mention all the stuff I needed to 'unlearn'. They also explained that crew looked after each other like a big family – which was not the same as the 'Qantas Family' line the company pushed. For one thing, there was no dobbing to management – under any circumstances. If something really bad happened, the crew would always find a way to get around it.

'We deal with problems on board, not in the office,' Eddie emphasised.

There was a lot to take in, but the most important thing I had to get into my head was the word 'seniority'. Everything in the company was driven by seniority. The rest of the crew on that flight had more than twenty years' experience over me; as I was on day one, I had to resign myself to dealing with the duties no one else wanted. On top of all the other tasks, I found myself running extra drinks and meals around the plane, collecting rubbish everywhere, checking the toilets were clean, and one job that looked easy but was a real pain – handing out immigration cards. Passengers would take that opportunity to ask you a million random questions or confess something to you while using you as the in-house maid, handing you rubbish, plates and anything else they had. Oh well, so be it; we all had to come through the ranks and one day I too would have people underneath me.

These two old camp guys were like something out of the 1970s Brit sit-com *Are You Being Served?*; for a young queen like me, it was just fabulous – what a workplace. Coming out as a gay man had been generally a bit tentative in any other place I'd worked. When anyone asked if I had a girlfriend and I 'confessed' I was gay, they'd usually go, 'Oh, okay.' At Qantas there were so many gay men, the only time someone would have to 'confess' their sexuality was if they were straight; then we'd go, 'Oh, okay.'

Having covered the company culture, Eddie and Brian moved on to talking about our destination. They told me a bit about LA and asked me what plans I had while we were there. I'd never been to LA before. All I really wanted to do was to visit a few gay bars and go to Hollywood. They said crew stayed at a hotel in Pasadena and we'd all go into Hollywood together. We'd hire a car with a driver for the night, they added – it was cheaper than taxis.

Even though I was interested in everything beyond belief, four hours into the flight I found myself leaning on the galley bench gently snoring.

'A bit tired, love? We're not even at Perth yet,' Brian said.

Even taking into account my partying the night before, I couldn't figure out why I was so tired. It's so obvious to me looking back: I was moving from hangover to jetlag.

Meantime, the others are all standing around lathering themselves with moisturiser. I asked how come they kept moisturising themselves. Brian took me into the toilet and told me to have a look at myself in the mirror, pointing out the dry 'T-spot' across your forehead and down the bridge of your nose; apparently it was where you aged the most if you didn't looked after it properly.

'Petal, you must keep yourself hydrated at all times otherwise you'll look sixty before you're even forty.'

Soon, Eddie came back and told me it was time for my five hours' rest. As a general rule, attendants work on either the left or right side of the plane with a partner. In economy, when the left side is off for a rest, the right side is on and vice versa; business and first are two-people operations – one is galley operator and the other cabin, and when galley was off cabin was on.

Being in the crew bunk for the first time was like being in a noisy, rocking coffin. And the assist's bunk was the worst because it was a bottom bunk and looked directly into the light from the stairwell, which had to stay on for safety reasons. Despite these impediments, I fell deeply asleep. It seemed as though only minutes had passed and I felt this soft gloved touch on my arm, stroking it. 'Darling,' a woman whispered. 'Darling,' a little louder. 'DARLING. Time to wake up, and here's a refresher towel. Time for breakfast.' It was one of the very senior crew from first class.

I felt like I'd been drugged. In the galley, crew were scrambling eggs and I was scared I was about to throw up. Somehow I managed to hand out the breakfasts despite feeling like a zombie. I wanted to lock myself in the toilet.

The others were enjoying a laugh at my expense and made a few funny remarks.

'Darling, have you arrived in Perth yet?'

'Oh, pet, would you like to sit down for a little rest?'

'I'm so tired,' I said.

'Mmm; it's called jetlag, petal. Get used to it.'

'Aren't you tired?' I asked – they all looked as fresh as daisies.

'God no.' They waved their hands dismissively.

What I didn't know was that these veterans of hundreds of long-haul flights had special little 'helpers' with which they knocked themselves out during the crew rest; I'd been welcomed into the 'family' but not yet to the inner sanctum and initiation into the real tricks of flying.

They had a few more tricks up their sleeves for me yet. When it was time to prepare for landing, we had to change from our serving vests back into full uniform for disembarkation. As I went to retrieve my jacket, a crew member came through holding out a bag full of beer to the other crew. 'Any beers? Any beers?' and held the bag out to me.

'What for?' I asked. It had been drummed into all of us during training that crew couldn't drink on board.

It was then explained to me that crew always had a couple of beers on the bus on the way from the airport to the hotel. After we'd checked into the hotel the procedure was to shower and change and then go to someone's room for a few debriefing beers; this was when everyone offloaded about what had gone on in other sections of the plane during the flight and company gossip or whatever else was on their minds.

Even though that sounded great, I was far more concerned with trying to find my jacket. I went up the stairs and down the stairs looking for it. In the end I was standing in the galley crying. I was beside myself; it was my first flight and I'd already lost my uniform.

The gay guys gathered around me offering sympathy. 'Owen, what's wrong?'

'I can't find my uniform.'

'Where did you put it?'

'In the cupboard; I'm sure I put it in the cupboard. Maybe I put it upstairs.' I raced back upstairs and came down empty-handed again.

'Maybe a passenger stole it,' Eddie said. 'They all love our uniforms. Didn't you lock it up?'

'Oh, my God! Really? They didn't teach us that in training.' I stood there with my hands over my face.

Someone said, 'Is this your uniform, Owen?' – just in the nick of time before the seatbelt sign went on.

'Thank you *so* much,' I said as I slipped my jacket on gratefully; then they all started laughing. It had never occurred to me that those lovely guys had hidden it. They were actually bitches but it was a strangely inclusive trick, a kind of initiation.

As I sat in the jump seat for landing I started to nod off again. This is the crucial phase, where flight attendants should be most alert. Next thing, someone was nudging me to wake up:

'Welcome to Perth, pet.'

GLOBETROTTING PRE-QANTAS

Ever since I can remember, I've loved travelling and meeting people from different walks of life. Even so, the idea of becoming a flight attendant never crossed my mind. I grew up in a country town and moved to Sydney at the end of 1994 to study law at the University of New South Wales.

During the summer break of my second year, I was excited when my friend Shaun was offered a job in Hong Kong. But I became even more excited when he said that they were looking for two others *and* – after he'd told them I was studying law and industrial relations – they were interested in seeing *me*. The job was with a recruitment agency in Hong Kong that was part of a range of companies.

I was interviewed for the position – at the Sheraton Hotel – by Michael Wong, a statuesque and extremely well-dressed Chinese man with an entourage. He had a friendly demeanour, spoke perfect English and seemed to pick up on my concerns before I raised them. To a nineteen-year-old, Mr Wong was a polished act. He looked at my thin curriculum vitae and offered me a job. Yippee.

Shaun and I flew to Hong Kong; I'd recommended another friend so there were three of us. We were put up in a 'luxury' apartment in the hills; well, actually, in the New Territories – just outside Hong Kong. The area was considered upmarket

Confessions of a Qantas Flight Attendant

by locals but 'far too Chinese' by expatriates. It stank of sewage and was crowded and scary.

Hong Kong bombarded the senses. There were telecommunications shops galore alongside open-air kitchens with hanging pigs and ducks; everywhere you looked there were masses of people wearing designer and sci-fi gear. But we scarcely had time to look or explore our new environment: it was off to work! Our suburb was at the end of the red MTR line, and it took over an hour to get to work in Wan Chai, on the fifteenth floor of a grotty high-rise. Almost straightaway, we realised Mr Wong's recruitment agency was a scam; we weren't helping people get jobs, we were recruiting investors for Mr Wong's various projects. It soon became apparent that we were also working illegally. Mr Wong was cagey about our work visas and every now and again instructed us to catch the ferry over to Macau for a day. At the time the island of Macau was a Portuguese colony, and spending a day there was a way of getting our passports stamped so we could extend our stay in Hong Kong.

Hong Kong was fabulous for all the things that made us scared and curious – it was fast and trendy, a city of indulgence that ran on sex, drugs and money. For young guys, it was exciting. And it was a visual delight. Incredibly modern buildings dotted the skyline, dwarfing the little traditional junk boats and villages.

Mr Wong paid us well – we even had cleaners to tidy up after us – but we knew something was off-centre. In the apartment, often we would find our things had been moved around. Our *Spartacus* – the gay bible – would be placed on the table, as if to signal that they knew we were gay. Shaun had hidden some pot, which also made its way onto display. It was all very

14

sinister. Were Mr Wong's people telling us that they knew what we were up to? There was a general sense of unease at the time because Hong Kong was about to be handed back to China by the British, and a lot of locals were on edge.

It all got too much for Shaun. He booked a ticket to Australia and left. Mr Wong invited me into his very grand office and asked me to stay, promising me promotion and the prospect of big money. I could be like him and his associates, he said, who all drove Lamborghinis and wore Rolexes. When I thanked him but declined, he shook my hand, gave me some money and warned me never to speak of his business dealings. So within twelve months, I had done the Hong Kong thing and returned home. It had been an interesting but crazy time.

Even though I returned to Sydney and resumed full-time study, my heart was never in it. I was more interested in travelling and experiencing life. With Hong Kong being so full of expatriates, I had met a lot of English people there and also dated a couple. So it didn't take much to entice me to base myself in London to do more travelling. In London at the end of 1997, I met Andrew, who became my first long-term partner, so we set up home. Ironically, in London I worked as a recruitment consultant.

In 2000, my father was diagnosed with an extremely aggressive brain tumour and given three weeks to live. This was when Sydney was hosting the 2000 Olympic Games and I arrived back on the day Australia's Cathy Freeman won the gold medal for the 400-metre sprint. Everyone seemed to be celebrating. I was so proud to be Indigenous, so proud to see her carrying the Aboriginal flag.

Dad was in intensive care in Sydney and I went straight to the hospital. Soon after, he returned home to the north coast for his last remaining weeks. Following the funeral, I stayed on for a few months and then rejoined Andrew in London, but within a year our relationship had disintegrated and I returned to Sydney.

ME, YOU AND THE FLYING KANGAROO

It was time to plan a career. Shaun had just been accepted as a Qantas international flight attendant and he urged me to try out too, telling me that it was a really good job; you got all this cash to fly free all over the world and stay in luxurious five-star hotels. Mmmm. Nothing not to like about that. The bonus was that it was one of the only jobs in the world that was completely 'gay friendly'; a sizeable percentage of Qantas flight attendants were gay. It sounded like a life of fun.

In late 2001 I applied to become an international flight attendant. The timing could have been better: there was an oversupply of people wanting flight attendant jobs at Qantas; their main competitor in the domestic market, Ansett, had just collapsed and the former Ansett employees were queuing up at Qantas's door.

It didn't bother me all that much whether or not I was accepted. Because I'd lived in Hong Kong and London, I con-sidered I'd already travelled extensively. Consequently, when I was called for an interview, I was fairly relaxed, even though it turned out to be a serious business. Qantas had a six-tier interview process; the vetting was full-on – they wanted to be sure the candidates they chose would fit into the 'Qantas Family'. It was more difficult than getting a spot in New

College, the prestigious on-campus dorm at the University of New South Wales.

On the interview day, in the waiting area there were a lot of obviously ex-Ansett crew – gay guys and women with their hair in buns wearing blue suits and pearls, looking as if they'd stepped out in their old Ansett uniform. I don't know how many people they were interviewing, but I was surprised how quickly the numbers thinned out. Our height was measured: height requirements – 163 centimetres to 183 centimetres – are related to safety and were clearly specified on the application form. Nevertheless hordes turned up under the minimum height. Women in particular thought they could sneak through if they wore high heels; naturally, we were asked to remove our shoes before measurements.

We also had to have the correct documentation, including a Responsible Service of Alcohol Certificate and an active passport with at least six months' validity, the latter being crucial for US visas. It was extraordinary how many people didn't even hold a valid passport. Incorrect height and incomplete documentation eliminated about a quarter of the applicants.

When I was informed I'd made it through the first round, I counted myself lucky. There were so many stories floating around about people who had applied to Qantas again and again and been knocked back every time.

The next round involved group exercises. One of the exercises was a test of communication skills that was like playing charades using Lego. One person at a table of eight had to look at a picture of an object, which only they were allowed to see, then demonstrate to everyone else how to put together the object, within a limited amount of time. There were certain words you couldn't use – they were on the card with the picture. This particular exercise was all about time management and communication. It tripped up a lot of recruits.

Another of the group exercise questions related to our decision-making capability in an emergency. We were asked to imagine a scenario where the plane was about to ditch in the sea, there were five passengers but only four of them could fit on the remaining life-raft. We had to work out who we would choose to leave behind from among a priest, a pregnant woman, a terrorist deportee, a police officer and a young child. Everyone else in my group chose either the terrorist – making a moral judgement about that person's right to live – or the priest (the more popular choice), reasoning that the priest already had a relationship with God and would be happy to go to a better place! My answer was the right one: I chose the police officer because I believed the police officer would be physically fit and most likely to have had survival training and was therefore the best equipped to stay alive longer until rescued. I went through to the next round.

At every stage in the interview process I was aware that we were being carefully watched and our conversations noted, even during our tea breaks. Knowing this, I engaged people in conversation in the manner I thought befitting of a flight attendant. 'Would you like a cup of coffee?' I'd ask. Because the recruiters wore badges indicating what other languages they spoke, I'd say something like, 'I see you speak French; did you learn that at school?'

In the very last round there was a tricky panel interview before three Qantas recruiters. They tried to lull applicants into a false sense of security and then see if they could catch us out. They would ask you about the destinations Qantas flew to and see if you knew each one's famous landmarks.

One of the crucial questions was why you wanted to work for Qantas and what you could bring to the airline. This was the question where many would-be flight attendants let down their guard and confided they'd heard it was a really good job where you got to travel the world on the cheap and shop in great places. Of course Qantas didn't care if you wanted to go to London to shop at Harrods, they just wanted to know you were going to be a responsible member of the Qantas Family.

After that session there was a psychometric test with questions like, 'Would you rather be alone or with a lot of people?' and 'Would you rather have a swim or sit and read in a corner?' It was pretty easy to figure all that out.

That was followed by a one-on-one interview with the most senior member of the selection team. By the end of the day, about fifty of us remained – the ones who got jobs, provided we passed the general health check, which included tests for drug and alcohol, bone density, sight and hearing.

Finally, I got the good news via email: 'Qantas accepts you as a flight attendant. Welcome. We'll be back to you within the next six months.'

I was in! The secret world of the flight attendant was about to be unveiled to me.

TRAINING

The six months became eight months; then nine months. While I was waiting to be called, ready to go as soon as that phone rang, I started to daydream about where I'd be off to first: Paris, Rome, New York. I used to gaze in the window of the travel agent's, looking at destinations and all the interesting things to do. I was in and life was about to begin. Why the delay? Well, after the attack on the Twin Towers, which happened on 11 September 2001, not surprisingly people all over the world were nervous about flying and consequently there was a downturn in demand in the international market that lasted for a couple of years.

As compensation, we as yet untrained recruits were each offered a role as a casual in the domestic division. I took it. Working casual jobs is fine for a while, but I needed to move on.

The training covered service and safety. You know the expression 'chalk and cheese', right? Well, those topics were that way: the service people were all about detail and passenger comfort and the safety department were about the emergency procedures if an accident occurred; service people were all 'darling this' and 'darling that' and the safety crew were commandos. In one safety training module – in which a plane had supposedly propelled towards the ground and crashed and we'd had to evacuate the passengers – there we all were with our torches out, looking under seats before we followed the passengers and disembarked down the slide. It's a steep drop, but we all made it and were feeling proud until a Gestapo-type training woman snapped, 'Fail!', which took the wind out of our sails. She certainly had our attention.

Had we gone through all the different checklists? Yes.

What about the second last one, checking all areas? Yes, we did that.

'NO!' she screamed. We had checked under the seats but not the lockers; what if someone's infant or child had flown up during the impact and got stuck in one of them!

'Shit,' I thought. But I never made that mistake again.

Despite the service training being all hot air and bullshit, I managed to make a big boo-boo there as well. A particularly intense service trainer – he was forever walking around straightening your suit jacket and fluffing you, staring you up and down – started quizzing us about managing strange passengers. Here's the question he directed at me: A passenger has boarded in business class and is nervous and visibly shaken; what would you do?

'Give them a drink,' I said.

'Now, Owen, do you think that would be the best, considering he is already upset? Wouldn't you talk calmly to him and reassure him?

I nodded compliantly.

We were all new to this game and couldn't wait to graduate. It was six hard weeks before we got a feel of those shiny new uniforms. And then boom, just like that, you were out of training one day and onto a flight the next.

Flying involved learning a new language and a lot of acronyms. For example, passengers were referred to as pax, so if you were passengering on a flight it was called paxing. Often, the CSM, or cabin service manager, would say to us we have paxing crew so make sure you show your best; they will be watching you. Paxing crew could be on staff travel or duty. Duty travel, or flying as a passenger en route to do your duty, was called deadheading. It was usually in domestic flying. For example, you might be working to Brisbane, deadheading to Melbourne and then working Melbourne to Perth. Then there was 'meet and assist' for disabled passengers, and economy was known as Y and Business as J. It all came pretty quickly. Imagine if a pax overhears a flight attendant say something like, 'I'm paxing to Brisbane tonight, slipping, signing on tomorrow in Melbourne, and then I do four sectors and end up deadheading back to Perth in J before I overnight and do one leg home.' To the untrained ear, 'one leg' and 'deadheads' could easily sound like what they talk about in a morgue.

When I first started, I loved the way you were treated in uniform. As you walked through the airport with puff-chested pride, people would stop and compliment you. And you would skip queues! No lining up at security. But the camaraderie among the crews was terrific. When one crew was coming off and you were coming on, as you passed on the aerobridge, the departing crew would give you that big smile and tell you about any problems with the aircraft and, especially, the IFE, or in-flight entertainment.

After I'd been working the flights and boarding the passengers for a while, I realised that I'd wised up a lot to human behaviour. It was easy to identify the inflated businessman trying for an upgrade, the nervous travellers and the holiday-makers ready to start their holiday right here on your flight. There were plenty of self-important celebrities who would be as nice as pie until you told them no, they were not getting upgraded, and suddenly you got the cold shoulder. Conversely, you could also tell the quiet and well-mannered passengers, patiently wanting to get where they were going.

Even though I did learn a lot doing domestic, it wasn't what I'd signed up for originally and I hankered for more. Everyone knows a flight attendant's job involves slog, but knowing you could unwind at a gorgeous hotel in a long-dreamt-of destination at the end of your shift is a handsome reward. I still wanted that opportunity to travel and explore, and I longed for the variety that international offered.

The Canberra flight was my least favourite. It was short but madly busy: it was only about thirty-five minutes in duration and you had to do a full service, so it was super-noticeable if you had difficult red-faced passengers wanting a glass of port at 7 am. You had to get up at 4 am on a Monday morning knowing you had to look after a posse of politicians, with their big suits and their dismissive hand gestures.

The pollies stood out; very tricky. Once I was on a flight with Tony Abbott – who has since become Australia's Prime Minister – before I knew who he was. He was no better: loud, self-assured and smirky. When we served him, he was rude and dismissive. We used to laugh in the galley at the irony: we had to treat these politicians with kid gloves even though they were only there because of us; they were travelling on taxpayers' money. Sometimes you itched for them to get a wake-up call of some sort. Unfortunately for us though, on this particular service, taking coffee from a minister's hands as we came in to land often resulted in a complaint and a 'please explain' in the office.

After almost two years flying domestic, I was finally able to transfer to the international division, and I was so ready.

LOS ANGELES

KANGAROOS AND COUNTRY CODES

'I'll sleep when I'm dead,' I thought, as I ordered a cocktail. I had just stepped into the magnificent bar of the Hilton Pasadena in Los Angeles after my first long-haul sector. Its décor was relatively plain but absolutely regal, and featured a grand collection of wines and champagne on mirrored shelves. The waiters – or servers as they are called in America – were in little vests; some wore gloves. It felt like I was in a movie.

Burning a hole in my pocket was US$400 – my allowance for three days in LA; at the time, this was equivalent to about AU$800. For someone as young as me, that was very good money.

After the debriefing beers on the bus into the hotel, I had gone to my room and flopped on my bed: I could have wept with relief, I was so exhausted. When the phone rang, I had studiously ignored it: one of the rules the boys had told me was 'never answer the phone' in the crew hotel in case it was Qantas ringing me and, as the most junior, they might want me to fly off somewhere. I'd just arrived in America and I wasn't going anywhere. I lay there until the phone stopped ringing and I felt my eyes closing. Next thing I saw the message light flashing; it was Eddie and Brian saying they were getting ready to go out and if I still wanted to go to Hollywood to let them know.

Hello! I flew out of bed like an Olympic sprinter exploding out of their starting blocks. Even after a cold shower I was feeling rather jetlagged, whereas Eddie and Brian were waiting, looking bright-eyed and fresh. But I wasn't about to give up Hollywood for sleep.

The hire car – a fresh-smelling big black vehicle with leather seats and a mini-bar – arrived, a uniformed driver behind the wheel. We began our tour with a lap of Hollywood, taking in all the stars' mansions, the Hollywood sign and other landmarks. Los Angeles turned out to be one heck of a spread-out city; the downtown area, which was the financial city part of LA, was about an hour from Hollywood and Beverley Hills in one direction, and Malibu was about an hour away in another. I didn't expect to find that vast, sprawling low-income suburbs were surrounded by ultra-rich areas.

It was time to leave the ultra-pads of Beverly Hills and get into the heart of the action. We went to Micky's, a well-known gay bar on Santa Monica Boulevard in West Hollywood. Eddie and Brian may have looked fresh, but I had the advantage of youth and people wanted to buy me drinks. We're at the bar and I ordered cocktails; the bartender asked me my name.

'Owen.'

'That sounds like an Australian accent.'

'Yes, it is.'

'Oh, my God; what are you doing over here in LA? Are you an actor?'

'No, I'm a flight attendant.'

'United or American?'

'I work for Qantas.'

'What's Qantas?'

'It's an Australian airline.'

'Get out! Australia has its own airline?' He was incredulous; I was incredulous that he was incredulous!

Then he said, 'Don't you Australians all ride around on kangaroos?'

I could see Eddie and Brian were enjoying this and nudging me to keep it going. Even though I was a bit suspicious of their intentions after the uniform prank, I felt like I'd just stepped into a comedy routine. I decided to play along.

'Of course we do but we leave them tied up at the airport when we fly our planes around the world.'

'Oh, my God. Chuck, did you hear that?' he called to another bartender. 'The Australians tie their kangaroos up at the airport and fly their planes over here.'

It was surreal. Did this guy really believe this? I asked him where he was from.

'LA born and bred,' he said proudly.

'And you found your way to Santa Monica Boulevard all by yourself?'

'I sure did,' he responded sincerely, not picking up my slightly sarcastic tone. That's when I discovered Americans don't do irony. It was so easy to have a lot fun with them; most of them were quite naive.

We chatted away and the guy told me his name was Steve. I said it must be fun working in Micky's – so many good-looking guys.

Steve leant across the bar conspiratorially and said, 'Oh no, I'm not a bartender, I'm an actor/singer/model/dancer.'

'Are we in a movie? I thought we were in a bar,' I said, looking around as if to find a camera pointing at us. 'Sorry, I'm awfully jetlagged.'

'No, silly; I'm just doing this part-time so I can fulfil my potential and my destiny.'

'Well, I'm actually a supermodel in Australia and I'm just a flight attendant part-time so I can pay the bills and fulfil my destiny too.'

'Really? When do you think your big contract is going to drop?' He was nice but a head case.

As we left the bar, Steve called out, 'I'll watch out for you on a poster. Come visit again soon, won't ya! And give that kangaroo a big hug from me.'

Eddie, Brian and I danced the night away at other clubs. When people asked me where I was from and I said Australia, they would ask how I got there. I'd say I flew with Qantas, Australia's airline. Invariably that person would turn to someone else and say, 'Did you hear that, Australia has its own airline!'

Hadn't everyone heard of Qantas – one of the biggest and best airlines in the world? Not in America; not even after the movie *Rain Man*, where Dustin Hoffman's character said he'd only fly Qantas because it was the safest airline.

That was my introduction to Americans. 'Don't Americans travel?' I asked Eddie and Brian on the way back to the Hilton Pasadena.

'No, darling, they don't; try and get some international news on the hotel TV.'

And I tried and no, I couldn't; there were about 500 channels, it was the twenty-first century and CNN was about as international as it got in 2004.

After a luxurious sleep, when I went down to breakfast I asked the concierge if I could get an Australian or British newspaper.

'We have the *New York Post*, the *LA Times*, the *Washington Post* and *USA Today*.' He told me I'd have to go to Hollywood for a European paper.

It occurred to me that America was so big that they were only interested in what went on in other states or, at a stretch, Mexico or Canada.

But what Americans lacked in world knowledge they made up for in food. I had never seen portion sizes so big. The breakfast buffet alone was enough to feed a small nation – cholesterol and cardiac central on a plate. Everything was bigger and better than whatever it was next to.

Over my three days in LA, the guys took me everywhere – to the huge malls with all the stores I'd long heard about, like Macy's and Bergdorf's, and I loved it all. Clothes were so much cheaper – I got a Calvin Klein shirt for US$20 that would have cost AU$200 at home. And when it was time to head back to Sydney, I couldn't believe how much of my allowance I still had. That's when the boys told me another trick of the trade: change my US currency into Australian dollars in the States because the country of the currency you exchange usually offers the best rate. If I was careful, I could live off my allowance and save most of my salary.

By the time we left LA, I'd adjusted to Californian time and I thought I was little Mister International. Wrong! On the trip to the States, you virtually arrived before you left, courtesy of the time zone. Returning home was like a two-day trip: we left LA late at night on a Thursday but didn't get to Sydney until 8 am on Saturday. And the jetlag was even worse than going over. I felt as if someone had picked up a brick and slapped me in the face with it.

When I got off that plane, the only thing I could think of was getting a bottle of duty-free vodka, climbing into a taxi and going home. I was so tired I slept for three days.

The more long-haul flights I flew, the more I learnt. In my first year of flying I was like a sponge absorbing everything I could from the more experienced crew. The more confident I became, the more fun I found I could have with the Americans on my US trips. Because LA was a senior route, I only got LA trips sporadically.

When I started flying to the US, people still remembered the 'Crocodile Dundee' movies and the Australian tourism ad campaign featuring its Australian star, Paul Hogan, with the phrase 'shrimp on the barbie' but it seemed that the only people who identified with Qantas were those who remembered Raymond's safety comments in *Rain Man*.

Americans loved to talk about kangaroos when they discovered I came from Australia and I played up the role of kangaroos in the lives of Australians. Yes, I had my own kangaroo; yes, I rode it. When they asked where I put my bag, I said I tied it to the saddle.

'Oh, my God, you tie your bag to the kangaroo! How cute.'

Most of the Americans I met in LA had never been anywhere outside the States – except perhaps Montreal and Acapulco. Going overseas was going to Hawaii. Only a small percentage of Americans even had passports. When other flight attendants and I talked about all the places we had been, they were not in the least bit interested.

'Wouldn't you like to go to Paris to see the Eiffel Tower or to Venice to go on a gondola?'

'Honey, I've seen the Eiffel Tower and I've been on a gondola.'

'If you've never been to Europe, how did you do that?'

'I've been to Las Vegas; they have an Eiffel Tower there and gondolas.'

Americans often appeared quite insulted if I suggested that they see the rest of the world. They lived in the greatest country in the planet; why would they want to go anywhere else? In a club one night when I was a bit drunk I asked the guy next to me at the bar how he determined America was the best country in the world.

'Honey, our dialling code is plus-one; what's Australia's?'

'Plus six one.'

'See, you're sixty-one, we're number one: America – plus one.'

It was hard to argue with that reckoning. The patriotism was mesmerising. LA people were completely off the planet. I was flying around the world on an airline they'd never heard of from a country that they believed ranked sixty-first on their country-code scale.

ANYONE FOR TENNIS?

The flight of all flights for me was a Sydney to LA in 2008, and it was all to do with tennis; I love the sport and am an avid follower. The day before this flight, I had attended the Australian Open at the Rod Laver Arena in Melbourne, where both the Williams sisters had been playing; Serena won her match but Venus lost hers. Once they lose, tennis players normally leave the next day, and I wondered if Venus would be on my flight. Just in case, I'd tossed my used Aussie Open tickets in my crew bag.

It turned out I was working as assist in first class and, sure enough, Venus and her mother, Oracene Price, were travelling in first class; and as a bonus, Lisa Raymond, the veteran American doubles player, was also on the flight. I was like a kid in a candy store and didn't know who to approach first! There were various other tennis people of interest, including coaches and hit partners and an agent or two, but it was Venus Williams herself – the real prize – I had my eye on.

I told Venus, who towered over me by at least a foot, that I'd watched her play the day before and showed her my ticket, which she later autographed. She confided that she was disappointed with the way she'd played but hoped Serena would go on to win. Serena's quarter-final was being played that day, and I promised I would bring updates on the competition from the pilot. When I found out that Jelena Jankovic had knocked Serena out of the tournament, winning in straight sets, and would be meeting Maria Sharapova in the semifinal, I passed this information on to Venus and her mother.

'I reckon it will be between Ana or Sharapova now. I love Ana,' I added nervously.

'Mmm,' Venus said, not looking especially pleased.

'Don't you like Ana?' I asked.

'Well, it's not that but she did knock me out of the tournament!'

Another 'oops' moment.

Later Venus came out to the galley and talked about her plans for life after tennis. She had studied fashion design because she wanted to create better tennis clothes for women. Recently she had started her fashion label, EleVen, and was manufacturing tennis apparel and casual sportswear, some of which she happened to be wearing. On top of that, she told me, she was also writing a book.

I asked Venus if she ever imagined she'd one day be one of the top tennis players in the world.

'Yes, I did,' she answered, surprising me somewhat with her frankness. She said she had trained long and hard and knew she would one day be a great player. She also predicted that Serena would go on to be one of the best women tennis players in history. At the time of writing, she is hot on the heels of Chris Evert and Martina Navratilova.

I was on a roll, and got chatting with the lovely Lisa Raymond, who had just competed in what she said felt like her one hundredth Australian Open; she still had no plans to slow down, she told me. Lisa couldn't believe I knew who she was; I said I was a genuine tennis fan. It felt like Lisa and I talked all the way to the States; we discussed sponsorship money and how lucrative the sport was. Although she was earning nowhere near the endorsement money of players like the Williams sisters or Maria Sharapova, Lisa said she didn't mind because their high profile had actually transcended sport and brought women's tennis to the world stage.

Lisa was a pioneer in her own right. She had been an accomplished singles player but she realised earlier than most that you could make a great lifestyle on the tour playing doubles exclusively. She has seventy-nine doubles titles to her credit and has played with everyone from former greats Martina

Navratilova and Lindsay Davenport through to today's Samantha Stosur and glamorous up-and-coming stars Laura Robson and Daniela Hantuchova. In fact, in the couple of years preceding our meeting, she had formed a strong and successful partnership with Australia's Sam Stosur, netting a Grand Slam and season-ending tournament glory. She had seen the game evolving and adapted with it.

Lisa confessed to me that coffee and Perez Hilton were her morning indulgences. After that, I started looking on the website at Perez, who is a notorious Hollywood internet gossip columnist.

Chatting with Lisa was so easy and enjoyable. In the tennis world, she is a veteran, an 'old school' player, but she recognised that times were changing and the sport had globalised; for instance, twenty years ago there were few Eastern bloc tennis players and now every second player had a name ending in 'ova' or 'vich'. According to Lisa, you either embraced the changes or you got out.

It was quite ironic that she was on the same flight as Venus Williams. Eight years earlier, the high-profile William sisters had been selected as doubles players to represent America on the 2000 Olympic tennis team, bypassing the number-one ranked Lisa and her doubles partner, Corina Morariu. Lisa sued the United States Tennis Association (USTA) and although she still didn't make it onto the team, the rules were changed so that the same situation would not arise in future Olympics.

Tennis is one of my great loves and before the start of the international tennis season – in late December, early January – I would always bid for LA, London and Frankfurt as I knew these were the flights the top players would be on if they were competing in Australia. Meeting these players was the ultimate!

In 2010 I was lucky enough to be on the London flight with German player Sabine Lisicki, who was coming to Australia to play in the Hopman Cup. She was lovely, and although I didn't manage to get her parents upgraded to business so they could sit with her (the CSM couldn't see it would be fruitful for the airline), I did look after them with some Dom Perignon. Sabine, like most of the players, really believed in her abilities and was not afraid to put that out there. She had achieved notoriety after an incident of shoulder bumping with Caroline Wozniacki the year before at Wimbledon. When I asked her about it, she said it was 'nothing really'. Our conversation covered the young clique of girls, including Wozniacki, Azarenka, the Radwanska sisters and a few others; Sabine said that she was not part of any group and really only hung out with the other German players. She was fun but very German in her sharp conversation.

The same year, surprisingly, I was on a flight with Danish player Caroline Wozniacki between Sydney and Melbourne, and even though it was only a forty-minute flight, it was a fantastic opportunity to talk tennis. Then we chatted a bit about Princess Mary being an Australian; Caroline said Prince Frederick was a very good tennis player and had helped her out with some sponsorship funding when she was younger.

Caroline was a pioneer of the group of young Gen Ys coming into tennis. She was fearless, attractive and happy to speak her mind. I really admired her and asked her what it was like for a slightly built people like herself and Aga Radwanska to handle the big Williams' serves.

She smiled. 'I have to be quicker and play smarter.'

With her athleticism and sun-kissed good looks, Caroline

is a sponsor's delight; even at that relatively early stage in her professional career, she was on her way that year to a season-ending number-one position. Although she led the young guns, she respected her forebears of the game. She told me she really admired the Williams sisters. She was all smiles and an absolute delight. A few years later, she became engaged to golf former number-one Rory McIlroy.

My friend Jeremy had an oops moment with Lleyton Hewitt in 2005. He and the former soapie star Bec Cartwright, whom he later married, were headed home from Wimbledon; the previous year, Lleyton had been dumped very publicly by his former fiancée, Belgian tennis star Kim Clijsters.

The three of them were chatting in the galley, and a stony-faced Bec turned on her heel and walked back to her seat.

'Nice one, mate,' Lleyton said, and followed her back to first class.

Something had gone wrong! Apparently Jeremy had told Lleyton how much he loved the women's tennis and asked him who he thought would win at Wimbledon. Lleyton had said he had no idea.

'I really hope Kim Clijsters wins. I really love her, don't you?' Jeremy asked, which was when Bec gave Jeremy a withering look, then turned and walked off. Only then did Jeremy realise he'd made a faux pas.

In late January 2013, I was at the door of the plane welcoming passengers when the last person to come on board was Casey Dellacqua. Only the day before, I'd been watching her and rising tennis star Ash Barty lose a nail-biting ladies doubles final at the Australian Open in Melbourne. As I welcomed her and looked at her boarding pass, I saw she was seated in economy.

I was working in her zone so I made sure she had a first-class service, with extra blankets, pillows and champagne. I found Casey interesting because she wasn't a 'show biz' professional athlete. When I asked why she was travelling in economy when she had just made nearly AU$120,000 in one tournament, she explained how expensive it was being on the professional circuit, with lots of massive overheads for competitors. I'd assumed the tennis pros were quite pampered; all the ones I'd seen had always been in business or first class. But she told me that when they played in tournaments, competitors only got one complimentary hotel room, so any others travelling in her team, such as her coach or family members, had to have their rooms, meals, and travel and transfers paid. There were also medical costs. Being an athlete, she could get injured at any time, so she needed to have something put away for the proverbial rainy day. Already she'd had several injuries and truly understood the value of professional tennis money. Without a sponsor the expenses were high.

Casey said a player had to be in the top fifty to get the lucrative endorsements, but she was not too perturbed by the few at the top taking all the spoils. Like Lisa Raymond, she too believed that if it grew women's tennis, it was fantastic. 'It's like this,' Casey explained. 'Say you have a sponsorship budget of ten dollars and one high-profile player wants six of it. That leaves four to go around everyone else. It starts to get a bit thin.' She didn't have a sponsor and had to pay for everything out of her own pocket. There were, she said, millions for the top few and a smattering for the rest. To put it in perspective, in 2013 she would earn over US$600,000 in prize money and Serena Williams earned over US$12 million in on-court prize money.

She told me she loved representing her country and loved being able to make a living out of doing what she loved, and that was the main thing.

Casey confided in me that she really wanted to do better in her singles. I gave her a bottle of champagne and said, 'Have that when you win.' She didn't win the Pattaya singles tournament but she did win the doubles so I sent her a message of congratulations and told her to enjoy the champagne.

NEW YORK

ANOTHER LESSON IN COUNTRY CODES

New York, New York! I had a love affair with that city. Although I found Californians friendly, in LA, people had their own friendship circles and were into their own things. In New York, everyone wanted to go out and do something. New Yorkers would open their doors to you. The people I met wanted to know who I was; they took me to underground parties, into their lives, and in return they made their way into my heart. But I should start my New York story from the beginning.

Going to New York had long been my dream and it was a dream I managed to realise fairly late in my career. Because it is part of the One World Alliance of international airlines, Qantas flies to few destinations in the States; American Airlines, its code-share partner in the Alliance, flies all the US domestic routes, including New York. When for various reasons Qantas negotiated to fly the LA–New York and New York–LA sectors itself, I rejoiced: woo hoo, the big Apple, here I come!

Funnily enough, I didn't have to fight my way onto the roster as it wasn't popular with the most senior crew. The typical New York crew pattern from Australia began with a flight from Sydney to LA, where you would spend two days, and then you'd do the sector to New York. Most senior crew preferred to do Sydney to LA, have two days there and then fly back to Sydney and have four days off.

Why? Well, the time difference was awkward. New York was three hours ahead of Los Angeles, so you'd leave LA early in the morning and arrive in New York at about 5 pm for an eight- or nine-hour day. The way flight attendants looked at it, the financial rewards via overtime and capacity to accrue leave doing LA to New York weren't up to scratch. However, on the plus side, because we didn't pick up domestic passengers in LA, and most passengers from Sydney disembarked at LA, the loads to New York were fairly light. But the biggest plus of all was the destination itself.

New York was so familiar. It was everything I'd ever heard about, read about or seen in movies, only more so. The lights seemed brighter, the buildings taller, the streets more exciting, the people friendlier. What struck me immediately was how different New Yorkers were from all other Americans. They seemed upbeat, refreshingly straight-talking and non-delusional.

Having said that, New Yorkers are still Americans. They don't mind having a dig at other Americans themselves, but God forbid an outsider should do the same thing. I was reminded of this when I was visiting on a personal trip with my friend Grant, another flight attendant (how we loved that staff travel). Our daylight hours were filled with shopping and taking in the sights, then we'd have a power nap and put our disco shoes on. After dark, being young and gay, we'd hit the nightlife.

One night we went to a very hip gay bar called Trade, later featured in an episode of *Sex and the City*. Oh, we were glamorous. Yes, we were. I was jetlagged and easily intoxicated, and let's say Grant was full of glee or something else that rhymes with that.

We met all kinds of interesting men with fabulous jobs in fashion and media. One guy was a colourist for one of the big designers. He could really read you the book on pink versus fuchsia. Imagine: your whole job was to decide the precise shade everyone would wear in the coming season.

We were invited to an after-party in a warehouse in Chelsea, an area that gays had made especially trendy. The music was pumping, the drinks flowing and I found myself happily chatting to a doctor; he seemed quite worldly and I let my guard down.

'It's so cool here; everyone collaborates; everyone is helping everyone else reach their dream.' On and on I rattled, and then started telling him how different New Yorkers were to people in LA.

Others in the group rolled their eyes in agreement: 'Oh yes, La La Land.'

Emboldened by their apparent agreement, I said quite loudly, commanding even more attention, 'Can you believe these people never leave Los Angeles? I never met anyone who had even been to Europe. They think that they know international culture because they've been to Las Vegas and seen a replica of the Eiffel Tower!'

The buzz in the room stopped; everyone went quiet and turned to look at me. I had made a fatal mistake.

'What's so strange about that?' someone asked.

'Well, for a start, the Eiffel Tower is in Paris, not in the middle of some desert. Don't you guys agree?' I said, drunkenly digging myself in deeper with every sentence.

'We all go to Las Vegas; honey, you've gotta get on the white parties [gay parties at all kinds of glamorous destinations where everyone wears white] – we go to Las Vegas, Palm Springs, the Bahamas, Miami . . . But I don't know if they do chubbies. Have you heard of the Atkins?'

I tried to explain I'd been living in London, but in a market that snorts their dinner, my defence fell on deaf ears.

Next minute, the thing I'd heard on the West Coast popped up here on the East: 'Honey, what's our dialling code? Plus one. We don't need to go anywhere else; the world comes to us.'

The epicentre of the world had just informed me that it is the epicentre of the world. It was another lesson in ranking. Sure, by fair means or foul, Australia could potentially make it to number two but America was number one. Always.

I did agree that New York attracted the best of the best in many fields, but a telecommunications country code equates to that country's world status? Really? That would mean Britain ranked 44th, Hong Kong 852nd and America's favourite holiday destination, Mexico, only ranked 52nd – how could that possibly be?

The more I tried to explain myself, the worse things became, and in the end Grant and I picked up on the signals that the party was over for us. Out on the road, we looked at each other, bewildered.

'What just happened there?' I asked.

'It's not like we said we were living in Brooklyn,' Grant giggled.

There we were, Carrie and Samantha – or possibly Miranda and Samantha. All I knew was that Grant was definitely

Samantha and we were out on the street with a glowstick and a Chupa Chup.

Clearly, if you're an American, you can take the piss out of other Americans but that behaviour is not acceptable for a foreigner. Americans generally don't get Australian humour; they definitely don't get it in LA. New Yorkers understand our humour but even they seem to find it rude. In the end, I put it down to cultural difference, relaxed and enjoyed all the good things that New York had to offer: they were there in abundance.

I savoured my love affair with New York. Just walking around was like being in a movie. Each corner brought someone who was amazing and a new visual treat: the United Nations HQ, Statue of Liberty, Supreme Court of America and, of course, Magnolia Bakery. On my last trip there, a shining bright beacon in the NYC night sky caught my attention. It was the light of the new Freedom Tower, which replaced the Twin Towers destroyed on 9/11, something that has much significance for flight attendants. Tanya, the CSM, and I both shed a tear. It was truly spectacular.

That evening I went to the Village with Tanya. The Village is an eclectic mix of new money, celebrities and the gay community. It's a place where you can meet intelligent and cultured people from all around the world. We spent an evening at my favourite bar, Monster, and while Tanya sat upstairs conversing with guys in the cabaret room, I chatted to guys on the downstairs dance floor.

Each time I went up to check on Tanya she would introduce me to someone new: 'Owen, this is Joe; he works at the UN', 'This is Bob, he's a classical musician', 'This is Jake, he's a lawyer and about to become a judge.' One of the men, a literary agent, insistently tried to arrange for me to go on a date with him the following night.

'That's fine, darling,' I said, 'but it will be a very expensive date as I'm flying to LA tomorrow and you'll have to get a ticket to come with me.'

His face fell.

'Such is the life of a flight attendant,' I thought.

New York is a city where everything happens and every time I went there was an adventure. Maybe there is something in the country coding after all – but if there is, that number-one status only applies to New York.

THE GALLEY

A galley can be like a small prison cell or confessional, depending on what stage of flight you are at and whether someone – be that passenger or colleague – needs to offload something from their conscience.

Within your typical galley there are wet areas, which deal with all the liquids – everything from tea, coffee and milk to juice, soft drink and alcohol – and then the dry areas, where all the food is managed. Up to eight people at a time work in a galley, loading up the double-ended carts. Each galley can hold as many as eight carts, and these are public enemy number one on wheels. They are tricky to move around and when they are stacked with piping hot meals, they are heavy. Pulling, turning and jamming those carts is one of the highest contributors to injuries on the job. That and burning yourself. There's nothing worse than standing in front of 300-plus people when you have burnt your finger and then jammed your hand, all in the space of thirty seconds.

Each cart does only one service; at the end of the first meal service, the economy operator has to exchange the used carts with the unused ones, which are stored on the upper deck. The carts are transported via a lift in the middle business-class galley and then manually moved around the plane. This entails collaborating with the crew on the upper deck: we had to wait until they were ready to move the carts out of the lifts and so on.

Preparing the meals can be tricky. The mains are colour coded; for example, red for chicken and orange for beef, but if you are preparing for a service in the dark, it can be hard to tell which is which. Actually, they tend to blur into one after a while – until the do-gooder flight attendant pops up and says, 'Remember: team red for red rooster and orange for our curry beef.'

While the hot food goes out, the galley operator is preparing second carts to go out, keeping meals warmed in the ovens to be reloaded halfway through or as needed. In first and business, this is a great job but in economy, it isn't: you have to do the full service as well as galley and it's for 315 passengers, not fourteen.

After the service is cleared away, the next job is the rubbish. Each galley contains a standard rubbish bin and rubbish compactor, which needs to be changed at least twice per flight. The big bags of rubbish are squished into empty carts. More often than not, they will be shoved in a vacant toilet for landing because by the end of a long flight, there's no space anywhere else.

When landing is imminent, in business and first class, there is a mad dash to roll up and stow blankets and doonas, push linen into linen bags, gather up cutlery, glasses and chinaware and discard large wine and champers bottles. Although it's totally against regulation, a lot of stuff invariably ends up stored in the toilet for landing. This is because on descent you are on a race against the clock. The plane is coming down whether or not you can get the linen packed and the garbage perfectly compacted.

During flight though, the galley is the heart of the aircraft. Flight attendants will gather in the first-class galley, stocking up on nice cheese and coffee or grabbing some breakfast prior to landing. The mid-galley – in the business-class section of the aircraft – is the biggest kitchen. All crew pass through this and it's where information about everything and anything is exchanged. No matter what the topic – from the best exchange rates to the cheapest tailor in Shanghai – pretty much any problem can be solved in this galley. It's where everyone will be talking and gossiping. It is the hub of the aircraft.

SAN FRANCISCO

A VERY BAD DREAM

All flights to the States were monopolised by senior crew, but San Francisco, as a bastion of gay culture, attracted the Jurassic Park gays; they were about as senior as it gets, old men with receding hair, moustaches and make-up. In flying terms, that's about as far along the yellow brick road you can go with Dorothy after collecting the Tin Man, Lion and Scarecrow.

To understand how senior crew get to monopolise certain flights, I need to explain rosters. As I've mentioned, in this game it's all about seniority, and all flight attendants are ranked from number 1 to x thousand. To give you an idea, a good friend of mine has been with Qantas for thirty years and she is roughly number 500 in seniority. Anyway, there's all this negotiation between us and the operations people: crew put in their preferences for destinations, days on and days off, and the more senior they are, the more likely they are to get the destination they want on the day they want to do it and have the days at home they want too. There's nothing worse than having something lovely taken away from you, so understandably the senior crew are super-protective of their privileges. If they had bid for a trip and not got it, and saw that someone junior to them was on it, they would head straight to operations for a 'Please explain.' At my seniority level, the roster was a lucky dip. In many ways it was good because it meant I got to go all over the network.

I kept putting San Francisco as my number-one bid but was unsuccessful until early in 2008, when lo and behold I achieved four trips in a row. On my first trip, I knew I'd be pretty much on my own once we landed. The crew on my flight were all much older than me; it was unlikely I'd be crossing paths with any of them. It wasn't as if every crew member was gay, but straight crews on the San Francisco flights usually liked to head to the Northern California ski resorts for a few days.

As soon as humanly possible, off I went exploring, as usual following my *Spartacus*, the gay guide to the world. The area known as the Castro was the heart of it all. You could look down the hill and see a big sign in red saying CASTRO, so you knew you were there! And then dotted along the road were cafés and bars with the rainbow flag. Lucky me: Joan Rivers was performing at the iconic Castro Theatre; many famous people and gay luminaries had taken to the stage there over the years.

Many people compare San Francisco to Sydney because of its similarities. San Francisco had a real buzz. In the background were sounds of cable cars intersecting and people generally having a good time. It was always busy and even in the day you would see the punks, the leather guys, the lesbians, transgenders and the posers all hanging around. In any of the cafés there was an array of gay literature and newspapers and a noticeable sense of strong HIV-positive support, which I thought was fantastic compared to other places.

I worked my way around San Francisco's tourist spots and experiences, such as Alcatraz, Lombard Street, the cable cars and Fisherman's Wharf. Over those four trips I saw them all. It was a relaxed and friendly city but very touristy. You would hear accents from all over America and a good sprinkling of European and British accents too. It was funny: I'd tell locals I was Australian and they'd all say that I sounded British.

The people I met in San Francisco were quite different from those I'd met in Los Angeles. They still had the Californian thing going on but they weren't predominantly singers/dancers/actors; they appeared to be well travelled and more socially aware. They were intellectual and seemed to be across many social issues.

As you will have gathered, I loved San Francisco; but of all the times in my career when I could have been sacked, what happened to me there was the most serious.

On this particular trip the gays on the crew, although all older than me, often partied in the same Sydney scene. As we knew each other quite well, we made plans to go off to the Castro together. Before I arrived I had been chatting with a guy online who wanted to meet me with a group of others at a bar in the Castro and then we would all go off to a warehouse party. Fabulous. By this stage in my career, I was well versed in the art of certain helpful pharmaceuticals – no more jetlag issues for this flight attendant – so I arrived in San Francisco rested, had the customary drinks with the crew and then off we went. As planned, I met my online contact and I don't remember much of what happened after that.

Our crew cards got us entry into the VIP area of the warehouse party and I remember dancing with some crew and a lot of other older guys. Hours later, not only was I feeling nauseous but I'd lost everyone I had arrived with. Somehow I made it back to the hotel and found myself sitting on the toilet and vomiting into the bath; I was also hallucinating. One of the rules was not to call the Qantas doctor unless you really needed to. I was so off my head and sick, I called the doctor.

When I opened the door to let him in, I was wearing a hotel robe – nothing on underneath, mind you – and smoking; I'm normally a non-smoker. He talked to me but God knows what I said. He said he needed to give me an injection. Just the thought of looking at myself naked in the mirror is enough to scare even me, let alone what I did next.

'Okay, give it to me,' I said and dropped down on all fours, pointing my dimpled bum at him like it was some golden dart board for him to practise on. He gave me an injection and a tablet and said he would be back in the morning to check on me.

When I woke up some hours later, it was as if someone had taken over my body the night before. My memories of what had happened were gone, though I had an awful feeling that something was wrong. I wondered if I'd had a really bad dream until I saw the evidence: vomit in the bath, cigarettes strewn around and open cans of beer. Straightaway, I believed that this would be the beginning of the end for me at Qantas because I knew what had befallen other flight attendants in similar situations. What on earth was I going to say to the doctor?

I rang the other crew members and found out they were all really sick too. What had we been given? None of us had any idea. Luckily none of us had been raped, robbed or bashed. No one else had rung the Qantas doctor because they knew the rules; we all knew Qantas would not be very sympathetic.

By the time the Qantas doctor returned to check on me, I was beside myself. He was a lovely man and introduced himself as Dr B. I suspected he was gay and was hoping he'd be sympathetic. He asked me how I was feeling. I told him I felt awful; I had no idea what had happened but I'd had a terrible dream that I was smoking.

'Yes, you were smoking and drinking and acting bizarrely.'

My mortification grew as I suddenly had an image of myself flashing my bum in his face. 'How bizarrely?' I asked; I had a feeling there was more.

And there was: it turned out I had asked him to go to bed with me; I had asked him to dance; I had jumped up on a chair and danced by myself! As if all this wasn't bad enough, I had done it stark naked – by then I'd put on weight, so try to picture 100 kilos of wobbling flesh. Up dancing on a chair. The thought curdles milk.

'Don't be alarmed but I think you may have been drugged,' Dr B said, gently taking my arm.

'What do you mean?' Of course, I knew exactly what he meant.

'You have all the signs – the sweating, chewing your top lip, memory loss. It's a real problem here in San Francisco.'

I knew I hadn't taken any drugs at the party. 'I'm not quite sure what you mean here from your comments,' I said. It wouldn't be something from Bangkok as the stuff we purchased there – perfectly legally, I might add – only put you to sleep, and if we'd struck a bad batch it would have been obvious on the flight over. It turned out the doctor was hinting about the drug G, which people can slip in your drink and is extremely dangerous. I used what I would now call the Nigella Lawson defence – the goddess's day in court happened years later: 'Look at my size – do I look like a drug taker?'

Dr B then questioned me tactfully about any sexual activity I might have indulged in while I'd been out of it, trying to determine whether I was at any risk. He informed me that there were new medications available should that be the case.

Oh, my God! Although I knew I wasn't at risk, the thought of Qantas prying into my sex life was enough to make me hyperventilate.

'What are we going to do? Shall I tell Qantas?' I asked. I was wondering if *he* would tell Qantas.

I gathered from his response that he wouldn't take that action. He had dealt with cases similar to mine in the past and seemed sure about that.

Dr B asked if I'd been out with other crew members; naturally I said that I hadn't. The golden rule: if you go down, you don't take the rest with you.

He then told me he'd heard reports from hotel staff of others acting crazy and running around the hotel corridors. Dr B thought we all may have been drugged. I told him I had no knowledge of the activities of the other crew.

By then I was coming down and must have looked woebegone. Dr B then starts apologising to me on behalf of San Francisco! I couldn't believe my ears: after having a wild night out, and being drugged, I had *danced naked in front of the Qantas doctor while smoking* and I was going to get away with it.

Then came the icing on the cake. He told me I would have to passenger back to Australia in first class.

How could you not love San Francisco? I got off my face, then had to passenger home in first-class service and was paid for it.

ONE FOR THE TEAM

After those four fun trips, I kept bidding for San Francisco but rarely got it. Then my luck changed and I was given a six-day San Francisco, later in 2008. I was very excited.

We weren't long out of Sydney, and I was working in a packed economy with five crew, including senior cabin supervisor Keith (and I mean *senior* – about thirty years more service than me senior). That's six of us working to move our carts out of the galley, which is a space about half the size of a prison cell. Believe me, it does feel like a prison cell when you're in it. Anyway, I pulled the cart out, sashayed down the aisle to the last row and began serving the food: 'Would you like the chicken or the beef?' Chris, another crew member, was behind the cart offering drinks: 'Can I get you something to drink?'

Halfway along the cabin, I looked down to see a really fat woman slumped in her seat; her bottom lip was practically dragging on the floor. When I asked her if she would like lunch, she went 'Mmm.'

'Would you like the chicken or the beef?'

'Just give me a fucking meal.' She was American, from the south – maybe Dallas, but she was definitely not of the JR Ewing dynasty.

'Pardon,' I said politely. Obviously there was something wrong with her so I bent down and quietly asked if she was all right.

She grabbed my arm, glaring at me: 'Just give me a fucking meal!' She then pushed hard against the cart, rattling the contents and almost toppling it onto a mum on the other side of the aisle bouncing a baby on her lap. Quickly I stood up and steadied the cart, smiling and ignoring the appalling display of manners – as I'd been trained to do.

During training we were also made aware that we could encounter aggression in people who were not intoxicated if they are diabetic and having blood sugar problems. So, keen to assess what was wrong, I knelt down and asked the question, 'Are you a diabetic?'

The woman then became even more agitated and angry and proceeded to deliver a full-on, extremely loud and vitriolic diatribe. Passengers near and far craned their necks. I stood up and signalled to Chris and we whizzed the cart back to the galley as fast as we could push it. A crew member in the opposite aisle sensed an escalating situation and alerted Keith, who also made his way back to the galley.

As we reached the galley, I became aware that the enraged passenger had followed us. When I started to turn around to face her, she grabbed me by the tie and punched me hard in the face; she packed a real whack!

Immediately Keith intervened and, using a 'let me handle this' tone, asked what had happened. Stunned, I explained, and she said loudly, 'I am not a fucking diabetic!'

Keith then apologised profusely to her before solicitously escorting her waddling mass back to her seat. I stood there, quite shaken. My head was pounding, my face burning and my lip was swelling. I had expected Keith to give her a bollocking, not the sweetness and light treatment.

'She's psychotic – she should be reported to the captain,' I told him when he returned to the galley.

'Owen, you cannot ask people if they're diabetic,' Keith

said, dismissively, an indication of the different eras in which we'd been trained. There'd been no Occupational Health & Safety rules back in his day; people still smoked on board.

Almost as if I had a tape recorder in my head, I rewound to a pre-flight comment he'd made when he saw I was part of the crew: 'Oh, look out, we've got a spring chicken on this flight and she's a tubby!' To be frank, all that first-class cheese had been wreaking havoc with my waistline. Keith's sense of humour was exactly the sort shared only by the dinosaurs who normally operated the San Francisco flights.

Well, if Keith had issues with me, there was nothing I could do about it. For the rest of the flight, I worked on the other side of the cabin, still smiling despite having a very sore jaw. On our approach to San Francisco, Keith asked me to swap with Tracy, the flight attendant on the upper deck, as he didn't want me to 'infuriate' the fat American as she disembarked.

Infuriate her? I was the one infuriated. And what was she infuriated about? It turns out that she and her friend or lover – not sure which – had somehow been allocated separate seating and crew had not been able to arrange a change of seating.

After leaving the plane, I was approaching the baggage carousel with the captain and other crew members when I spotted the fat American woman pulling Tracy's ponytail, trying to get her attention. Although she wasn't being as aggro to Tracy as she had been to me, it was still out of the ordinary. Fortunately for Tracy, she managed to deftly shake off the perpetrator of this deed and move away. With the exception of Keith, the whole crew thought the passenger was a nutter.

'What's going on there?' the captain asked.

'Oh, that's the woman who hit Owen,' another crew member said.

'What do you mean, "That's the woman who hit Owen"?' The captain stopped dead in his tracks and turned to the crew member for an explanation.

'She's a corn-fed lunatic who couldn't sit with her lover for fifteen hours because they got separate seating or something.'

'I should have been told about this,' the captain said. Indeed he should; the captain is supposed to be notified of any acts of aggression by anyone on a flight.

Within hours there were emails flying around like bats at sunset: Keith had filed an account of the incident with Michelle, my cabin crew ground manager in Sydney. He must have had way too many gins when he wrote it – he was accusing me of provoking the woman into hitting me. I was incredulous when I heard about this. In response, the captain sent a scathing report to management.

Keith and I had a frank exchange about the matter when our paths next crossed, and I pointed out how out of balance what he had taken to be my 'provocation' and her reaction were: 'That's the rapist's defence – she provoked me so I raped her! If I'd been working in a bank and she'd punched me in the face, she'd be arrested,' I told him. I also raised the fact that it was against guidelines not to have reported it to the company or to the captain as an injury.

The dream trip had turned into a nightmare and as I rested in the hotel with a cold pack on my jaw, I felt quite stressed during what should have been a pleasant five-day layover in one of the most fun cities in the world.

Upon my return to Sydney I went to see Michelle to complain. On her desk she had laid out the two reports – the captain's one supporting me and the crew senior supervisor accusing me of provocation. Because the captain is at the top of the seniority heap, I was expecting at the very least a feigned duty of care from Michelle – possibly a medical question. Instead she told me I should be on a disciplinary charge for provoking a passenger into assaulting me.

'Michelle, I have been assaulted in my workplace and you are telling me *I* should be given a disciplinary? Didn't anyone think to ask about my welfare? Shouldn't I have got a call from compliance asking if I was okay? I could have had a broken jaw or been depressed in my hotel room knocking back gins and Valium for the past five days.'

Michelle started talking about 'procedures'.

'Darl, if you want to go through all the procedures that were broken, we'll start with the fact that the captain wasn't informed of the incident immediately—'

'Do you know what, Owen?' she interrupted, deftly changing tack because she knew that her argument had broken down. 'It's a recession – a global financial crisis – and we all just have to take one for the team sometimes. Let's just learn our lessons and leave it at that.'

One for the team?

This incident didn't turn me off San Francisco; however, I had now experienced firsthand some questionable decision-making by management. I walked away with a nasty dent in my devotion to Qantas.

DALLAS

WHERE EVERYTHING IS BIGGER
AND BETTER

Dallas became a Qantas destination in mid-2011 so I only went there once or twice. Because it was the longest direct flight Qantas did from Australia – about seventeen hours – it was another flight that attracted senior staff. On a Dallas flight, crew would earn a motza. There would often be extra time as there were frequently delays out of Dallas. It was the epi-hub of Qantas's co-chair partner American Airlines, so any weather-related delays encountered at regional airports caused knock-on effects in Dallas.

Americans make jokes about Texans and Texans make their own jokes about themselves but by the time I got to do Dallas, I knew not to criticise anything American. By then I'd been flying internationally for nearly ten years and conse-quently was a lot wiser about all manner of things, including flying.

It was funny to look back on all I'd learnt. On the US flights I'd discovered Americans use strange language to order bever-ages: 'Excuse me, can I have a half-and-half frappacino but easy on the cream.' I'd never heard of a half-and-half before this request but I discovered it was half cream, half milk and we had cream on the US flights especially for this purpose.

I'd figured out how to handle the relentless requests: 'I can have a weakened decaf latte, and do you do soy milk?'

'Darl, this is not Starbucks; here's decaf; it's in a cup; now sit down.'

Initially it was a shock when people buzzed for coffee all night long; one of the tricks if you were working in economy was to give them the decaf from business class. They'd complain that the coffee was 'horrible', which was perfect as it had served its purpose and it killed two birds with one stone – they wouldn't be asking for coffee again and they wouldn't be staying awake.

Yes, there were plenty of tricks I'd picked up in the call of duty.

It can be lonely being in a foreign city where you don't know anyone except the crew; you might not know the crew particularly well, or even like them enough to want to socialise with them, so sometimes you had to make your own fun. Luckily I could always rely on my trusty *Spartacus* to find great local clubs or bars; sometimes I'd go online and arrange to meet people at a hotel or a café.

In Dallas the crew hotel was the lavish Worthington Renaissance in Fort Worth; very nice. As towns go, Fort Worth – the cultural gateway to the American Midwest – reminded me of a carefully laid out movie-set town: everything was picture perfect and manicured. Texans, I discovered, are extremely proud of their heritage and their place in history.

Dallas has some of the longest established Mexican restaurants in America, and in my opinion, Joe T. Garcia's was the most authentic of them all. There are few places in the world where I'd go back for a meal, but I'd go back happily to Fort Worth for the food at Garcia's, and also the Tex Mex across the road from the hotel. Of course, you'd never tell a Mexican you'd been for a 'Mexican meal' if you'd been to a Tex-Mex – they'd get offended, because it's nothing like real Mexican food, only a Texan variation. This place served margaritas in glasses the size of salad bowls, and after such a long flight, it was the place that undid many a flight attendant.

Everything is bigger and better in Dallas. People drive around in cars more like removalist's vans or army tanks with tractor wheels. Men have spreading tattoos, big moustaches and enormous cowboy hats. Women look like they've stepped straight off the set of *Dynasty* or *The Jerry Springer Show*. The supermarkets are the size of a suburban block and have massive trolleys holding enough groceries for a year and car parks with spaces for 5000 cars. I began to understand why it was called 'flyover country' – meaning somewhere most airlines flew straight over – but I wasn't about to say a word.

On one Dallas trip, I made another discovery: not only is everything bigger and better there, but everything is louder, too. After spending the whole day with the crew, starting with shopping and finishing with dinner, I consulted my *Spartacus* for a local gay bar. Everybody else was planning on heading back to their rooms, resting up for the flight out, but I wanted to slip out quietly and have a bit of fun. When I told the concierge which address I wanted to go to – I was trying to be discreet – I was in for a shock.

'Oh, you know that's a *gay bar*?' the concierge asked, with certain emphasis.

'Yes, I know.'

'It's for *gays*; lots of *gays* and *lesbians*!'

'Right.'

'Are you *gay?*'

'Yes, I am,' I almost whispered. It was one of those moments where the whole place stops and goes quiet and you can feel your cheeks burning with embarrassment.

'Okay, that's cool then. I'm going to come out and give the taxi driver instructions how to get there.'

So he walked me over to the taxi and gave the Mexican driver some long-winded instructions. The driver said he knew where it was. We drove for a long time until he pulled up in front of what looked like a school demountable in the middle of an industrial estate surrounded by cars. It looked nothing like any gay bar I'd ever been to anywhere in the world.

'Where's the bar?' I said, getting a little worried.

'In there.'

I paid the fare and the taxi sped off into the dark. I walked into the building and, sure enough, it was a gay bar but, hysterically, everyone was in checked shirts, boots and cowboy hats. I wondered if I'd just walked onto another movie set.

A tall cowboy with blond curly hair greeted me. 'Well, hi there, sir. How you goin'? You look like a fine little filly,' and he gives me a friendly pat on the arse. 'Are you boot-scooting tonight?'

'Um, I don't think so.' No offence to all you line-dancers out there, but I didn't fancy myself as a Jessica Simpson–Daisy Duke type.

The dance floor, I quickly realised, was crowded with people of all ages and sizes boot-scooting. Every so often the African-Americans among the cowboys would spin off and bust out their own ghetto moves and then move back into the boot-scoot; it was absolutely mesmerising but also slightly weird.

Everyone was so friendly; talk about southern hospitality. The guy who had asked me if I was boot-scooting introduced himself as Aaron and acted as if it was his personal duty to welcome me to Texas. He pulled out a chair for me.

'Now, what can I get you to drink, sir?'

By then, I'd become almost addicted to American margaritas, so that's what I asked for. While Aaron headed for the bar, I sat back to soak up the surreal atmosphere. It was like a caricature of the American Deep South; I was half-expecting Hanna Montana or maybe even Dolly Parton to appear on a hay bale any minute, strumming a banjo. Around me was everything you see Americans themselves making fun of, but I'd learnt my lesson well – no making fun of it myself. When the extremely well-mannered Aaron rejoined me, I told him how fabulous I thought the boot-scooting was but again declined to join in.

'Do you want a game of darts?' he asked.

Darts? This was not some English pub but a gay bar in a shed on a quadrangle in the Deep South of the United States. Anyway, minutes later, there I was in my Ralph Lauren Polo shirt throwing darts; mind you, the darts were lucky to hit the wall and not some cowboy.

Aaron seemed to be pretty serious about his aim: 'You gotta hit the squirrel.'

Turns out, he was referring to the bullseye. An image of alligators and banjos and tumbleweed entered my mind but I was certainly not about to say anything.

Later he drove me back to the hotel in his extremely large pick-up truck.

'Y'know, you're really sweet,' he said. 'If I didn't have manners I might try to get up to your hotel room.'

By then I was a bit giddy and drunk and when he said something about showing me round and finished with the words, 'I'll see you tomorrow,' I replied automatically, 'Yes, see you tomorrow. Thanks for a great night.'

In the morning the phone rang and naturally I didn't answer. Next I received a message to contact guest relations. Usually, this was not a good sign; it often meant someone wanted to have a talk about some problem. I rang reception and immediately recognised the voice of the 'Are you *gay*?' concierge who'd put me in the taxi.

'You have a guest at reception. His name is Aaron.'

'Aaron who?'

I heard the concierge ask Aaron, 'What's your other name?'

'From the bar last night,' came the reply.

'You know, from the *gay* bar you went to last night,' the concierge said loudly into the phone.

'Yes, I know. Tell him I'll be there in five minutes,' I said, slamming down the phone.

Speedily, I showered and dressed and went down. Aaron, wearing his cowboy hat, was waiting patiently.

'Did you forget about our arrangement from last night?' he asked politely.

To be honest, I was so used to meeting people and making plans only for them not to turn up the next day that I had long ago stopped taking that sort of thing seriously. But here was Aaron, ready to show me Dallas. I apologised profusely and blamed jetlag. Jetlag can explain away most things, I find.

Aaron showed me all around Dallas – the baseball stadium, the Dallas mansions and he even took me to a rodeo. That night he invited me to dinner at a famous Mexican restaurant that had photos on the wall of just about every well-known actor and personality you could think of – all taken at the restaurant.

Over dinner, a few generous-sized margaritas loosened my tongue and I confessed that the reason I'd forgotten about our arrangements was that I hadn't expected him to keep them, and that flight attendants got fed so much bullshit and received so many invitations that weren't honoured that I no longer took them seriously.

'In Australia, if you invited a visitor somewhere and arranged to take them, you'd turn up,' I added.

Poor Aaron was mortified and apologetic on behalf of any Americans who might have been rude enough to stand me up. He was a gentle, well-mannered young man and I thought he was lovely. He told me I should come and live in Dallas. Suddenly I pictured myself moving to Dallas and becoming a fixture at the Kentucky Derby. Obviously too many margaritas – the whole idea of me in the Deep South was pretty ridiculous.

When Aaron dropped me back at the hotel he told me that when I came back to Dallas he would like to take me out on a 'proper date'. I told him I'd like that and we parted amicably.

Dallas had turned out to be all the things I'd expected and a lot of things I hadn't. It was the real heartland of the south and I felt like I'd had a glimpse of some genuine American history and met some down-home southerners along the way. Unfortunately, that was the last Dallas trip I ever did.

HAWAII

NOT WORTH THE LEI-OVER
(LAY-OVER – GEDDIT?)

It should come as no surprise that Hawaii was another destination that attracted senior crew, probably the most senior of any route, especially the five-day trips. There were four-day and five-day trips to Hawaii: you could fly up Sunday night, be back on Thursday or Friday and then have a four-day break. Doesn't it sound fabulous? But although Hawaii is a stunning destination with a lot of things to do, for me, it wasn't worth the hassle.

I hated the Sydney–Hawaii flight and did it as rarely as possible. Qantas used an ageing 767 on this route; it was a very old plane with cramped galleys and there were only seven crew. There was a small curtained-off seated crew rest at the back of economy, and man were the seats uncomfortable. It was a twelve-hour flight and the crew break was spent in an economy chair.

The flight left Sydney at 8 pm but flew into daylight very quickly so it was important to make sure all the blinds were down before daylight hit. It was a two-class flight, economy and business, and they didn't even have flat beds in business class. There was no back-seat in-flight entertainment, just a movie screen at the front of the cabins. This was terrible because it meant passengers were easily distracted and fidgety. And because they were also mainly holiday passengers, they were looking to start their good times in the cabin. For me and my colleagues, that flight could be a nightmare.

Qantas also did a three-day trip to Hawaii and this was not at all popular with senior crew (or junior crew, who were the ones most likely to get it). If you were on a three-day, you flew over, had one night in Honolulu and were up at 6 am for the return flight back to Sydney. It was daylight for the whole return flight, which arrived in Sydney at about 6 pm, so you were on your feet all the way. Hawaii attracts families, so there would always be lots of children on board, along with the backpackers and surfers and the all-inclusive packaged holidaymakers, and the call button never stopped. It was common to run out of everything, and by the end of the flight the cabin looked like a rubbish tip.

Okay, that is a long list of complaints. The good part was that if you had enough time in Hawaii, it was so relaxing you'd almost forget how hideous the flight was. *Almost*. Don't forget that Hawaii was the 'international' destination of choice for Americans with passports. Seriously though, apart from lazing on the beach or around the hotel pool, there were plenty of things for tourists to do. You could have a day out on the water whale-watching and seeing dolphins. Another flight attendant and I took a helicopter ride over all the islands once and it was really stunning.

Perhaps even more memorably, in Hawaii I learnt a lesson about giving opinions about individual crew members to other crew members. How did that come about? Well, being a holiday destination, Hawaiian happy hour was really 'happy hours', and because it is a state of America, the drinks were generous so it was very easy to get drunk while bonding with other flight attendants you don't know well. It was a warm summer night and I was kicking back at a bar on the beach-front with Mary-Kate, who I'd worked with on the flight over. She asked me what I thought of a flight attendant I knew called Alex. I knew him because he had a reputation as a sleaze bag and was dating Sue, a friend of mine.

In a warm, friendly gossip session, jetlag and alcohol came together and I happily imparted this information to Mary-Kate. She was egging me on, saying she had heard that he was not to be trusted and she knew someone who had been on a date with him recently. He was one of the few straight men among the crew, so naturally he was dating a lot of the girls.

Back in my room, Alex called me from Sydney.

'What have you being telling Mary-Kate? I haven't dated Sue for a long time. Mary-Kate is very insecure and this has really upset her.'

I apologised profusely and said I'd fix it up with Mary-Kate on the way back. It was a long flight back, with Mary-Kate going on about how she couldn't trust Alex, and me frantically back-tracking and explaining that I didn't really know him that well and I didn't think Sue was still seeing him. This epi-sode came back to haunt me later when I introduced myself to someone who said, 'Oh, you're the guy who dobbed Alex in.' It turned out that Alex had been dating both of them after all.

While Hawaii was a beautiful destination it was nowhere near beautiful enough to keep enticing me back. Not for a working trip. If it came down to it, I'd rather go to India than Hawaii.

LONDON

CHIN SLINGS

Early on, I realised that flying was going to be a lot of fun. 'Are we actually getting paid for this?' I would ask myself frequently. While the ordinary travelling public needed to save all year to travel in economy for a couple of weeks' holiday in a three-star resort, I was flying all over the place, staying in luxurious hotels, collecting cash allowances then returning home – for a rest – where my actual salary was waiting for me in the bank. How lucky was I?

In 2004 I came online, that is I went onto the regular roster system. Once online, you bid for your trips and could find out exactly where you were in the seniority rankings. Our rosters were worked out over two months, in which we had to work a minimum of 155 hours; hours were capped at 180–190.

When I drew three London trips on my first roster, I was super-excited. The newest recruits in long-haul were right at the bottom of the list, and London was regarded as a junior trip. But I saw a big upside. London trips were either nine or ten days and equated to about fifty hours' duty flying time, after which you had a week off. By doing three Londons during this period, I'd worked almost all my hours for the whole two months. All I needed was one other trip, such as a four-day Africa or Jakarta, and voilà, hours done! Effectively, I'd only had to go to work four times in eight or nine weeks. Granted, when I worked it was for days at a stretch, not hours, but it seemed great at the time.

In those days, Qantas had various types of London route, known collectively as the 'kangaroo route'. You would start in Sydney or Melbourne and go via Bangkok or Singapore to London. Singapore intersected with so many other Qantas flights to Europe and regionally around Asia that it was like a massive second base for the company. Hong Kong–London was added a little later.

London trips were split, with stays in Asia either side. Crew spent forty-eight hours in Singapore on their way up to London and forty-eight hours there on the way back, with either thirty-six hours or fifty-six hours in London. On the Sydney–London via Bangkok, crew spent the same length of time in Bangkok but it was a little less junior than via Singapore.

The main reason most senior crew didn't bid for London was because they were older, often had families, and that route took them away from home for too long. In the time it took to do one London, they could work three LAs, so they could touch base with home in between but still experience the fun of LA – and get six sectors of long-range overtime pay. Crew who frequently drew London were known as 'pound hounds' because of the generous £150 allowance to cover thirty-six hours. This was extremely lucrative when the pound was high against the Aussie dollar. So I became a pound hound.

There was the odd downside. Because Qantas didn't have a long-haul Melbourne base in 2004, Sydney crew who were allotted a Melbourne–London would have to work on a 747 down to Melbourne the day before. Those flights left early morning, which we all hated, and because it was an international flight, there was all the kerfuffle associated with getting through customs and quarantine just to do a short domestic flight. And even though we were put up at the old but not too shabby Hilton on the Park and received an overnight allowance of about AU\$250, we didn't get enough hours up so considered it a bit of a waste of time. Most of us preferred to fly Sydney to Singapore direct and have two days lazing around the pool. On the Melbourne to Singapore flight, we had one day in Melbourne and only one day in Singapore to laze around the pool.

I often didn't get beyond the crew hotel, especially if it was luxurious. In Melbourne, the Emirates crew were put up at the same hotel as us and we had lots of parties. This was before Emirates became a Qantas partner. The Emirates people liked to party hard. They were all nationalities – Australian, English, New Zealanders, American, European – and the poor pets would have been stuck up in Dubai with no alcohol, plenty of money and nothing to spend it on. They practically had 'Get me to a pool bar' signs on their foreheads, especially the girls, because they were strictly supervised in Dubai. Ironically, this worked to Emirates' advantage as the crew couldn't wait to go to work to get out of Dubai. Nevertheless, Emirates is one of the most sought-after employers in the world – in 2012, over 100,000 people applied for just 4000 flight attendants' jobs.

Qantas, British Airways and Emirates crew were always trying to one-up each other. In Melbourne, Qantas crew would arrive at the hotel with Moet lifted from first class, and the Emirates crew, always immaculately turned out, would check in with bottles of Dom Perignon or Krug, which was more prestigious. Picture us, trotting meekly through the hotel foyer, our crew bags clink, clinking – it's amazing what came out of those bags!

One of the more senior Qantas crew members once hosted a memorable hotel-room party. Arrayed on the bench were an entire Qantas first-class cheese platter surrounded by all sorts of other top-end goodies; as everyone entered, he sprayed them from a can of refreshing cologne mist. It was the only time I've ever seen the Emirates crew upstaged.

When I started the London trips, one of the first things I learnt was how important it was to get your work position on the flight sorted quick smart so you didn't get stuck next to someone you clashed with; there was only a limited amount of time before you departed. Flying attracts all sorts of personalities and there's no escape once you're in the air. Flight attendants smiling sweetly as they swan through the cabins attending to the demands of the flying public are often secretly gritting their teeth while they cope with major personality 'issues' behind the scenes.

Positions available on each flight are decided on seniority. Surprise, surprise: seniors usually worked in first and business, with the positions being cabin and galley. In economy, the positions were the galley, duty-free, cabin or 'assist' – all with varying degrees of annoyance factors. After the 8 am sign-on at the Qantas HQ, everyone would go into the briefing where positions were distributed from top down. Because many of the crew on those early London flights had trained together, there were often four or five of us at the same level.

A lot of double standards applied, a hangover from the

days when the older male 'stewards' traditionally worked in the galley and the carefully manicured and made-up 'hosties' worked in the cabin, on display as if they were the demure cousins of Playboy bunnies. Some of that thinking had remained; for example, you might get the straight guys pushing for the girls to work in the cabin. Mind you, on the flip side of the coin, a female flight attendant only had to appear a bit teary if she was about to be allocated the economy galley and someone would come to her rescue and find her another spot.

Working in the economy galley was the most manual position and the most hated because the entire meal service was driven by the galley operator: the loading of carts, popping the bread rolls in the oven, working out special meals and distributing the carts and meals evenly for the left- and right-hand side of the plane. After the service, the poor operator was left with all the rubbish and cleaning up the galley; suddenly the rest of the economy crew would be off doing 'something else'. Then they had to get the galley ready to do the second service all over again.

Fortunately, I usually managed to steer myself away from galley duty and mainly did cabin work. My favourite gig was looking after the first three rows in economy, a position that has since become 'premium economy'. Passengers in these seats were generally considered a bit 'special'; they may have been frequent flyers or from companies that had a contract with Qantas, so they tended to be a little more sophisticated than the average economy traveller.

During the flights, the more experienced crew would pass on tips to the junior crew. One piece of advice I picked up on the London flights was not to engage with the British passengers too much because they all think they're 'royal' – they'd take a friendly chat as an opportunity to whinge and complain about anything, often how they were supposed to be on a British Airways flight and how 'frightfully inconvenienced' they were to have to travel on Qantas; the seating was inferior and the service 'awfully common'. Weather conditions were also good fodder for a whinge: 'Can you believe we had rain on our campervan trip around New Zealand?' They also seemed to expect they should be treated at a higher level and took forever to order something quite simple: 'Excuse me, sir. I was wondering, if there was any chance, if you have a moment, when you aren't busy, if I may have a tea – no, a water – no a tea please . . . Only when it's convenient.' I mean, really!

On one of my first stopovers in Singapore I was approached by a senior flight attendant who asked me nicely what I was going to do in London. What a caring thing for the old darling to do, I thought, but what she really wanted was to know if I was taking any cigarettes to London. I wasn't, so she asked me if I could use my cigarette allowance to take some duty-free cigarettes in for her. After doing the rounds, she ended up with about six crew members carrying in the cartons of cigarettes she'd bought cheaply in Singapore (then about AU$15 a pop). She collected them from us later at the hotel then disappeared – to her waiting customers at the pub across the road! A little extra cash here and there made quite a lot of difference to some of the older crew, who had waterfront homes and investment properties to maintain all over the place. And the demand for cheap fags would surprise you. If people knew there were crew about with cigarettes, they would literally start lining up in the pub waiting to purchase them. Some crew sold duty-free liquor as well, but the real money-maker was the ciggies. It was a thriving hidden economy.

London was where I discovered that the more expensive the city, the worse the accommodation. The cabin crew stayed at a Holiday Inn in Gloucester Road; my room was so compact I had to wheel my Samsonite suitcase in sideways and I could only open it if I put it on the bed. The bathroom consisted of tiny shower, a bath, a toilet and a small mirror. If you turned around you'd bang into something. Later, I found out that this was not a problem for everyone; the pilots stayed at the more upmarket Millennium Hotel down the road, and half the female cabin crew ended up at the Millennium because they were shagging the pilots.

On my first London trip, after the customary debrief over some beers in someone else's matchbox, the junior crew followed the senior crew to the supermarket under the hotel, where we were advised to buy everything we needed for the next couple of days. On the old kangaroo route, most flights from Sydney arrived at Heathrow in the early hours of the morning and we would need food and drinks to sustain us when we woke up in the middle of the night unable to sleep and there wasn't much to watch on television. It was not wise to run up the room-service bill. I can't count the times I'd wake at 3 am and watch mindless TV, eating egg and cress sandwiches, waiting for 6 am so I could go down to breakfast and chat to the other crew.

Over time I'd realised that while the crew socialised well together in Melbourne and Singapore, many went their own way once we hit Heathrow; some didn't even leave the airport but transited through and went off to Scotland, down to Brighton or over to Europe for a couple of days. On my first trip, however, there was a group of us who decided to stay and party together.

As I'd lived in London before, I knew my way about a bit, but it was the first time in London for a few of the others so we did some touristy things. We went over to Greenwich Village and had a pub lunch, visited the Greenwich museum, Kensington Palace, checked out Big Ben and Westminster Abbey.

Later a couple of us gays went on to the massive nightclub G-A-Y at the Astoria, where well-known entertainers used to make appearances. Dannii Minogue was performing that night. It was like New Year's Eve, with hot guys dancing with shirts off, horns going and whistles blaring – all of which confirmed that, indeed, flying was fun!

Having partied hard, I arrived back at the hotel in the early hours of the morning a little the worse for wear. I decided to have a shower to freshen up and, while trying to manipulate my body in the tiny space, slipped over, fell out of the shower and smashed my jaw open on the toilet. I lay there literally stunned and it took me about half an hour to get up. There was blood everywhere – in the shower, all over the floor, toilet and towels.

On my first Los Angeles flight, I'd had drummed into me the golden rule – never ring Qantas management. Once away, the crew mantra was, 'Have no contact with management'; if you were in trouble, you contacted other crew. The first thing you did when you checked into the hotel was write crew room numbers on the back of your allowance envelope. Pulling on a terry towelling robe, I managed to crawl out of the bathroom to get the envelope and called Mandy, one of the junior girls I'd made friends with.

'Darl, I need you. I have a problem. I'm bleeding.'

'God, Owen, what have you done – it's 2 am!'

'Darl, I slipped over and hit my head. It looks like Courtney Love has been having a room party in here.'

A few minutes later, Mandy arrived with Kate, another junior crew member; they took one look at the blood all over the room and freaked out – none of us knew what to do. Mandy sat next to me on the bed.

'Shit, Owen, are you okay?'

'You look like you've broken your jaw; your face is starting to bruise,' Kate said, concerned, as she peered at me. 'Oh, my God, there is no way you can hide this. Shit. What'll we do?'

Eventually Mandy called reception and organised for a black cab to take me to the nearest hospital. Even though it was the middle of winter, in my pain and grogginess I barely managed to drag on some shorts and shoes; it was agony. Mandy and Kate helped me into the lift then walked me through the hotel lobby, clutching a blood-soaked towel to my chin, trying not to attract too much attention. Mandy came with me to the hospital and once she'd delivered me into the safety of the emergency room, she had to go back to the hotel and get some sleep for the flight later that day.

The hotel contacted the medical service that deals with Qantas crew overseas and the girls took care of contacting everyone else. In the morning, the CSM came to see me in hospital. By then I'd come to my senses but I was full of Pethidine, which was fortunate because the Irish nurse told me Qantas had wanted a drug and alcohol test but it wasn't possible because the hospital had already doped me up.

'Been out on the bikkies, darlin'?' asked the nurse, appearing to find much about the situation amusing. Presumably I wasn't the first casualty from Soho she'd tended to in

Emergency. Falling over in the shower didn't have quite the same cachet as falling over in the gutter.

Meanwhile, unbeknown to me, the situation was a drama for Qantas. I was so wet behind the ears I just thought I'd get patched up and then work normally on the flight home. All I wanted was to get out of hospital as soon as I could. For Qantas, however, it was cheaper to keep an injured or sick crew member in hospital because it saved paying the £150 meal allowance crew received while staying in the hotel. Obviously I missed the return flight but I managed to get back to the hotel to recuperate until I was fit to travel.

The Qantas doctor was cautious about giving me the all-clear to fly the long distance back to Australia with a head injury, thanks to the legal ramifications should anything have gone wrong; there was even talk about returning me as a passenger accompanied by a nurse.

After five days I was allowed to fly home – first class, but with my chin in a sling, a bag full of pills, plenty of champagne and some extremely attentive crew. A few of the more experienced flight attendants reminded me how important it was to get my story straight for Qantas management when I got home. Essentially it was a safety issue about the accommodation, and in fact I would be well advised to call the flight attendants' union and make no mention of nightclubbing outside the hotel. It was best to stick to the story that I'd had dinner with friends, gone back to the hotel and, being tired and jetlagged, had slipped over in the shower. End of story. Everyone knew how ridiculously small the bathrooms were in London.

By the time we landed in Sydney I was well prepared for the Qantas 'kangaroo court', as it was uniformly termed by crew. To my surprise Qantas handled the issue with great kindness and said I should have some time off. Still very green, it didn't occur to me that I was within my rights to make a much bigger deal of the accident, make a claim and get plastic surgery for the scarring under my chin. If you were injured at work, the company was supposed to make sure you were returned to work physically as close as possible to how you were pre-injury. It would have taken a bit of work to return me to being a Brad Pitt lookalike, but at any rate I had a few days off and that was that the end of the matter.

A PERMANENT POUND HOUND

Throughout 2004, London pretty much became my base every two weeks. It was routine to come home to Sydney, have six days off and then go back to London. I'd arrive at the hotel and, after the customary debrief, do a supermarket shop and return to my room, where I'd watch the previous night's episodes of *Eastenders* and *Coronation Street*. Afterwards, I'd sleep a bit then meet everyone at the local pub, following which we'd all go off and do our own thing.

Talk about living high on the hog. Where, previously, I had lived here with Andrew on 150 quid a week, as a flight attendant, I was on an allowance of 150 quid a day! Wandsworth, where Andrew and I had shared a flat, was a far cry from affluent Gloucester Road and, believe me, I made the most of my new lifestyle.

Flight attendants who jet all over the world, stay in five-star hotels and have money to spend, find it quite easy to act as though they are first-class passengers themselves. London

offered lots of fabulous clubs, restaurants, festivals and con-
certs and I didn't think twice about hopping into a cab to go
somewhere, even though I knew the tube would have been a
fraction of the cost of a taxi. It was actually about a year before
I took advantage of the underground right beside the hotel.

But of course, it's when you think you have something
down pat that the change you never saw coming turns up.
Qantas had been planning for years to open a London base
so it could reduce costs by cutting out the hotels and allowances and reducing the wages it had to pay for the long-range
flying. The idea was to have Australian-based crews flying up
to Asia from Australia and the London-based crews flying
down to Asia. So in 2005, Qantas announced the opening of
the London base with tremendous fanfare and ran a sort of
'Quick, quick, get in now for the London experience; don't
miss this great chance to live in London for two years – shop
at Harrods, catch the Eurostar to Paris . . .' campaign. They
needed around 200 cabin crew to open the base and tried
to interest the older crew on the higher pay scales – keen to
maximise the cost savings.

It wasn't exactly an appetising deal – with a base salary of
about £12,000 a year, the pay was about a third, and instead
of flying 180 hours per two-month roster, the hours required
were 240 over the same period. Added to that, a return flight
between London and Asia was only worth about thirty hours,
so a flight attendant would have to do about eight flights a
roster without the benefits of long-range sector pay. Another
disincentive was the high cost of living in London, even
though Qantas offered a relocation fee.

Next, Qantas tried to attract local Australian crew with
British passports, but again there were few applicants. The

ones who did respond to the job offer tended to be people already in the UK working in bars on holiday-work visas.

Then this wonderful magical London offer was extended to short-haul crew; then to casuals; then to everybody, including the lower ranks on long-haul. That yielded only about a hundred staff. People like me – young, single and still quite green – were called in to management one by one and sold the 'fantastic opportunity' of being based in London. I was told I had 'amazing potential', even though I'd used up all my sick days for an entire year on my first London flight.

I was hesitant. My resistance mainly came from having lived in London before; I knew too much about contending with harsh weather and the loneliness of being surrounded by millions of people. The money was an issue as well – I was still paying off my debts from when I'd lived there with Andrew. Then the subtlety of the corporate push diminished: it was no longer about the wonderful opportunity for me but about what I owed Qantas. The company wasn't investing millions of dollars setting up the London base only to have it fail. Didn't I know I'd been picked from thousands of people? I needed to be pulling my weight and representing the Qantas brand. Then came the final smack of the kangaroo's tail: if I didn't go to London, I might just be out of a job.

It boiled down to a choice between basing myself in London, staying permanent, keeping my seniority and working business and first class or staying in Sydney but going back to short-haul casual, with no rights and no guarantee of hours – maybe no position either. With an incentive like that, who could say no?

I know it doesn't sound at all good – effectively accepting much less pay to work much more – but I could see an upside.

For me it was the chance to work exclusively in first and business class, which I loved, and travel around Europe, this time as a single man.

Qantas finally scraped up the numbers – mostly juniors and couples; so we were all off to Old Blighty.

Once I had resigned myself to the fact that I would be living in London for two years, I needed to find somewhere to live. Eamon, an older flight attendant who was also taking up the London posting, and I decided we'd get a place together and I would do the flat-hunting. That meant arranging open inspections to coincide with my trips to London. I found us a place in Ealing, a nice suburb in West London that was full of Poles. The rent was £1200 a month and another £200 extra in council tax (£700 each) plus extras like a TV licence; so that was £700 pounds to come out of my monthly pay of £1100 pounds before I even ate or we heated the house. That's London for you. 'We'll take it,' I said; the landlord wanted a month's rent in advance.

Off I went to a bank in Knightsbridge and told the teller I would like to open an account with £10,000 and that I would also be depositing my monthly salary into it; as a sweetener, Qantas had given us £10,000 relocation money – £5000 for each year of the posting – to compensate for the lower wages and higher cost of living; after tax that dropped to about £6000. When the teller asked me if I had an address, it transpired that I couldn't open a bank account without an address and I couldn't get an address until I paid the landlord some money. I explained that I was currently staying at the Gloucester Road Hotel. He looked me up and down then proceeded to have a whispered conversation with another teller.

'Would you kindly accompany me?' he asked, indicating an office where another little bank person waited behind a desk.

'Mmm, getting the royal treatment here,' I thought and contemplated giving a queenly wave to the line of people waiting to see a teller – Brits do love a queue.

'Please don't be alarmed. We would just like to ask you a few questions,' the more senior bank person said after I was comfortably seated. 'Under what terms are you living at the hotel?'

'I work for Qantas and I'm transferring to work at the new London base.'

This news was received with blank looks. How come these people didn't know about the new base? I was so indoctrinated into viewing Qantas as the epicentre of the world, I didn't realise it meant nothing to everyone else.

'I'm sorry, we won't be able to help you,' my interrogator said. 'In fact, we're going to have to put a security alert on you with other banks.'

'What for?' I said, completely taken aback.

'We're concerned that you might be money-laundering. There have been a lot of Russians laundering money in the UK recently.'

The total ridiculousness of the thought!

'Well, darl,' I said, 'I'm not Russian, I'm Australian. And besides, if I *was* money-laundering, I wouldn't be standing in the middle of your bank trying to open a bank account, I'd be at the money exchange, changing it into roubles or pounds or whatever.' I huffed my way out.

Fortunately, I remembered I already had a UK bank account from when I'd lived in London previously, so I went down the road to the other bank and re-opened the account, with no questions asked. They were happy to take my money, dirty or clean.

UP IN LIGHTS WITH CATE

Cate Blanchett came on board a London to Sydney flight in late 2005 with her two little children and their New Zealand nanny and they all settled into the whole back row of first class. The Oscar-winning actress was returning to Australia from London. Her luggage included some massive designer gowns for an event and we made sure the gowns were laid out flat so as not to crush them, moving a lot of luggage around to accommodate them. Cate, me and Alice, the other attendant in first class, went to have a peek and they were gorgeous. After that, she put on her night cream and went to bed.

The children, Roman – then about eighteen months old – and Dashiell, aged four, slept beautifully but in the middle of the night Dashiell came out to the galley and started telling me about Superman. Next minute Cate appeared and asked if he was okay. 'He's fine,' I assured her, 'I've only lightly roasted him.' The nanny, who was an absolute hoot of a girl, did not appear, and Cate was wondering where she had got to. I peeled back the curtain and there she was, fast asleep and no doubt dreaming about the mud pools of Rotorua. While Cate tucked her son back into bed, I made her a cup of tea.

Over tea in the galley, we had a wide-ranging conversation, touching on such diverse topics as Labor politics, the union movement and Aboriginal issues. Although I chatted about it with Cate, my Aboriginality is something I rarely talk about because I don't look Indigenous. Often, if I do mention it, people assume I am trying to get some benefit from it. Cate mentioned that she had worked with the Aboriginal actor Ernie Dingo and had huge respect for him.

It also came up that we both liked intellectual men (her husband, theatre director and playwright Andrew Upton, is known for his intellect). Plucking up my courage, I told Cate I was sorry she missed out on an Oscar for her role as Elizabeth the First in the 1998 film *Elizabeth*. With a shrug, she replied that Andrew had told her that at her age then, it was better to still be heading towards the peak of her career rather than to have reached it. Then we shared a laugh at the irony of her being a Labor-voting gay supporter and Aboriginal rights activist from the country originally populated by whores and thieves and playing Queen Elizabeth the First.

I asked Cate why she did endorsements because I'd always thought she was 'above' such commercialism. She explained that actors weren't always guaranteed work, let alone well-paid work and endorsements were a good way to earn extra cash. Mind you, it was important to her that she believed in the products. Also, she said, when companies put money into making a film, there were sometimes reciprocal agreements that required an actor in the film to endorse the company's products.

Before Cate left the flight, she complimented me and Alice to our CSM, a lovely touch; I found her such a down-to-earth person. Later, I saw her wheeling her luggage through the arrivals hall and asked if she needed any help. 'Thanks, but I'm okay,' she said, with a smile, and as we parted, I told her I'd see her again one day when my own name would be up in lights. She winked.

RUNNING TO RUSSIA

Hong Kong, Singapore and Bangkok were the three destinations Qantas flew from London. Singapore was popular
because it offered the highest allowance and we stayed at
a lovely hotel. Prior to taking up the London posting I had
to learn everything about flying first and business class on
these routes. This is when I discovered how cruisey it was
to work in first class, which had very few passengers to look
after – a ratio of fourteen passengers to three cabin crew on
a 747.

On one trip, service in first was finished in about forty
minutes and they weren't even halfway through handing out
meals in economy. Another more junior flight attendant suggested we go down and help them. The senior crew member
said firmly, 'No way.'

We were able to pass our 'free' time in various ways – talking, eating, faffing about. If it wasn't for the CSM wandering
around checking on us, we could have probably had a sleep
on the floor.

It was on the London to Singapore flight that one of the
senior crew told me we had to 'run to Russia'.

'What do you mean we have to run to Russia?'

Hadn't I noticed there was always increased turbulence as
we finished flying over Russia, she asked.

Thanks to the map on the in-flight screen which tracks the
flight progress, I knew roughly how long it took to get over
Russia, but I'd always been too busy to stand around studying
the maps in any detail. I thought the flights were just bumpy
on that particular flight.

She explained that as soon as we hit Russia – a few hours into the flight, more or less when you are frantic finishing doing bar, service, collection and getting passengers' beds made or carts exchanged in economy – we had about half an hour to round everything up and put it all away and get up into the crew rest before we flew over the mountainous terrain of Afghanistan, Kazakhstan, Turkmenistan and all those other stans. For the almost two hours we flew over this mountainous region, the plane experienced turbulence.

'But half the plane is still in service.'

'Not in first class; we'll have everyone battened down then it's straight up into the crew rest.'

Escape entailed slipping past the still working crew in economy and up into the bunks; the trick was getting past the CSM in business class. At the front of economy, there were three curtained-off seats with business-class headsets and blankets for crew. If economy was still too busy, we could slip in there.

In short order, we had all the first and business people comfortably bedded down and the lights out, while in economy, lights were still blazing. Senior crew knew they had to go on their break before the turbulence hit, otherwise the seat-belt signs would go on and they'd have to sit in the crew seats for ages.

In economy, there was no way junior crew could race off early – there were too many people to look after; when the seat-belt sign came on, they would just have to sit it out, further prolonging the time needed to finish service.

On another flight, I saw for myself how close the mountains over Afghanistan were; I was servicing business and I went into the cockpit to give the captain some refreshments. I could see the mountains not far below and they seemed too close for comfort.

'Are you flying at the right altitude?' I asked him.

'Are you questioning me?' the captain asked, a trifle indignantly.

'Well yes, I am. I'm not used to seeing people standing on top of mountains,' I said, referring to the ant-like dots below.

He showed me the instruments and explained that the ground level was truly 40,000 feet below us; the height of the mountains reduced the apparent altitude.

Eamon and I moved into our London flat in February 2005; the temperature was sub-zero and it was snowing and raining black misery. Apart from the foul weather, getting to and from work with luggage was a nightmare either side of very long flights. The Terminal 4 underground railway station was being renovated, so anyone trying to get to Qantas had to take the Piccadilly Line to Hatton Cross, wait for a shuttle bus to Heathrow Terminal 4 and then make their way upstairs through the masses to sign on.

I found the atmosphere of the London base considerably different to that of Sydney, but not in a good way. While the general manager referred to us as 'family', to me his use of the word had uncomfortable religious sect overtones. It did nothing to allay my concerns when impressionable young crew eager to get some notice found they could do so by dobbing in colleagues. Before long, I called attention to myself in London by not toeing the company line.

At a crew introduction and briefing at the London office, the company's advertising agency presented their campaign for a new self-service bar in business class. In a nutshell, this was supposed to be a refreshment bar stocked with fruit and chocolates to encourage people to get up and walk around. But the image proudly displayed on the creative director's story board was of a smiling flight attendant watching a self-satisfied man in a business suit pouring himself what looked like a large Scotch. I put my hand up.

'Excuse me; that's not a bar; people can't just go and help themselves to a drink. We have a duty to provide responsible service of alcohol.' Uncomfortable looks all round.

Afterwards, another vocal crew member and I were ushered into the manager's office and told in no uncertain terms how insulted the advertising people had been. Didn't I know it was an exciting time for Qantas, with lots of new initiatives? I'd been plain rude and consequently I was being placed on notice. My response was that I'd potentially saved the company millions in lawsuits, not to mention in-air problems, and they should be thanking me. Presumably, they didn't want some flight attendant bursting their bubble; they didn't thank me but the ad never saw the light of day.

While the Australian Qantas Family was urged to feel warm and fuzzy about spreading the Qantas love to the UK, the new British recruits didn't give a toss. They were not about to treat Qantas with any great reverence; to them it was just another low-paid job on an airline, and they had many others to choose from, including their national carrier British Airways. It is interesting to note that ten years on from the base opening, very few of the original British recruits remained, whereas Qantas crew in Australia are often still working after forty years.

My colleagues and I were still babes in the wood ourselves – newly out of our first- and business-class training. We'd always been looked after by the older flight attendants and now we were the most senior at the base and mentoring the new recruits, or retraining them if they'd come from other airlines and had brought their bad habits with them. We had our own bad habits to teach them.

It was the blind leading the blind on most of those early flights, with a minority of the crew being transplanted Australians and the rest being the new British recruits. I believe the entire operation was kept together by the unflappable, Thai-based crew, who worked seamlessly with everyone and never made a fuss.

Half of the new Brits didn't know the difference between dry and sweet wine, and hardly any of them had even been to Australia. It was excruciating to hear these young Gen Y Poms, with their blonde hair and orange spray tans, their big tits rubbing against the shoulders of business-class passengers, saying in their Essex accents, 'Y'know wot I mean?'

Strangely enough, they were a favourite with the pilots, particularly the younger second officers.

There's a well-known Essex-girl joke: 'How does an Essex girl turn on the light after sex? She opens the car door.' 'Cheryl' became our generic codename for the Brit girls, and more often than not, when someone asked, 'Where's Cheryl?' the answer was, 'Try the pilots' crew rest.'

When leaving a destination, service is not limited by time but when coming into land, there's a fixed time to get everything stowed away. When we were about to land and the Gen Ys were complaining they didn't have enough time to get all the glasses, plates and cutlery stashed safely back in the service trolleys, I'd repeat something more senior crew had taught me: 'If you can't fit it in, throw it in the bin.' And those young Brits sure did.

That practice worked brilliantly for about six months until someone in catering complained they'd cut their hands on glass in the bin. A check of business-class rubbish turned up bags full of china plates, linen, glasses, knives and forks and food scraps, all mixed together. After that, we had to beware of possible spot checks and were forced to find other ways of disposing of things we didn't have time to stow – which was really anywhere except your own bin. The next best thing was the lift that took the carts from the economy-class service on the lower deck to the extra storage area on the upper deck.

PASSENGERS AT THE POINTY END

In my first months in the London base, I had a funny exchange with a passenger. On this particular flight, I was working with a friend and colleague. I was busily preparing meals in the galley when she came out of the crew rest with her hair and make-up in a mess. I told her to pop into the toilet and freshen up and began handing out the breakfast, starting at the back of first class. An elderly Joh Bjelke-Petersen looka-like – the late Joh was a colourful, conservative Queensland politician – took that opportunity to chat with me about the London basing.

'What a great opportunity for a young man. Did you bring your wife?' he asked.

My colleague appeared right at that moment with the bakery selection and commented, 'Are you blind?'

The gentleman looked perplexed. To distract him and defuse the situation, I said, 'No, I'm single.'

'You should try and tame that little firecracker,' the man quipped, indicating my friend.

We laughed and laughed.

At that stage, I was still adjusting to the culture of first and business class; that is where the weirdest, most unexpected passenger behaviour occurs. In business class, more so than in first, people seem to need to tell you of their importance. Business class is like being in Martin Place, in the heart of Sydney's CBD, on a Friday afternoon with a bunch of middle-aged suited types stroking their own egos and running their own PR campaigns. Both men and women will announce to you that they hold this or that corporate role, and that they always sit in a particular area of the aircraft. Then they will tell you they drink a certain wine and all about the company they work for and its relationship with Qantas. This is in the attempt to get upgraded and preferentially treated. Or, at least, so they think.

People who sit on the 747 upper-deck act as though they are elite as they are in a more private cabin. Often they will come on board dressed up to the nines, only to hand you every skerrick of their clothing to hang up for them and get straight into their complimentary PJs.

Celebrities and guests in first class can go a bit nuts mid-flight. Generally, in their daily lives celebs are surrounded by lots of people and receive lots of calls, emails, Tweets and posts on Facebook and the like. On board, it's only you and them, and they often try and strike up a friendship and will even confess their secrets to you. Flight attendants will almost always go along with it all; usually celebs have influence in our industry and hence it is in our best interests to make sure they feel good.

According to a story that did the rounds for a while, a crew member who was passing through first class in the dead of night went ass over tit; they hadn't seen a passenger who was crawling around on hands and knees. The passenger was Grace Jones, and she was looking for her dropped 'medication'. The flight attendant said that at first all she could see were the whites of the singer's eyes. Naturally though, she dropped to the floor and crawled around the first-class cabin looking for this pill too.

You can always tell the upgrades and the newbies from the frequent flyers. Those who travel a lot offer minimal fuss and have a routine. They know when they want to eat and sleep and watch movies they like and when they want to wake. The newbies or the upgrades want to try everything. They will guzzle through the wines and the food and they will want an extra amenity kit or extra pyjamas. They want to experience it all; they want to make a big deal about the fact they are there. They want to be seen.

Travellers will often come into the galley and want to talk. In fact, I met one of my longstanding friends that way. I had finished the service in business class and was preparing some snacks for crew. Smoked salmon and cheese toasted crackers with lemon and cracked pepper. Scott from first class came wandering through, and in his big Texan accent, he asked what they were and I offered him some. He loved them and we had a bit of conversation. Later, he asked the first-class hostess about gay bars in Melbourne and she directed him to me. This time Scott and I had a camp old chat and I told him that I would take him and his partner for a drink in Melbourne. We became great friends after our night out. Since then I have visited them in Texas and vice versa.

DIPLOMATS, WHIPS AND WAFFLES

After a couple of months living in London, it became obvious that it was not a good idea to mix my flying life with my private life. My housemate, Eamon, was even more pedantic than me, but what was worse, he didn't like partying or socialising. Obviously that wasn't going to work for me. So after six months I made the decision to move out of London. A lot of London-based crew were living in Europe; Paris and Spain were popular but Paris was almost as expensive as London, and getting to London from Spain was risky during holiday periods.

I'd been to Brussels on a visit and fallen in love with the city; it seemed like a workable compromise. My good friend Cameron from Sydney, who had been living in Ireland, decided he'd join me. I found a fantastic mansion handy to the city centre and with easy access to the airport which cost 200 Euros a month, not even half the rent of the much smaller Ealing flat. It was a three-storey Dutch provincial house in a town called Schaarbeek, which has the nickname 'the city of donkeys'. Apparently the name dates back to when Schaarbeek farmers cultivated sour cherries to make Kriek beer, and transported them by donkey to the nearby Brussels marketplace. Donkeys are still kept in the enormous Josaphat Park, in the centre of town, and sour cherry trees grow in the streets of Schaarbeek's upmarket Diamant Quarter.

Friends would come to stay with us for the house alone. The dining room had an enormous marble dining table and a fireplace. The kitchen had huge double doors opening onto

a massive loungeroom with a balcony. There were two bed-
rooms upstairs; I took the one in the attic, which although
bigger was freezing; I discovered the reason for this much
later – it wasn't insulated.

For the next eighteen months I had a beautiful life in
Brussels. I'd arrive off the London flight early in the morning
and transfer to a flight to Brussels. Those Belgians were super
sophisticated; they would serve champagne on the flight and,
on arrival in Brussels later in the morning, you'd find them
having a glass of champagne and a chocolate croissant at the
airport and in cafés.

Brussels was so close to everywhere: you could lunch and
dine in Paris, stay overnight somewhere then return home
by train the next morning. Once I even went to a party in
Cologne without so much as a driver's licence, let alone a
passport. When I wasn't flying I was having the best time,
travelling to neighbouring countries and partying. As Brussels
is where the European Union (EU) is headquartered, I ended
up dating a lot of diplomats. Plenty of guys with wives and
families back in their home countries were having affairs; if
not with women, with men.

After some dates, I did not go back for seconds. I spent
an evening with a particularly boring Austrian called Fritz;
he wasn't a diplomat but worked for the EU on Europe's
transport system, trying to develop one effective set of road
rules. We went to a top restaurant in what had been an old
library; the steaks were magnificent but the conversation was
not. While listening to Fritz's extremely detailed description
of licence plate systems, I was frantically mapping an escape.

Out of the blue, in between mouthfuls of prime beef, Fritz
announced that he had a leather fetish and liked S&M. Ah,

now this sounded a little more interesting, so I told him I also 'indulged'. He told me of his preference for submission and how he liked to be punished.

'I like S&M too and I'm quite happy to slap the shit out of you but you're not coming near me with any whips and chains,' I said.

'You Australians are not free in the mind.'

'Well, you people are the ones fond of locking up young girls in underground dungeons for sick reasons; don't talk to me about free in the mind,' I said as I got up and left, excusing myself on the grounds of being unwell.

A few weeks later, Cameron came home from a dinner party accompanied by some high-ranking EU people.

'Well, well, well, you've certainly made a name for yourself,' he told me.

'Why?'

'I was talking to some people about living here with my friend who was a Qantas flight attendant. Then this guy across the table who'd been boring everyone witless about the unification of licence plates asks, "His name isn't Owen, is it?" and when I replied that it was, he said he'd had a date with you and you'd left abruptly in the middle of dinner because you were sick and he hasn't seen you since.' Cameron knew all about the dreadful date with Fritz and it took a great deal of willpower not to burst out laughing when he realised it was him.

Summer in Belgium lasts about two days; the temperature rarely climbs over 20 degrees Celcius, but as soon as it does, everyone packs their picnic baskets, sunscreen and beach gear and travels up to the beach at Ostend. On one occasion, Cameron and I spent a day there sunning ourselves, drinking beer and eating seafood. We got chatting to some locals and after a few beers, we were fluent in Flemish. The locals were so much fun and enjoyed treating themselves to a high-calorie, high-alcohol lifestyle about as much as I did. Armed with a six-pack of beer, we got on the train back to Brussels. After about forty minutes, we realised we were no closer to Brussels but the names on the stations were looking more French: we were on the train to Luxembourg.

There was never a shortage of things to do, especially eating. Since I'd been flying I'd gained a few kilograms, and in Belgium I put on even more weight, eating lots of lovely waffles with lashings of cream and, naturally, sampling lots of beautiful Belgian chocolate.

Ben, one of my spray-tanned and trim Qantas friends, also living in Brussels, was somewhat obsessed with looking good and he extended his obsession to me; he decided I had to go on a diet. He was a keen cook and while he was making up luscious pots of food and pouring champagne he'd serve me steamed broccoli and a glass of water and try to console me with a home spray tan.

'You're on your way to looking stunning, darl,' Ben assured me. I did lose weight but I was miserable.

There was a men's club in Brussels that a crowd of us liked to frequent, but it was more the sort of club best visited alone. On the way there, I'd excuse myself and take a detour to an Irish pub, where I could fill up on delicious fish and chips. One day I was sitting there minding my own business, reading a European magazine, drinking a pint of Guinness and eating fish and chips with lashings of tomato sauce when a thump on the table woke me up. It was Ben. I'd been sprung.

'Right, Owen. I'm going to have to lock you up in that apartment,' he screamed.

I didn't know which would have been less appealing: a life with Ben or a life with someone like Fritz. At least I got food and wine with Fritz. I simply couldn't diet in Brussels.

GERMANY

A LESSON IN TAXIDERMY

I should have loved Germany. Everything I'd read about it made me think I'd love it. Although I had found some German passengers hard going, I wanted to love the country.

Frankfurt is the financial centre of Europe and has one of the world's busiest airports. After Qantas stopped flying to Paris in 2004, Frankfurt became its European hub. I started doing Frankfurt trips once I'd returned to Sydney after my two-year London posting. It was a junior trip overall but the 'language speakers' would be the most senior and it was popular because of its proximity to the rest of Europe. We had three days in Frankfurt and as soon as we hit the tarmac, half the crew took off again for somewhere else. I did like Frankfurt but after I'd been there a few times, I too would take off – perhaps head to Brussels to catch up with old friends or spend a couple of days in Paris.

Frankfurt is a modern, high-rise city with a skyline reminiscent of Manhattan – sometimes referred to as 'Mainhattan' because it's situated on the River Mainz. Crew stayed at the Hilton on the Rhine in Mainz, a village about 40 kilometres from the centre of Frankfurt. The rooms had the most uncomfortable beds – two singles pushed together with the European-style pillows. TV had rotating CNN or BBC news or local German channels and I didn't speak German. If you woke up in the middle of the night and flipped through the channels, you mostly got porn. It seemed like an incredible amount of voyeurism for such a serious culture. Somewhat eccentric in design, the hotel straddled a road and the two sides were connected by an overhead walkway. One part of the hotel always seemed to be undergoing renovations and the general feeling of the hotel was spooky – doors closing unexpectedly and windows slamming on their own; it was widely reputed to be haunted.

Room parties were popular because there wasn't much else to do to relieve the boredom in Mainz; crews were a mix from different incoming flights and some you might know and others it was an opportunity to bond with.

Frankfurt is also one of the most expensive cities in the world but we got a really good allowance to offset this. German food proved to be problematic. Its staples are potatoes, cabbage and pork. Unfortunately, I don't eat pork and everywhere I went I was offered huge pork schnitzels. But there was a wonderful selection of cheeses and other deli goodies. There was a good Mexican restaurant across from the crew hotel and a Thai restaurant up the road.

In most cities Qantas flew to, crew wouldn't get up for breakfast but breakfast time in Frankfurt would coincide with early dinner-time back home, so crew would be in the restaurant for the incredible buffet of European-style foods. The restaurant looked out over the Rhine and we could happily stay there for hours, chatting about crew and company politics.

A lot of the European language speakers chose the Frankfurt trip so they could visit their families in the various countries, so for crew interaction it was a hit-and-miss destination. However, 'as soon as I arrived I'd know if there was a room party at the hotel – people smoking out of the French-style windows of the hotel or a message at the desk; crew already in the hotel would usually know who was coming off the next flight.

In Frankfurt, I had a brief affair with a man called Horst. I met him in a sauna. Bear in mind that saunas in Europe are different to saunas in Australia, where an operator would need to have separate licences to have sex and sell alcohol on the same premises. European saunas tend not to be frowned upon like they might be in Australia. They are usually situated in well-appointed premises in the nicer parts of town. While there are big sauna areas and smaller private rooms, the concentration was not on sex alone; people could sit around on comfortable lounges, chatting, having a few drinks or a meal. There was a mix of clientele – ages and occupations – and for gay men it was safe way to meet other men and get up-to-date information on social events.

I met Horst at the bar. Between his limited English and my limited German, we managed to communicate and he told me he was a delivery man. Later, he drove me back to the hotel in his delivery van. After that, we met at a café in Mainz and a restaurant in the nearby upmarket neighbouring town of Wiesbaden. The next time he asked me back to his place for dinner.

I got a weird feeling as soon as I stepped inside Horst's apartment; it was dark and airless and smelt of kitty-litter even though he didn't have a cat. It had a strong smell of damp, which is common in European homes because of the weather and closed windows. But then I discovered Horst's hobby was taxidermy, which made me very nervous about the delivery van. His place was full of stuffed owls and small stuffed furry animals: Horst was a nut case!

Compounding my unease were gloomy portraits on his walls – of people with eyes that followed you around the room. Oh, my God, *this is it*, I thought; was I next for the stuffing? Would I become one of those flight attendants who disappear in foreign ports?

Dinner was quite unnerving. He told me he was into hunting and I cast my eyes about for guns and trapdoors in the floor. He told me he hadn't had a boyfriend for a long time.

And your next one won't be me.

Thoughts raced through my head, like the fact that I had never had the best of relations with German passengers; they were so serious and humourless. Now Horst's creepiness was not helping. I was going off Germans!

Soon after being frightened half to death by my encounter with the taxidermist, there was an incident in Berlin that turned me right off Germany for good. Everyone said I'd love Berlin. What an exciting city! I stayed in Nordenplaz, a leafy and wealthy gay area of Berlin. I didn't experience any pulse-quickening immediately but I found a bar which was full of hot guys and great music and, feeling mellow, I thought perhaps I could love this city after all.

Next minute the owner rushed out from behind the bar and pulled down the roller doors in front of the hotel and the blinds on the windows. I had no idea what was going on but I had a crazy idea that maybe we were all going to be part of a porno movie. Turned out the owner was getting prepared for approaching trouble outside; it was the day of street demonstrations against the unification of Europe which rapidly became riots.

The scene became surreal; while the riots raged outside I was stuck inside with a bunch of Berliners for hours and hours; the more beer they drank the more indignant they became about the unfairness of the taxes the West Germans had to pay to rebuild East Germany. They moaned that the East Germans had never had it so good. I was arguing for the other side.

'But they were locked behind a wall for forty years, for God's sake.' I could not understand how these privileged men could think that way after all the East Germans had suffered. To me, Germans had weird views; I couldn't get their humour and they couldn't get mine.

I did want to love Germany but I just couldn't.

THE GAY GAME

In a workforce where every other male flight attendant was gay, it was inevitable that gay crew would hook up. And then after they did, the rest of them would bitch about it. The 'gay mafia', as it was referred to, infiltrated all areas of the Qantas cabin crew department. And because they had the friendship and support of all the pretty female flight attendants the rest of the company wanted to shag, they were in quite a powerful position.

However, when it came to hooking up, the general rule was: don't shit where you eat! Literally. Unless you want your performance, proportions and the details of any individual behaviours or fetishes spread across the 'kangaroo news', then it was always wise to follow this rule. Just as the girls graded the pilots, the gays graded the gays. In a shallow, self-indulgent, body-conscious judiciary, more often than not it was the embarrassing stories we heard.

I was with a good friend Jason, another flight attendant, when his phone was running hot with that annoying smart-phone sound that lets you know you have mail. The pair of us were scrutinising the messages of a guy who seemed nice and said he worked in 'hospitality'. Messages were whizzing back and forth, and this correspondent was telling Jason what he did and didn't like in bed and that he was 'looking for love but happy for NSA fun'. (In gay terms, 'NSA fun' pretty much means let's just fuck until the fantasy and the profile match up.) He sent Jason some rather revealing photos and certain potentially embarrassing personal information.

I left Jason to get on with hooking up with this guy. He called me a short while later.

'Don't tell me it wasn't George Clooney when you opened the door?' I teased.

Jason, normally extremely level-headed and undramatic, said dramatically, 'It was Kurt.'

'Kurt who?'

'You know, Kurt from A380 and good friends with Rowena.' Rowena is another flight attendant and a close friend of mine.

'Oh, my God! What did you do?'

'I invited him in and we had a glass of wine. Then I said I had an early flight in the morning.'

Mmm, there I was in possession of all this intimate knowl-edge of a colleague simply by association. I rang Rowena, who told me Kurt had called her all embarrassed because he knew I had been with Jason earlier and was worried that I'd viewed the photos.

'Honey, trust me, I know all the goss – who pitches and who catches and everything else in between.'

Kurt was mortified, and although we have never officially discussed it, every time I see him I give him a knowing raised eyebrow. Without fail, he goes red.

They say there are six degrees of separation between people; in the flying world, especially the gay flying world, I reckon it's more like two degrees.

The internet comes in very handy for gay flight attendants who want to hook up but not with crew. There are plenty of international gay dating sites; I could go onto one and click on the country I was visiting, pick the type of guy I wanted, and up would come all these profiles. Click, click, click and send a message off and I'd have someone to hook up with once there.

Gaydar was one of the original sites and today there's also Grindr, which is an iPhone app. Gone are the days when you sent someone a coy message saying they looked nice and you would be in LA on such and such date and wouldn't it be great to meet. Now you can press the app and get an instant message telling you how far away an available date happens to be – one metre or one mile. Hilariously, with my own eyes I've observed two guys in a hotel foyer bar, both flight attendants, busy on their iPhones, then suddenly waking up to the fact that they are talking to each other.

I'd been chatting on the internet, with messages rapidly shuttling back and forth, for about a week with one guy in Santiago; his written English was broken but I could understand enough of it. His photos looked amazing and we arranged to meet. With expectations high, I had the whole weekend all planned out. After I met him, I realised he couldn't speak any English. He held his phone up and I saw he had written to me in English. I wondered if he was deaf, so I wrote, 'Are you deaf?' He took the phone away and came back with the message 'No'. He was putting what I wrote in English into Google Translate to get it in Spanish; he would then translate his reply from Spanish back into English. That relationship was obviously not going anywhere. It was just one of the problems with internet dating.

Most gay flight attendants are not looking for long-term relationships in overseas countries, they simply want to hook up with someone. Sometimes you don't get what you expect. Once I met a guy in Africa who advertised himself as Middle Eastern Afrikaans; his photos looked promising and he claimed he was an officer in the army. To be honest, I didn't know what to expect but I assumed he'd be at least six foot (183 cm) tall. When I opened the hotel door and looked down, I thought he'd sent someone else; the guy was a 5'2' (157 cm) weedy Pakistani. I asked him when he'd had the photos taken and how he'd figured out he was Middle Eastern. Apparently the photos were taken when he was in the army twenty years earlier in the Middle East. He was certainly no Arabian general and there was no Arabian night!

HONG KONG

RICH ME, POOR ME

By the time I was flying regularly to Hong Kong, I'd wised up to why the older crew always looked so well-rested while I'd been walking around like a speared African animal: they were all dropping nice little 'helpers' during the crew rest and at our destinations to make them sleep. It is particularly hard to sleep on demand; when you were working, your adrenaline would be running; the endless supply of coffee in the galley, which we all poured down our throats, heightened the effect. Naturally, that made it hard to nod off when you needed to. Once I was in on the secret, though, I didn't look back.

In Hong Kong we used to stay at the fabulous Langham Hotel in Mong Kok, which was situated near the Ladies Market, a mecca for bargain shoppers. The area behind the markets was full of pharmacies where you could get sleeping tablets and all sorts of other pills, with no questions asked. The transactions were interesting, to put it mildly: I had a limited idea of what the pharmaceutical names meant; I'd tell the pharmacist what I wanted and they'd bring me back something labelled totally in Chinese script. It always seemed to do the trick.

At the markets, the locals got to know me and would call

out, 'Qantas, Qantas, how are you?' or pat my expanding waistline and say, 'Very rich man.' This was part of the artful game of bartering, which I loved.

My housemate, Cameron, came to Hong Kong with me once; he wanted to shop so I took him to the markets. Bartering was alien to him and he was nervous about trying it. Not for the first time, I was surprised about something that seemed so straightforward to me being well out of the realm of other people's experiences; as a flight attendant, perhaps you took aspects of travelling for granted after a while. Anyway, one of the traders I knew said he could show Cameron and me the 'triple-A' quality stuff; he promised us it was streets ahead of the cheap knock-offs sold to other tourists on the street. Next minute, Cameron and I are following him down a side alley, through a wire gate, up several flights of stairs, along a corridor, and then we're being ushered into a room full of the triple-A goods. Arrayed before us was practically every designer label in existence. It was more expensive because it was the real deal supplied by the factories that made the originals. Apparently, the factories double the quantity of material needed for an order and then sell the surplus finished goods on the side; they're distributed to special outlets around Asia and sold well below normal retail price.

I was in heaven; Cameron, being in unfamiliar territory, was not. Totally ill at ease, he kept edging towards the door while I haggled loudly with a Chinese woman. I kept telling him not to worry – it was all part of the game. It was hot and the barter process even hotter, but after about twenty minutes we got what we wanted and headed back to the hotel, much to Cameron's relief. After this experience, he became more confident about bartering.

Hong Kong is a heady mix of East and West. It has a stunning harbour, dotted with junk boats and surrounded by towering high-rises – a mix of modern architecture and traditional old Chinese buildings. The disparity between rich and poor is stark; the average Chinese worker will be housed in a couple of tiny rooms while the Westerners live in luxurious towers designed for expatriates, and Chinese who've made it big in the new economy also live like colonial kings.

When I'd worked in Hong Kong for Mr Woo in 1996, I'd struck up a friendship with a senior banker, a 45-year-old Englishman called Toby Thomas. I looked him up when I started to fly the London–Hong Kong route and we started a relationship. From then on, I flew to Hong Kong as often as I could.

Many a time I did rosters with back-to-back flying to Hong Kong so I could be with Toby. Such is the price of love because the flying was horrendous. Hong Kong wasn't as popular as Singapore and Bangkok. For starters, it was day-flying both ways; the passengers were usually awake for the whole trip, giving them more time to ding for attention and more things to complain about. With a full lunch service and bar, we never had a chance to sit down; we were virtually walking all the way. And did I mention that the sign-on time for the return was 4 am?

Toby worked in both London and Hong Kong and he and I enjoyed a lovely relationship. He had a palatial home at The Peak, the best part of Hong Kong, and he lived an openly gay life. We spent a lot of time in the popular ex-pat area called Lan Kwai Fong – it wasn't a gay area but there were men at various bars who to me were obviously gay but pretending to be straight. There were plenty of gay bars in Hong Kong. At one called Propaganda, if you flashed your crew ID, bingo, you found yourself at the front of the queue and entry was free.

Being gay wasn't a problem for the ex-pats but it was for the local Chinese. That was the tricky thing about Hong Kong: if you were Western and had money, you could buy anyone's silence – people would look away; greasing palms was much more prominent than you would think. Toby told me that his 'welcome to the bank' indoctrination consisted of being taken by one of the managers to a Chinese strip club where the girls offered him a lap dance. Having women on your lap (or anywhere in your vicinity) and being able to splash your money around signalled that you were a powerful, strong heterosexual man.

There was no hiding our relationship; we often went out with other crew members while we were in Hong Kong. We frequented the races and the Hong Kong Yacht Club; we would often take a shopping trip to Macau. I sometimes daydreamed that I could get used to life as a banker's 'wife'.

We'd started our relationship while I was still living in London, and when I moved to Brussels, Toby would visit me there when he came over to London. He asked me to give him my roster so that we could align our times together in Hong Kong and London. I thought this was a sweet and thoughtful gesture. The old Qantas computer system allowed crew to log in from anywhere in the world and check their roster; I uploaded the software and gave Toby my log-in access code so he would always be able to plan ahead for our encounters.

Every once in a while, you'd be given a call-out day; you'd be on standby in case someone fell sick. It so happened that I was staying in London on one of these days when I found myself called out for a Hong Kong flight. 'Ooh, goodie,' I said to myself, thinking how I could surprise Toby. The previous day I'd seen him and I knew he was heading back home – on that flight; he had no idea about this turn of events. Toby always flew first class and I knew I would be working the first-class cabin so I was quite excited; I thought it would be a nice surprise when I greeted him off the aerobridge.

As the first-class passengers started to board, I caught sight of Toby coming down the aerobridge and my heart went flutter. He arrived at the door of the aircraft immediately behind a smartly turned out woman. When he realised it was me, he registered shock and went red in the face. Myra, the other flight attendant in first, said, 'Welcome, Mrs Thomas,' to the well-dressed woman as she stepped on board, but it still didn't click with me. Toby followed her in and stuck his hand straight out to shake mine before I could say a single word.

'Hi, Owen.'

'Hi, Toby. How are you?' Momentarily, I was slightly off-balance; something wasn't right. What was it?

He then said quickly, 'Owen, I'd like you to meet my wife.'

'Nice to meet you, Mrs Thomas,' I said, without missing a beat.

'Owen. How lovely to meet you; I've heard so much about you from Toby. He says you're often on this flight and you look after him so well . . .' Mrs Thomas then proceeded to prattle on about how she was looking forward to going back to Hong Kong and how she hadn't visited for ages. On and on she went, completely oblivious to the expression of strain on her husband's face and on mine. The pair of them were still standing at the entrance to the plane. Toby was looking shell-shocked. I only heard white noise.

'Let me show you to your seat,' I said, finally finding my voice. I was stuck; there was nothing I could do – I *had* to serve them.

Still she made small talk: 'Oh, you must come and have dinner with us in Hong Kong; we have a beautiful house at The Peak.'

Darling, I've been handcuffed to your bed – I know all about your beautiful house.

I looked across her to Toby and he looked back at me. I was a metre away and it took supreme effort on my part not to reach over and smack him.

Toby's wife was lovely; she'd done nothing wrong. Later, she came out to the first-class galley and nattered away about all kinds of things, including what a special celebration they were going to have for their wedding anniversary, how she was planning to redecorate the Hong Kong house – she had this gay friend who was a fabulous decorator, she informed me. I nodded and smiled and kept her talking. All the while, thousands of thoughts, memories and questions were running through my mind, such as how the hell Toby had managed to keep the apartment free of anything feminine – there was not one thing in the wardrobe or bathroom to suggest the presence of a woman. Nothing. Did he have a secret cupboard? Eventually, to my relief, she returned to her seat and after a while she fell asleep. Grabbing the opportunity, Toby come up to the galley to try to talk to me.

'Please, let me explain.'

'Toby, I suggest you take your seat, otherwise you're going to lose your life and I'm going to lose my job.'

Looking inconsolable, he went back to his seat and I never spoke to him again.

By halfway through the flight, the entire crew knew all about what was going on and were gossiping about my love life from one end of the plane to the other. Crew were sneaking up from business and economy to have a peek at Toby and wife. The CSM said it would be too weird to move me so I had to stick it out. It was the longest, most horrendous flight I've ever done. Unfortunately, this time the subject of the galley gossip was me!

PILOTS AND FLIGHT ATTENDANTS

The symbiotic relationship between flight attendants and pilots is as old as doctors and nurses. Female flight attendants wanting to be a pilot's wife can be found on flights all over the world every day – on every airline and from all cultures.

The majority of Qantas pilots – or tech crew – are men; they're not always attractive looking but the lure of the uniform is. At school, they would have been the smart maths and science dorks, and they come out of aviation school with all the other dorks in their snappy uniforms, shoulder stripes and spray tans and they're instant chick magnets, flying around with beauty queens. They cannot believe their luck.

Flight attendants who specifically target pilots are known as TCMs – 'tech crew molls' – and they normally try to work on the upper deck, which services (ahem) the cockpit. They were easy to spot and blatantly predatory; they walked with an air of purpose about what they wanted: becoming a pilot's wife. I really noticed it when I was working out of London with the new crew of typical young Brit girls, who were flying abroad to party – only this time with young second officers.

They were so keen to work upstairs I could practically name my price to swap positions.

'I'll give you 20 quid if you'll let me work upstairs,' they'd plead.

'Okay.' That would help with the bar bill.

There are four pilots on a 747. A crew rest in the cockpit is for the use of the captain and the first officer. There is an aft flight crew rest for the (usually very young) second officers, located conveniently near the upper-deck galley, where the two flight attendants work. Some of these girls found their way into the crew rest with the second officers; if they weren't there when you were looking for them, they'd be in the cockpit with the pilots.

There was one notorious TCM called Kasey, who was believed to have slept with almost every pilot known to man – and not just the Qantas ones. And she would spread stories about their performance. One pilot's dick, she disclosed, was so small that she took one look, got dressed and said she was going home; it was hard not to laugh every time we saw this poor pilot afterwards because we all knew he had a little stump. On one flight, an argument broke out in the cockpit when one pilot said he was dating Kasey and another pilot said he was dating her too; then the captain piped up and said he'd been out with her in Hong Kong the week before. Three straight men – all married – all shagging the same flight attendant.

TCMs were also numbers driven – the wider they cast their net, the greater the chance of a catch; the looser the net, the bigger likelihood of getting a prize catch – a captain. Although generally less physically desirable, captains had command, earnt the big bucks and their partners had access to first-class staff travel. The down side is that they were usually divorced more than once and therefore had to pay out a lot of exes and probably had ongoing child support commitments.

When the new London base opened and a whole lot of junior crew joined the airline, this was very exciting for the pilots; there was a lot of talk about 'fresh calamari'. Apparently this expression referred to a particular part of a woman's anatomy. While the young girls might have been mesmerised by the pilots, the pilots weren't always mesmerised by the young girls and would often deride them as being 'as dumb as dog shit'. Talk about high-level misogyny! (That's the advantage of being gay by the way; you get the inside on what both sides are saying.)

Penny, one of the young Pommie flight attendants, a real Essex girl if ever there was one, with big tits that she used to thrust into people's faces, was quite brazen about slipping into the crew rest with pilots. Once, Sylvia, a very senior flight attendant with an extremely regal manner came up the stairs looking for Penny.

'Owen. Have you seen Penny?'

'No, Sylvia,' I lied. I knew Penny was in the crew rest because I could hear the thumping and giggling. Sylvia went back down the stairs. I knocked quietly on the door. 'Penny, Sylvia's looking for you.' A few moments later she emerged nonchalantly and started straightening her hair.

'Ah, there you are, Penny.' Sylvia was back. 'I've been looking for you.'

'I've been looking for you too, Sylvia.'

I said Penny was brazen.

'Really? Well I hope you haven't been walking around

looking for me with your skirt up around your thighs; I'd pull it down if I was you.'

Pilots would often get the gay guys to play intermediary in setting up dates with female flight attendants. A pilot would get a glint in his eye even before he boarded the plane if he saw a flight attendant who took his fancy at the crew briefing. So we'd be flying along and next minute I'd get a call from the cockpit.

'Hi, Owen, this is James, the second officer. How are you?'

'Good thank you, James.'

'You know that young blonde . . .'

'Well, that's half the crew. Can you be more specific?'

'You know, blue eyes. Cute.'

'Oh yes, that's Justine. She's doing duty free.'

Next minute the phone down the back is ringing and James is telling them he's thinking of getting some duty free; can they send someone up. Justine comes up with the duty-free brochure.

'One of the pilots wants duty free,' she says coyly to me.

'James; duty free is coming in,' I tell him on the interphone and let her into the cockpit. In she'd go, and he'd give her the chat about taking her to the best bar in Singapore, which would probably be the one the crew hung out in anyway.

Occasionally, however, the conversation would go something like this:

'Owen,' the second officer would say, falling into step with me as we trundled our crew bags through some foreign airport, 'are you going out tonight?'

'Yeah, probably.'

'Are you bringing Justine?'

'Yeah, she's probably coming.'

'Can you find out if she's coming?'

I'd move to catch up with Justine and call out, 'Justine, are you going to come out for a few drinks?' Then, lowering my voice conspiratorially, I'd add, 'That pilot is interested in you.'

'Really? What did he say?'

'He just wanted to know if you're going out for drinks. Come on, sweetie, we'll go out and have a few drinks and make him pay for everything.'

'Oh, I couldn't do that though . . .'

'Yes, you can. I'll show you the ropes.' And that's how it all starts.

At most destinations there was a bar the crew frequented; often it was in the crew hotel. On the more traditional routes, such as Singapore and London, tech crew and cabin crew stayed at separate hotels that were close to each other but there always a well-worn path between them. A plus B equals C.

When they first start flying the girls all want to marry pilots and actively hunt for them; they tell you they're dating a pilot but he's 'one of the good ones'. After ten years and they've married and divorced one, they're no longer interested because they know what goes on and that their pilot husbands will be shagging the next crop of young flight attendants. Pilots are only married when they're home.

Crew tended to get together on the longer flights, such as London, Frankfurt, the regionals that intersected Singapore and Hong Kong and, believe it or not, Mumbai (a place that makes me more inclined to think of E-coli and dysentery rather than bar-hopping and shagging) because there was more time to get to know each other and more opportunities to go out together. A friend of mine met a pilot on a Sydney to London flight; by the end of the stopover in Singapore they were insep-arable, holding hands, spending every moment together – a real couple. They go off to London and it's all love and light; on the stopover in Singapore on the way back, she's got the tissues out and he's putting his wedding ring back on.

Another friend was having an affair with a married pilot and he was always trying to keep her at a distance in overseas ports so as not to 'blow his cover'. He was treating her quite badly and she finally asked him why she was getting mixed messages from him. 'There are no mixed messages; I'm hap-pily married with three kids.' The message doesn't get much blunter than that.

Often when flight attendants didn't want to fly anymore, because, say, they wanted to spend more time with their family, they would get jobs on the ground, sometimes as managers. It wasn't uncommon for those still flying to end up with one of the grounded crew as their manager; if it was known that the manager had had an affair with someone's pilot husband it got very delicate. Or less delicate, more, 'That fucking bitch had an affair with my husband and broke up my marriage – she's not going to be my manager.' Flight attendants married to pilots finding out they're having affairs with other flight attendants – well, that's a recipe for a plane crash.

When you are a flight attendant, the challenges of main-taining normal relationships at home are tough enough. For those very young female flight attendants, the allure of a love affair with a pilot can be so strong, it can turn them into masochists. It may have been a romantic notion – five-star hotels, cash allowances, straight men in command and exotic foreign ports – but very rarely was there a Julia Roberts *Pretty Woman* ending.

HOW TO DRIVE A FLIGHT ATTENDANT INSANE

The acronym BOB, shorthand for best on board, should really stand for batty on board. The vast majority of people, especially those who don't travel frequently, adopt the most bizarre behaviour and ask the stupidest questions. The more insane the travelling public is, the more insane flight attendants go. While still smiling, albeit more tightly.

One thing drives flight attendants insane above all else: it's when passengers are still boarding the plane and someone barges back against the flow and calls for your attention:

'Excuse me, excuse me, I need to speak to you.'

Thinking something's wrong, I'd ask the anxious passenger what they wanted.

'I'm going to Geneva and I only have an hour's transit time at Heathrow. Am I going to make it? Because I'm just texting my husband before we leave.' She's holding up the mobile phone to my face, in case I don't quite get it. Meanwhile, I'm desperate for her to switch it off. This person wants me to predict weather conditions on arrival at Heathrow and we haven't even left the tarmac in Sydney.

'Don't worry, they book flights tightly together but your luggage will go on automatically; they will wait within reason, and if you miss the flight, there are flights going to Geneva every hour.'

'No, no. I'm on the 7.05 flight.'

'Don't worry; if you're not on the 7.05, you'll be on the 8.05. It will all be sorted out at Heathrow.'

'No, I'm on the 7.05.' An indignant tone will creep in about now. 'Where will my luggage go?'

'Your luggage will arrive before you. Don't worry; it will all sort itself out. Please take your seat.'

I mean *really*? All things being equal, I have a rough idea how long it will take to get to Heathrow. Pilots will do everything possible to hit the on-time destination arrival time – they'll speed up the plane, fly above the clouds, fly beneath the clouds. *And guess what, madam – all that effort is not for the sake of your 7.05 connection to Geneva but to make sure the flight is as cost-effective as possible for the company.*

Questions about arrival time typically go on and on throughout the flight.

Medical emergencies are another instance where people do odd things; crew handle most medical problems quietly among themselves but when they can't, they advise the captain and will ring around the other galleys and ask the other crew if they have a doctor in their zone as it will be on their list of passengers.

I was working in premium economy on a London flight once and the CSM made an announcement: 'We need a doctor immediately.' This signified something pretty bad had happened – a fall, a fit or a heart attack. A couple of bells dinged; one was a guy sitting in the exit row in economy and I went down and asked him if he was a doctor.

'Yes, I am. I'm a doctor of ancient history. Do you know I'm actually on my way to Cairo for the Cleopatra exhibition?'

'Sir, congratulations on getting your PhD but I actually need a medical doctor.'

People on planes feel compelled to tell you their life stories, as if by doing so you will protect them from some terrible event.

'I was on a flight once that got hit by lightning.' *And you're still here to tell the story?*

Or their every movement.

'I'm just letting you know that there's a row free up there and I'm going to move into it.'

'Well, it's probably best that you move into it now, as I'm sure that other people have their eye on it.'

Tantrums on board are one of the biggest problems for crew and they even happen up the pointy end of the aircraft – in the supposedly civil business and first class. In business class, the seats are two abreast and suddenly there's a war over who sits where.

'I'm in an aisle seat and I want a window.'

'Okay, sir. Did you request a window at check-in or did you do pre-boarding on the internet?' Bear in mind this man had probably been in the airport for three hours prior to boarding and most likely lounging in the Qantas Club; plenty of time to check seating while waiting.

'No. I expect to have a window; I *always* have a window.'

I would still be seating people and trying to work out if someone was prepared to move to accommodate the window Nazi. What a pointless argument – all the seats turn into beds anyway and no one looks out the window when they're asleep. But it wouldn't stop there; male passengers battling over entitlement to a seat would then try to up the ante in an airline class war in which they showed off their peacock feathers to each other.

'I'm a chairman's lounge.'

'Well, I'm a chairman's lounge platinum.'

'Well, I'm a chairman's lounge platinum and my friend is a OneWorld Emerald.'

'Well, I'm also in the Star Alliance.'

'Well, I know George Bush.'

Well, I don't give a shit who you are or who you know; just sit down and I'll find you a window if I can, not that we have a huge selection to choose from. Anyway, if you're such a frequent flyer, wouldn't you know how the allocating of seats works?

All this is happening while the plane is boarding and the crew is doing its best to make sure we have an on-time departure. So having someone sitting with their arms folded high across a puffed out chest, announcing, 'I'm going to be complaining about this,' you know you have the longest fifteen hours ahead of you.

Sometimes it seems that the wealthier the passenger, the more bizarre the behaviour. Once when I was working in first on a London flight and I thought everyone was asleep, I heard a rustling and shuffling. It was impossible to see where it was coming from. I walked through the cabin with my torch and literally tripped over this woman on the floor rummaging in the first-class amenities storage cupboard. Immediately I recognised her: the tiny woman in seat in 3F with bouffant dyed blonde hair who looked like an older version of Bette Midler (sorry, Bette) and clutched an enormous designer handbag that appeared to contain a huge amount of stuff. I apologised for tripping over her and she whispered to me, 'I just wanted to get a few extra amenities to give out as gifts when I get home.'

You're paying $20,000 for this flight; you can have them all if you want – just ask me.

It was amazing how many silver salt and pepper shakers disappeared from first class; I guess it was simply the upmarket equivalent of souveniring pens.

Another irritant that you often strike in the wealthiest section of the plane is the middle-aged men who are constantly pressing their buzzers and asking for another landing card. They forever make mistakes. Why? Could it be that they're used to having other people fill out forms for them? Or perhaps it's a pretext for checking out the female crew? Or maybe they're plain stupid?

Alcohol is another thing that sends people batty on planes and teamwork was used to handle difficult situations. If someone was going on holiday and wanted to unwind with a couple of cocktails, I liked to have a bit of fun with them too, making them drinks, chatting and having a joke. Most passengers enjoyed this but others could take it to another level.

A very nice man became rather drunk on a Frankfurt flight and I was standing in the galley when I felt a pinch on the bum. I turned around to see this man standing in the toilet with the door open, with his crotch fully exposed and his hand on his dick, inviting me to join him in the economy toilet.

'Do you realise I'm at work?' I asked, with as much sang-froid as I could muster.

The CSM was sitting at his work station behind the stairs up to business class and out of view of the man in the toilet with his hand on his dick, but the CSM was staring at me wondering what I was staring at. Of course there was no point in reporting it to management; if I complained, the passenger was just as likely to I say got him so intoxicated he couldn't help getting amorous.

SINGAPORE

THE GENIUS OF CARRIE BRADSHAW

After I broke up with Toby, going to Hong Kong lost its appeal and Singapore became more of a staple in my life. All the flights up to London used to stop there before the London base opened, and even after it had opened, two out of the four weekly flights out of London passed through Singapore. Qantas flights to Frankfurt, Paris and regional centres also intersected with Singapore, and the city was awash with flight attendants. Although this wasn't always a positive thing, there were compensations. One was the crew hotel, the Swissôtel Stamford, which was very centrally located; the historic Raffles Hotel was right next door. The Stamford was a brilliant place for room parties and for feeling the pulse of the 'family' workforce.

It was also the crew hotel for a lot of other airlines, such as Etihad and British Airways, so it was common to run into other crews. It was fun mixing with them because we shared a lot of common experiences. In Singapore, you would hear and learn things about the airline business before the airline business had even issued their press release about it.

Singapore was a hive of activity for the airline. If someone became sick, crew would be turned around quickly; you might arrive one day and find yourself going back to London or Frankfurt the following day. Consequently, it was a place where answering the hotel phone was a definite no no.

By Asian standards, Singapore is a very expensive city. Locals are not encouraged to drink so alcohol is pricey. At most places, not only did they try to discourage you from drinking, but they'd charge outrageous prices for a teaspoon of vodka in a big glass of soda, which was somewhat off-putting. The Raffles has history and bucketloads of charm but it's way too expensive to hang out in; one Christmas some of us had an à la carte meal there and it cost us about AU$400 each; a bottle of wine alone was about AU$160, and there were taxes on top.

The worst thing about the place was that there wasn't much to do there, which is why it's called Singabore. It's a very efficient city but sterile. There aren't even any interesting industries – it's either banking, shipping or information technology. So I'd spend days lazing by the pool with other crews. We'd meet in someone's room or at the pool bar and maybe go off to Fatty's, a little Chinese restaurant. Even eating out in Singapore was strictly controlled; everything is from a set menu; there's no deviating or doing things like swapping beef for chicken. 'No, no, no. Set menu.' And when you placed your order, it was very literal; you could take nothing for granted. If you were eating in an Italian restaurant and assumed bread would come automatically, you were wrong.

Restrictions were a big part of daily life for Singaporeans. Spitting is a serious crime which can incur an instant penalty. Homosexuality is not illegal in Singapore but buggery is and gay locals lived with a certain amount of fear. What was kind of weird was that the prancing Asian queens – and there were plenty of them in Singapore – were largely ignored. It seemed as though Singaporean gays could have a gay life so long as they kept it low key and didn't ruffle any feathers. Gay Qantas crew had few qualms about being open; their behaviour sometimes verged on the outrageous, with things like table-top dancing in bars (occasionally with the captain). There was nothing flamboyant about the behaviour of gay crew from the Arabic airlines, who had to be cautious about being open anywhere they flew. In Singapore, they felt every bit at risk as they were in their own countries.

All this goes to explain why the gay scene in Singapore was not exactly flourishing; there were only two well-known gay bars and one was tiny and dark. Instead, we usually ended up with the straights at a fabulous bar called Chimes, which catered for Australians and Brits and was popular with airline crews. It had a fantastic live band and sold drinks to the Australian measure. It was a honey pot for pilots and flight attendants. After a night at Chimes, there was many a morning walk of shame from the Fairmont Hotel, where the pilots stayed, to the Stamford, where the cabin crew stayed.

Asian men had never held much interest for me. In Singapore, if you talked to them in a gay bar, they'd freeze up and deny they were gay when you knew they were; they were too concerned about the consequences if they were caught, and I suppose I wasn't patient about all that. One night there was a bit of a fight in a gay bar and someone called the cops. When the police arrived en masse, you've never seen so many Asian men flee; such was the fear factor. Of course, none of the rest of us flinched. We knew that in Singapore, you had to play by their rules; there was no bribing the police or anything like that. Nothing happened except that we were asked for ID. Fortunately I had my crew ID.

That particular night, one of the Qantas crew didn't have any ID on him so he was escorted back to the hotel to get it – somewhat humiliating for him. Somehow, management must have found out because shortly after that episode, we got a Qantas directive that we must take ID wherever we went, such as a copy of our passport.

I'd met Aidan, a Chinese Singaporean, when I was still flying out of Sydney. He was fairly high up with a Singapore bank and was well-dressed and very well-mannered; a gentle soul with a strong presence. He and I had caught up for coffee several times. Initially I didn't realise he was gay: Singaporeans will ask you out for coffee and because they don't admit they're gay, you might not realise. Many Asians can appear effeminate and you might think they're gay but they're not, so no one knows who's who at the zoo.

I ran into Aidan again in Singapore when I was flying out of London. I needed to get some paperwork off to Qantas and he offered to fax it from his office and bring it back to the hotel for me. When he arrived, I was hungover and lying on my bed in my room with the air-conditioning blasting. I'd been watching a *Sex and the City* marathon session on TV and contemplating the words of Carrie Bradshaw: 'You only get two great loves in your life.' I'd already experienced that with Andrew; I didn't count Toby; and I was thinking I was going have to make my second one really count.

When Aidan pushed the envelope with my papers in it under the door with one gentle knock, I opened the door and invited him to come in. We had a beer and a chat, and although nothing was said, I somehow figured he was gay. From then on we started seeing each other; soon Aidan and I were partners.

Aidan showed me all the local eateries and we had some amazing dining experiences. The more I got to know Aidan, the more impressive I found him. He spoke nine languages. I discovered that Aidan could conduct meetings in the board-room, with simultaneous conference calls going in two or three other countries, and he would be slipping between languages and speaking English to everyone else in the boardroom.

One night, we were out to dinner with a few of the young English crew – you know, those Essex girls – and Aidan, who was by nature very quiet, had had a couple of drinks so was more talkative than usual. One of the English girls seemed to have trouble with his accent and suddenly piped up and said, 'Talk English.' It was such a rude remark that the table went quiet.

'Excuse me; English is one of nine languages I speak. Would you prefer we spoke in Hokkien, the native language of the country you are in, or perhaps Cantonese, Japanese, French, Malay or are you happy just for me to speak my English?'

It was the only time I ever heard Aidan raise his voice. Everyone except the rude girl started laughing in support of his response. She didn't utter another word all night and he never mentioned the incident again. It was a perfect example of how Asians can make a strong point quietly and quickly.

And it'd be a mistake to think being quiet means being weak. Everywhere we went together, it turned into a meeting of the United Nations. I took Aidan on a Frankfurt trip and he picked up German in about two days. While we were on a cruise down the Rhine, of course Aidan found a handful of Asian tourists and started talking to them in Cantonese. Then he starts a conversation with a German guy, who spoke to Aidan in German, with Aidan answering the man's questions in perfect English.

There were more surprises in store in this relationship; I couldn't get over the fact that a grown intelligent Chinese man like Aidan could watch cartoons on TV for hours; apparently it is quite common in his culture. When I quizzed him about it, his response was that cartoons were an Asian's version of science fiction because they were so far beyond the realms of possibility. A Singaporean guy who was married to an Australian told me once that I should never judge another country by my own perceptions or standards. I could understand cultural differences but going to sleep every night listening to cartoons took some adjustment.

'WHO'S LILY ALLEN?'

On one Singapore–London flight in 2006, there was a bit of a fuss among the English first- and business-class crew: 'Oh, my God, it's Lily Allen!' This was apparently a reference to the pretty young girl in the last row of business.

'Who's Lily Allen?' I asked, because I'd never heard of her.

'She's a star!' The Essex girls were positively frothing with excitement. I was working in first so I thought I'd wander down to business to catch a glimpse of the star. She was sitting with her assistant and had an earphone in one ear that connected with an iPod.

'Hi,' I said. 'The girls are all fainting in first. I hear you're a star; what do you do?'

'I'm a singer. I'm Lily Allen. I'm number one in the UK right now,' she said.

I apologised for my ignorance, explaining that I was living in Brussels and commuted a lot. Later, I found out that her father was the British actor and comedian Keith Allen and her mother, Alison Owen, was a film producer.

'Oh, my God. I don't believe you don't know who I am. I'm number one in Belgium too and the rest of Europe,' she laughed, clearly finding it hilarious.

'Well, you'll have to let me have a listen to you on your iPod.'

She handed it over, at the same time introducing me to her record label assistant, who just happened to be the sister of William Baker, the guy who reinvented Kylie Minogue by putting her in the gold hot pants.

So that's how I ended up preparing the first-class meals while listening to Lily's album with her hit 'Smile' on it. I was quite impressed.

Later, when service was over and beds had been made up for passengers, I invited Lily up to the first-class galley for a drink and a gossip. What a delight! She was a proud Londoner and happily chatted about her life.

The conversation turned to the music industry. She told me she was returning to the UK after visiting Australia for a promotional tour – that was what an artist had to do if their first release was a hit.

'It's about establishing yourself internationally and creating a buzz with flow-on effects,' she explained.

At the time Lily was twenty-one and said she was finding

the whole celebrity thing pretty funny. She also told me the business was incredibly incestuous.

Although fairly new to stardom, she came across as very confident, and even had a few predictions. Amy Winehouse, she was sure, would be as big as her one day. (Of course, about a year later, Amy's hit 'Rehab' made number one on the British charts; Lily didn't predict Amy's 2013 death following an alcohol binge, after she'd kicked drugs.) The two of them would change the Brit girl-band image, she added. That could have been a Spice Girls dig; I didn't like to ask.

We were having a good old laugh in the first-class galley and she asked, 'What you gotta do to get up here?'

Quietly, I pulled aside the curtain that separated first class from business class so she could peep at the stretched-out sleeping passengers. 'Darl, this is what you can look forward to when you have a few more number-one hits.'

To reinforce the point, I loaded her up with first-class goodies – some La Prairie cream, a bottle of Dom Perignon and some Qantas pyjamas – and told her to remember me when she was a *big* star. Laughingly, she said would never forget me.

As I was leaving Heathrow, I saw Lily again: she was crossing the road and getting into a waiting car. She saw me, took a swig out of the $300 bottle of Dom Perignon, and yelled, 'Nice one, Owen!'

I blew her a kiss and headed home to bed; although I was living in Brussels I was overnighting in London. Later that afternoon, I received phone calls from two Qantas crew asking me if I'd seen the *Metro* newspaper, a free London publication that was read by millions.

'My God, Owen you're in the newspaper! Lily's thanking you for all the first-class goodies you gave her.'

My immediate reaction was that I could lose my job – that expensive bottle of Dom alone would be grounds for dismissal! Until I could get a copy of the paper, I was sweating on it, wondering what exactly the singer had said. Management was bound to be in touch so I worked out how I'd plead my case: Lily was a rising star and I was upselling, I'd say.

When finally I read the article, which turned out to be one of several artists' blog entries and appeared under the heading 'They're blog'n'roll stars', I was relieved and pleasantly surprised. She'd written, 'big up to Owen' and only mentioned the pyjamas. How flattering that of all the people Lily Allen had met, she mentioned me, and she'd gone out of her way to do so.

Management didn't call; they probably figured the publicity was good. They didn't seem to ever realise how close we flight attendants sometimes got to passengers in a single flight and what an asset we could be.

Lily had told me that she was scheduled to appear in Brussels a few weeks later and invited me to her concert. Unfortunately, I never made it as I was on a flight to Singapore at the time. But we stayed in touch for a while and, last I heard, she now lives in LA with her husband, Sam Cooper, and two children. Lily has recently come out of self-imposed retirement and is notching up number-one hits again; she had two songs in the UK Top 10 at the end of November 2013.

ALL AUSTRALIANS ARE ALCOHOLICS

A few years into my flying career, I knew all about the pills flight attendants carried around in their little black bags; my flying friends affectionately termed these their 'doctor's bag'. They contained uppers, downers, pills for pain, pills for diarrhoea, pills for constipation, antibiotics, sleeping pills – you name it.

When Aidan first saw me open my little black bag, he freaked out. You can get your hands chopped off in Singapore if caught with anything illegal.

'They're just antibiotics and Panadol,' I assured him.

'No, no. Illegal. Must put them in the safe.'

Aidan was extremely cautious; even being on the hotel balcony made him feel uncomfortable. I guess the combination of my little black bag, the fear factor from being gay and being indoctrinated in the ways of decadent foreigners didn't help his paranoia.

He and I were like chalk and cheese. Two drinks for Aidan and he would be dancing on tables as merry as a sailor, his cheeks glowing red; two drinks for me and the party hadn't even started. No wonder he thought all Australians were alcoholics.

'How many drinks you have?' he'd ask.

'I don't know; ten, maybe more.'

'Alcoholic.'

Aidan was also quite shocked at the way Qantas crew partied and how we all undermined management. 'You are saying yes, yes, to Qantas managers and then you close the cabin doors and tear up their rules. I've been on flights with you guys and I've seen what you do.' Although he was a stickler in many ways, I could usually win him over.

Ours was a very grown-up relationship. Aidan was holding down a responsible job in Singapore and I was living in Brussels and flying. We'd do our own thing and meet up when we could. Aidan was on my staff travel benefit so he could jump on a plane at a whim and join me for days away. A lot of the time we met in hotels; you have more time for romance in an air-conditioned five-star hotel with room service at your beck and call, clean sheets daily, someone to polish your shoes and three pools and six bars to choose from.

To mark our fourth anniversary, we wanted to do something special and decided to go to Bali. If Singaporeans are going to do anything naughty, they leave the country because at home they worry about being watched. I'd booked us into a very nice hotel in Legian and flew in on a Garuda flight to meet Aidan there. For the evening of our actual anniversary, unbeknown to Aidan I had splurged out and booked an evening at the Bvlgari Resort – a place with a nightly rate of AU$1000. I decided on a day package that included a spa and dinner. We needed to get ourselves out to the promontory in south Bali where the resort was, and I explained to the woman at our hotel desk that I'd planned an anniversary surprise for my partner and asked her to organise a driver to take us. I understood the journey was about an hour and a half and my instructions were specific: under no circumstances was the driver to give any indication of our destination during the trip, either when talking on the phone or to us; I added that my partner could speak Indonesian and could pick up anything the driver might say. Assurances were given.

We got in the car without so much as a word being spoken between us and the driver and we set off. About ten minutes into the drive Aidan said, 'Did you lock the safe?'

'I can't remember – no, you were in it last.'

'I've got my money, credit cards and passport in there.'

'Don't worry about it.'

But Aidan kept going on about being fleeced. 'We'll have everything stolen. You don't know what these Balinese are like,' he said, seemingly forgetting he was creating a laughable double standard.

I suggested we call the hotel. No, that was the worst thing we could do because that would only alert them to whatever was available in the safe. So we argued backwards and forward for the next hour until we were nearly there.

'Aidan, forget it. If we've been robbed, then it's already happened. Please let it go.'

'Anyway, where are we going, Owen? Why are we driving so long in the dark?'

'Oh, shut up,' I said finally. 'You work at a bank, I'm sure we'll figure it out.'

I was desperately trying to settle him down because his anxiety looked like spoiling my surprise. On arrival, as Aidan got out of the car I asked the driver if he spoke English; I wanted to confirm that he was going to wait to take us back.

'Yes, I speak English,' he said in perfect English.

'Oh, my God,' I thought, 'he heard everything we said; he's going to be straight on the phone calling the hotel.' No way could I say anything to Aidan; that would just ruin everything. In spite of a nagging feeling in the back of my mind about what might await us on our return, we had a wonderful day and magical evening and reconfirmed our commitment to each other.

True to his word, our driver was ready and waiting to take us back to our accommodation in Legian. Ten minutes before we got to the hotel, at about the exact same place where the issue of the safe first arose, Aidan suddenly remembered and started to fret.

'I bet we got no money. How are we going to pay for the hotel? I have to ring the bank in Singapore.'

We arrived to a room with red frangipanis in the shape of a heart on the bed, welcome drinks and a card that read 'Happy anniversary'. The safe was locked.

ODOUR ALERT

It goes without saying that smells and flying go hand in hand. In our training manuals there is an entire section dedicated to gas and sites of trapped gasses. While that pertains more to *medical* emergencies, some of the pongs I've experienced are simply out of this world.

The doozie of them all happened when I was doing a Frankfurt to Singapore and working in economy on the back left-hand section of the plane. A very friendly and lively Scottish couple seated in the last row of economy kept me steadily amused with their banter; they were about to spend several months in Thailand and were in high spirits.

After a while, a rather unpleasant pong arose. People were squirming in their seats; it was uncomfortable for everyone. Puzzled, I checked the loos at the back of economy, which was where the smell seemed strongest. There was no obvious source; what was I to do? After the meal service prior to landing into Singapore, the smell reached its most potent heights; it was definitely poo. By now it was unmistakable. My Scottish friend asked for a beer and I passed it to him, trying not to grimace from the dreadful stench.

As I sat in my jump seat as we were preparing to land,

I noticed my pal glancing around uncomfortably and with a definite expression of guilt. When the safety belt sign went off and he stood up, it was apparent that his adult diaper had burst and he had shite running all down his linen trousers.

Long after he disembarked, the whole plane was filled with a strong waft. I felt sorry for the cleaners coming on in Singapore; all of them were holding their nose.

BANGKOK

THE SECRET IS REVEALED

Bangkok was the third city that intersected the London route. Unlike Hong Kong, it had always been part of the kangaroo route. Before I was posted to London, I'd only done a few Sydney–Bangkok flights; it was popular with more senior crew, which I assumed in my naivety was because the hotels were gorgeous, the food was good and the Thai people were lovely. It was also a terrific place for having clothes tailored or altered and getting pampered for next to nothing. It was like a dream holiday after cold old London.

But there was another reason Bangkok was popular: it was where the crew topped up their little black bags with pills and potions. There were two particular pharmacies that supplied crew: one was near the crew hotel, which was the delightful old Queens Park Hotel, and one was in Siam, another part of the city. Both sold a range of goodies over the counter – Valium, Xanex, antibiotics, pain relievers and treatments for any sort of infection; name it and you could pretty well get it.

Finding out about the pharmaceutical bonanza didn't happen overnight. The details of how the older crew always slept so well in the crew rest and didn't appear to have the jetlag issues I had were closely guarded. Obviously there was stuff to be had somewhere; flight attendants would talk about it but you had to be in the confidence of the crew in the know; they weren't volunteering to take you to where you could get it. When asked where the place was, answers were vague but I did hear the name of one of the pharmacies. I paid it a visit but the pharmacist wouldn't sell to me because he didn't know me; I needed to be introduced by someone the pharmacist knew.

Finally, I was given the nod by some older flight attendants. One of them took me to the pharmacy and introduced me for my 'trial run' that night.

The pharmacist scrutinised me.

'Between us, between us?'

'Yes, yes.' I was told then that he would remember me. He instructed me to take half a Valium, half a Xanax and a Panadol when I went to bed that night. When I questioned taking the Panadol, he said it would prevent a headache from developing and explained that it would keep the blood flowing, so I wouldn't wake up feeling like I had a hangover.

Back at the hotel I confided in Natasha, another flight attendant whom I'd become quite friendly with. Although we were both a little bit scared, we decided to take the plunge together. My room had two double beds and so we took the prescribed dose of tablets, put on eye masks and lay down waiting for something to happen. It was not unlike a death pact – if one of us died, we would both die.

Many hours later we woke up, looked at each other and it was like, 'Oh. My. God!' Both of us felt as if we had been in a deep coma and had awoken from it completely refreshed. When we looked at ourselves in the mirror, our facial skin looked rejuvenated. We thought we'd hit the jackpot – no wonder the older crew always looked so fresh. We had stumbled across something precious in flying – a deep sleep – and it was worth its weight in gold. Of course that works for the first couple of months – until the body adjusts to the dose and you needed to start upping the dosage. But more about that later.

Now I had the secret, I had to pass it on. But I was told I had to be careful taking my little helpers into Australia. My instructions were to buy a bottle of something innocuous, like iron tablets, that wouldn't attract the attention of customs, ditch the contents and replace them with my special prescription. It all seemed like a lot of fun. I was in possession of the secret, woo hoo! It never crossed my mind that the supply was answering a demand, and that it may have been fuelling a fully fledged addiction in the workforce. In effect, we were all running drugs.

If we were caught, all of us had our explanation ready: we had bought them over the counter in Bangkok and had been naive. When you looked at the bigger picture, what we were doing didn't seem that bad: there were flight attendants running stronger drugs than these, not to mention passengers trying to bring in all sorts. In my entire career I was never pulled up, fortunately.

The secret spread fast. When I got home, I passed the information to other flight attendants, explaining where they had to go and to say they knew me or one of a few other names I gave them. It became routine: you'd get off the flight, get on the crew bus and share a couple of wind-down beers, check in to the hotel, walk across to the pharmacy and get your goods and then go and have a beautiful Thai dinner and a massage.

After I went to London, where I became one of the most senior crew, I shared the pills and potions information with the UK crew, who took to it like ducks to water. We all knew it was illegal but we were all looking after each other; if one of us got caught, we could all be in trouble. Crew were carting Valium out of Bangkok and into London or Sydney. No one gave much thought to customs because of the good trust relationship flight attendants usually had with customs and we were confident nothing would happen to us; we knew the customs officers were more interested in the trade of illicit drugs. If they looked in my toiletry bag and saw a medicine bottle with my name on it and the name of some antibiotic, there would be no questions asked. Besides, passing through customs was a quirky process. Once I saw a crew member with sixty DVDs get checked and walk through without so much as a question. For personal use? I think not.

Some flight attendants started selling the little helpers. Some guy who was a friend of a friend approached me and asked if I could bring in a batch of Valium for him; he could get AU$50 a tablet. When I asked why they fetched so much, he told me that there was a market in people who went out partying all weekend and got high and who then wanted something to come down on so they'd be able to go to work on Monday. I declined the request. I was okay about taking a few pills myself but I was not prepared to start selling them.

Unfortunately some of the young crew threw caution to the wind and started advertising the availability of these pills on social media; they were also indiscreet about mentioning the names of the pharmacies. Consequently, the pharmacists stopped selling to them and even started to refuse some of the regular old faithfuls. When the young ones complained to me that the pharmacists weren't supplying anymore, I expressed my opinion that it was their own fault. When I spoke to one of the pharmacists about it, he said, 'Too young and too loud. I can get shut down.' It was big business but it was becoming harder and harder.

WHAT GOES UP MUST COME DOWN

Being a flight attendant means being part of an ever-changing workforce. In most jobs, people work nine to five with the same people. In a workforce of 8000 flight attendants, you are rarely working with the same people; you get off one flight and you might not see the people you worked with on that flight for another two years. It was nearly ten years before I flew with one particular crew member again. I never flew with some of the people I trained with.

Half the reason crew go out drinking all the time is to get to know the new colleagues, which they wouldn't do in a 'normal' workforce. It's a social job and very gossipy and everyone loves to hear the gossip. There are always funny stories that crew like to share among each other, and this would extend to crew from other airlines if they were staying at the same hotel or drinking at the same bars. There was an immediate simpatico because they understood the lingo and the myriad of things a flight attendant sees and situations they face.

Once a flight is finished, it's the time find out what went on in various parts of the plane. Mostly it starts on the crew bus to the hotel, when we all opened a beer; then we carried on with the debriefing in someone's hotel room once we'd checked in. Debriefing was usually followed by a bit of a rest or freshening up then it was off out to bars, restaurants or parties.

Nevertheless, being regularly away from friends and family can play havoc with your mind and your relationships. You send a text message to someone at home and they don't text you back and you wonder what they're doing and who they're doing it with. Of course you're probably in a completely different time zone and the person you want to get in touch with has quite innocently just switched their phone off. International time zones can seriously fuck up relationships; eventually, with reluctance, Aidan and I agreed to call it quits. If something goes pear-shaped with the one you love while you are away and you haven't had a text, email or phone call to sort it out from wherever you are in the world before you fly out again, you could be in a high state of anxiety until you get home. This will certainly affect your mood on the plane. It was not uncommon for a flight attendant to come on board crying because she'd had a fight with her partner; this situation would affect the other crew on the flight.

Even though we're constantly with other people, the life of a flight attendant can be surprisingly lonely. You may be in a country with people you like but you don't like the country; you may be in a country you like but you don't like the people you are working with. Pilots in particular may feel more isolated because they are seen at the 'father' of the team and won't talk about their problems to anyone. Most pilots are heterosexual males and feel they have to be strong leaders; anything less will be seen as weakness.

People can feel very fragile away from home. Little things can turn into big things. You can talk about things with other crew on the plane but once you get to your hotel room you are on your own. Believe it or not, the two most reliable things for flight crew away from home are switching on the hotel TV and getting CNN and BBC World News.

Occasionally crew members crack up in spectacular fashion. In one famous incident, a flight attendant on an American airline couldn't stand the pressure and flipped out on landing; he went to the galley, got a beer, opened the exit door, activated the emergency chute and slid to the ground and took off – goodbye everyone! We all understood exactly where that guy was coming from. He's probably in a nut house now. But we all see him as a champion because there isn't one flight attendant I've talked to who hasn't wanted to do the same thing at some point. And yes, we do all dream of screaming those evacuation commands and jumping down the slide. The chances of needing to do something like that have increased over recent years.

All of these factors contributed to the popularity of 'little helpers'. Rather than confess to management that they have stress or injury issues and risk being in the spotlight for removal, it was easier to find a pharmaceutical solution. Whatever drugs you got your hands on freely overseas, would not be reflected on your medical records at home.

Through Qantas's Employee Assistance Program (EAP), we'd all attended lectures on such enthralling topics as 'Getting a good night's sleep', 'Not your normal 9 to 5' and 'How to relax and stop worrying'. Seriously? I mean being advised to get a good night's sleep is about as useful as reading *The Satanic Verses* before a flight.

Respect between management and crew hit an all-time low in 2008 after the Qantas CEO, Geoff Dixon, referred to cabin crew as 'bun tossers'. It would take more than a series of uplifting EAP sessions to repair that damage.

LOVELY ONES AND LOUTS

One day in 2005, all the attendants on the flight from London to Bangkok were nervous. Among the passengers were both the British band Oasis and the Scottish indie band Franz Ferdinand.

Carrying Oasis was a clear risk; in 1998, on a Cathay Pacific flight from Hong Kong to Perth, the wild boys from Manchester had famously got blind drunk then started hurling objects around the cabin, verbally abusing passengers and crew and smoking. When the captain threatened to divert the plane and off-load Oasis and their thirty-member entourage, they threatened him (with a scone). Subsequently Cathay Pacific banned the lead singer Liam Gallagher and any other associates or members of the band who had caused trouble from setting foot on their planes. Gallagher's response was that he'd rather walk anyway. The ban on Oasis extended to all OneWorld airlines (apart from Cathay Pacific, that's twelve other major airlines, including Qantas). Now, it seemed that Qantas was happy to take the money and so we had Oasis on board as our guests.

Franz Ferdinand, who were about to appear at a music festival in Bangkok, were seated in business class upstairs, where I was working. They were no trouble. There were only the five band members and their manager; perfectly lovely people – they drank a lot of scotch but I wouldn't hold that against them.

Meanwhile Oasis was in business class downstairs, which was situated between first class, at the front, and the main galley so it was fairly well supervised. Alice, one of two petite female flight attendants looking after them, kept running up the stairs telling me what was going on; evidently they were drinking a lot, but that was about it. On about her fourth visit, Alice whispered that one of the Gallagher brothers had offered the attendants a thousand pounds apiece to turn a blind eye while he smoked a joint in the toilet; what should she do?

'Get the money up front,' I suggested. 'Let him smoke the bloody joint – it will set the smoke alarms off and then maybe they'll go to sleep and leave you alone.'

How ballsy was this band even asking the question, knowing that flight attendants were the very people who could have them arrested. The transaction was never made, as it turned out.

Later on, when I went downstairs, fortunately, the hell-raisers were all tucked up asleep.

A SURPRISE IN THE PANTS

On one of my very first Bangkok flights out of London, the crew were all good friends. Brett, the CSM, had a Thai partner and consequently knew the city really well. When he offered to take us all out and show us the real sights of Bangkok, we all jumped at the chance. In the end, about seven of us went with Brett to a show in Patpong. It was very explicit; one girl asked one the guys in our party to pull on her finger;

next minute a banana shot out of her pussy and landed in my friend's drink. Another guy was asked to hold a threaded needle and as he did, she stepped back and razor blades on a piece of string emerged from her vagina. The performers even wrote their names holding the pencil in their vagina. Tourists from all over the world were there to watch these tricks; I had one eye looking in amazement and the other turned away in horror.

Of course there were plenty of bars where gay boys performed. These were also a little creepy as some boys were just that – skinny and undernourished kids standing around in Speedos with a number attached, waiting for someone to show interest. There was a more masculine show on offer too, featuring guys from the mountain regions; they did S&M shows and fully fledged porn. Most of these guys say they are straight but do this work for easy money. They were not places to take women.

In the straight bars, beautiful young girls paraded around dancing and singing under the fluorescent lighting; it was like watching a Victoria's Secret show. The straight guys in our group all had their tongues hanging out. One of the girls came over and approached our friend Paulo. Her name was Candy and she was stunning, with perfect-looking boobs and blue contact lenses; she looked a million bucks. Paulo's eyes were on stalks and he was obviously smitten. She was giggling, softening him up further while the rest of us kept our eyes on the show. After a while, Candy went off to get us all drinks.

'I am in love,' Paulo declared. 'I have found the girl of my dreams.'

He explained that Candy wanted 1000 baht (about AU$30 at the time) to take him upstairs. Paulo said he would have to get her out of that place. He wanted to take her back to London.

When Brett told him to calm down and be careful, Paulo was unmoved.

'She's a bloke, mate,' Brett said, bluntly.

Paulo didn't believe him. The rest of us were also finding it hard to believe our eyes; we stared at Candy, waiting patiently at the bar. Her bikini bottom was practically translucent – where would she hide a penis?

Brett reminded us that Thailand is the land of the 'Kinder Surprise' – crack open the egg and you never know what you'll get. At this bar, he said, the performers were all men who'd had 'the works': hormone treatment, plastic surgery, silicone breasts, Botox and even rib-removal to get the hour-glass figure – all were part of the make-over.

'If that's a bloke, then I'm gay,' Paulo said.

After Candy came back with our drinks, we passed the hat around to come up with the 1000 baht she was asking for; we were all curious by now. Shortly afterwards, she and Paulo headed upstairs. They were hardly out of sight when we heard the pounding of big feet running back down again; it was Paulo, white-faced. He streaked past us and hit the street running.

Candy tore down the stairs after him, calling, 'Paulo, Paulo.'

Brett raced after Paulo, and then we all sculled our drinks and followed them down the road to an Australian bar. Paulo said he was too traumatised to tell us what happened. After a couple of stiff drinks, we persuaded him to spill the beans: when Candy had removed her panties to reveal what he thought would be the honey-pot, he was confronted with a minuscule penis, about the size of the tip of his pinkie finger. Paulo said it was like looking at a baby's penis.

Brett explained these boy–girls were considered a 'delicacy' by some men. In reality, the whole thing was obvious when we thought about it later, but poor Paulo hyperventilated for two hours.

Brett repeated that nothing is as it seems in Thailand; if it looks too good to be true, it probably is. 'They call Thailand the land of a thousand smiles; I call it the land of a thousand lies.'

It will come as no surprise that I ended up preferring the liveliness of Bangkok to the sedateness of Singapore. When Aidan and I were still together, he would regularly fly across to meet me there instead. In terms of the roster, I was getting the flights and work positions the seniority system in Australia excluded me from. First class was luxury flying and didn't really seem like a job. The London–Bangkok flights were night services and landed at the perfect time of 3 pm. The passengers on that flight were usually easy too – mostly a lot of relaxed holiday-makers. Bangkok offered so much, apart from the pills.

An unexpected bonus was a fabulous laundry I found in an alleyway beside the hotel. That came about because one time I turned up and I'd forgotten to take a spare clean shirt; I was told I could have my shirt laundered there for 20 baht. Even though I had a perfectly good washing machine at home, it was hard to get anything to dry in the Brussels weather, so I ended up taking all my dirty laundry with me whenever I went to Bangkok. It cost me the equivalent of £8 for about 20 kilos. The word spread and the crew became a good supply of business for the laundry – so much so that they'd know when we were arriving and they'd be waiting in the hotel foyer for us, saying, 'Laundry, laundry?'

After crew went partying or shopping, they could usually be found recovering at a day spa. An establishment called Lek was the spa of choice with both Qantas and British Airways crew. It was about 100 metres from the hotel; there they did a cucumber peel-off facial followed by neck, head, back and foot massage all for about 400 baht (about AU$12). You could easily spend hours there. The bars next to Lek would bring us beer and we would lie there talking and drinking and having our feet and legs massaged. This was one thing that was not too good to be true; it was cabin crew heaven.

One thing the female flight attendants wouldn't get done in Bangkok was waxing; surprisingly, the Thais didn't do waxing well. One memorable night, a flight attendant came down for a briefing walking like she'd been riding a horse bareback for two days. She had rashes all down her bare legs, courtesy of a disastrous leg and bikini wax.

'Don't ask,' she said to the CSM, apologising for not wearing panty-hose. 'I've just had the most traumatic fucking experience. The girl's stripping off the wax and the next thing she has her head down a couple of inches from my jacksie, blowing into my crotch, saying, 'Hot, hot, hot' and when I look down I can see my skin is blistering and I'm practically on fire!'

Despite the poor girl's discomfort, we couldn't help but laugh all the way home; that story gave a new meaning to the expression 'emergency landing'.

I loved Bangkok so much that I wanted to live there. Apart from trying to fly there as much as possible, I used to holiday in Thailand as well. Some years later, when I was once again based in Australia, I had a shocking experience while holidaying with friends and some of the crew. We were at Jomtien Beach, a segregated beach: different nationalities inhabited different sections of the beach; there were colourful deckchairs under beach umbrellas all along the beach, where you sat and relaxed while attendants brought you cocktails.

I ventured into the ocean, which felt like a lukewarm bath; part of it was sectioned off with nets to keep out floating debris. When I felt a light prick on my leg I thought nothing of it. Afterwards, as I was putting on my sarong, one of the girls said, 'Oh, my God, Owen, look at your leg.' There was a big brown mark on my leg with a little spike sticking out of it, which I flicked, then I started rubbing the area. Immediately the affected skin started to blister and weep. Aghast, I asked a local beach attendant what it was.

He said, 'Snake bite. Don't worry. Follow me.'

He took me to the back of the bar which fronted the beach, where the owner of the bar, another Thai, said 'Leg up, leg up.' He then proceeded to scrape the area and tip gin over it. He called for some bandaids and covered the area with them.

'All good now. Want drink?'

Soon after, we returned to Bangkok but I couldn't sleep that night; my leg was throbbing. Next day, the brown stain had spread and swollen up. We were flying back to Australia that night and I thought I'd better get it seen to. I went across the road to the pharmacy where we got our pills. The pharmacist took one look at my leg.

'Ah, snake bite.'

By this stage, I'd been going to Thailand for twelve years and had never been bitten by a snake before. It unnerved me that everyone seemed to know about sea snake bites; how fucking common was this?

149

'Take this. Drink.' He held up a vial with some wormy thing floating in it.

'What is it?'

'Snake venom.'

'I don't think so,' I said, declining the potion.

'It good for bite. Otherwise you could lose leg. Chop off!'

If it was coursing through my veins already, there was no way I was going to drink the stuff. I decided to wait until I got back to Australia. But I couldn't tell Qantas because I knew they wouldn't let me fly.

As I walked out of the pharmacy, I noticed people sitting with their feet in two big fish tanks while little baby fish ate the dead skin off their legs. I decided I'd like to give it a go, snake-bite or not, made the necessary arrangements and then plunged my legs in; it was the most therapeutic feeling, a bit like having a mini electric shock.

Once home, I went straight to the doctor; she took one look at the mess on my leg and said, 'Oh, my God, you've been bitten by a snake.'

'Am I dying?' I asked. It wasn't that I felt particularly unwell, but people's reactions were freaking me out.

She circled the area on my leg with a felt-tip pen, gave me an intravenous shot of antibiotic and prescribed megadoses of another strong oral antibiotic.

'If this discoloured area hasn't shrunk away from the circle I've drawn by tomorrow night, then you'll have to go into hospital.'

'Why? What's going on – is there some flesh-eating bug in there?'

She explained that if the antibiotics hadn't started working in twenty-four hours then they would have to do some investigations. For the next twenty-four hours I kept staring at my leg wondering if the infected area would go beyond or shrink from the black line.

In the meantime it was a rally call for the Australian gambling spirit: 'friends and acquaintances' from far and wide were taking bets on which way things would go. Fortunately, the area did start to shrink the first day and continued to do so over the next few days. The doctor said the remaining stained area would disappear in a couple of months. But it never did – I still have a small discoloured area on my leg.

OLYMPIC HERO LOSES IT

It was 11 pm in Bangkok and the passengers connecting with the flight to London started piling onto the plane. It was one of the rare occasions that I was rostered on with both my two close friends, Malcolm and Marcus – they were working in business and I was working in first class. We'd just come off a riotous thirty-six hours in Bangkok and I was feeling like death warmed up. Between the heat of Bangkok and the whingeing of the boarding passengers, I wished I could click my heels and be back in Brussels.

Everything was running as it usually did in first – champagne corks popping, canapés flowing and passengers complaining before they even had their seatbelt buckled! As we settled the precious ones into their seats, there was a buzz from business class. Australia's Olympic swimming hero, Grant Hackett, and his singer girlfriend, Candice Alley – soon to be wife;

now ex-wife – were seated in 25J and 25K. There was general excitement from crew and passengers alike.

After the first- and business-class passengers were all put to bed, crew grabbed the cheese boards and gathered in the business-class galley on the main deck for our customary goss. The light over 25J went on and it was Candice. Grant was asleep. She handed us a packet of the sleeping sedative, Stilnox, and asked us to please hide it, explaining that they reacted badly with him; he'd just taken some. Thus instructed, we did as she asked. About two hours later, I was standing alone in the first-class galley flipping through a magazine when, smack bang, Grant Hackett came flying out of business class and through the first-class curtain followed closely by Malcolm and Marcus, who were desperately trying to restrain him.

'I should be in here,' he slurred. He then stepped towards the front right door and started to unzip his fly. Eventually, we wrestled him into the toilet; let's just say it was like getting a thoroughbred horse into a racing barrier. Although I'd heard that some people had bad reactions to Stilnox – even sleepwalking – this was truly bizarre behaviour.

Grant Hackett is slightly shy of two metres tall. Somehow, when he emerged, we managed to steer him back to his seat; that was a lengthy struggle. Minutes later, he was amorously kissing Candice. While we found that amusing, Candice was clearly embarrassed. We were trying to assess what she wanted us to do when his behaviour suddenly became a great deal more intimate. Quick as a flash, we removed her from the situation by taking her to the business-class refreshment bar then I raced to get Grant some water.

When I returned with the water, he was laughing to himself while hop-scotching over Candice's reclined seat. Everyone around him was shocked; our Olympic hero off his head on sleeping pills? Of course, years later, his battle with sleeping pill addiction would become public. Fortunately he settled, and during the breakfast service in the morning he appeared quite sheepish.

Before they disembarked, I quietly slipped Candice the Stilnox as she exited the toilet and she thanked me. Back in business class, Grant was looking under his seat and shaking out his blanket. When I enquired whether everything was all right, he told me rather abruptly that he was *looking for something*.

Marcus travelled in to central London on the same Heathrow Express train as the celebrity couple and reported that Grant still looked upset about losing 'something'.

He must have got over it because Malcolm, who was working on Grant's return flight to Australia, told me it was uneventful.

WHEN NOT EVEN JIMMY CHOOS COUNT

My friend Sally is really adventurous. She worked at Emirates for many years; heaven knows why but she almost knows the gay scene better than I do. The pair of us have worked many trips together and we've even holidayed together. This time, we were in Bangkok and Sally was keen to see a particular gay male strip show.

'Sally, I couldn't possibly take you – it's full-on S&M, with guys wearing freaky face masks; a lot of them are guys from the poorly paid armed forces and they get paid to shag other guys on stage. The show is absolutely shocking.'

'Owen, I want to go; I've seen it all before.'

'Sally, I can't take you.'

Sally is a stunning dresser. That evening she fronted up for dinner at the Sofitel Sky Bar in a beautiful Dolce & Gabbana dress and Jimmy Choo shoes, accessorised with a Stella McCartney handbag, and with her blonde hair piled up on her head. After dinner she still wanted to see the strip show and threatened to go on her own. To keep the peace, I took her to a male strip show but nothing as full-on as the S&M stuff she'd had in mind.

In these places they don't care if the patrons are male, female or donkey – you're just a walking ATM. When the two of us took seats at the bar, one guy sat down beside me and another sat beside Sally; her host was very handsome and splendidly muscled. All the young men working in this establishment wore tight underpants; each one had a number.

Sally's man says to her, 'You're very beautiful. Which country?' then asked her what she would like to drink – as if he was offering to buy. She requested champagne. I opted for bottled beer. Both men went off to get the drinks and Sally turned to me, smiling.

'You'll never guess what . . . he's straight!'

'Sally, don't be delusional; he's working in a fucking gay go-go bar in Thailand! Wouldn't you think he'd choose a straight bar if he preferred women?'

'He's an engineer called Ricky and a student, and he does this because it's better pay.'

'Come on, darl. How many other girls do you see in here? He's a hooker. He fucks guys.' I was getting a bit impatient.

'No. He doesn't do the fucking. He just does the entertaining.'

Ricky came back with a red plastic rose and presented it

to Sally, along with the champagne and lovingly lingering words about how beautiful she was. The guy sitting next to me started trying to feel me up.

'He's gay,' I said to Sally; Ricky was getting very close to her.

'I straight,' he says, looking at me.

'I gay,' the guy with his hand on my thigh offers.

'Yes, I know *you* are; so is *he*,' and I pointed to Ricky.

'He like both.'

The show started. In the darkness I could see Ricky whispering to Sally and when the lights came back on, she was rubbing his biceps. Getting to my feet, I announced that we had to go and Sally stood up and told him we were leaving. Ricky looked crestfallen (money was walking out the door) and asked where we were headed. She told him we were going to a gay bar down the road.

'I like you. I straight. Can I come?' he asked.

'Yes, sure,' Sally replied. She told me Ricky wanted to knock off early and take her for a drink, but obviously could not do so dressed just in his underpants. We prepared to leave. Surprise, surprise: that's when we found out the champagne wasn't a gift for Sally after all. We paid the bar bill and headed for the door. My guy, whose name I hadn't bothered to get, was calling out to me that he loved me.

'Yes, I love you too,' I said and dragged Sally out.

She toddles unsteadily down the cobbled street in her Jimmy Choos, and then turns and starts berating me:

'I can get picked up in a gay bar and you don't like it.'

'Sally, he's fucking gay; he's probably riddled with disease and you're sitting there rubbing his hand while he's telling you how beautiful you are and that he's only ever fucks women.

Right. And he's telling you this in a gay go-go bar while wearing red underpants with number twenty-seven on them.'

'It's all right for you to pick up but you won't let me pick up—'

'Sally, you've got a boyfriend!'

'I wasn't going to do anything,' she said indignantly. 'You just can't handle me getting the attention.'

'Well, I didn't see him buy you a drink,' I sniffed.

Next thing, we were caught unawares by one of those typically Thai tropical downpours. Then, while we were standing under some awnings still arguing, something loomed out of the darkness and stood blocking our way. Right in front of us was an elephant! A small man was walking him around and people were paying him to feed the elephant bananas. God, could this night get any more bizarre! Sally and I hooted with laughter, friends again.

At the next bar we ordered some drinks then hit the dance floor. Not much later, I got a tap on the shoulder; it was Sally, who pointed across the room. And there was Ricky sitting at the bar.

'See, he is straight. I told you he liked me,' she triumphantly declared.

Off she went to have a drink with him, giggling happily.

I was starting to reassess my own judgement when, next minute, Sally comes up to me and asks if I can get rid of *him*.

'Why?'

'Just get him to go. I want him to go.' She stomped off up some stairs then stared down at me with a face like thunder.

I told Ricky he'd better go.

'She owe me 2000 baht.'

'What for?'

'I came out for her.'

Then it clicked: he thinks he's on a call-out. As quick as I could, I shuffled him out to the street.

'He wanted 2000 baht!' Sally was indignant. 'If anyone was to pay anyone, shouldn't he be paying me?'

'Darl, he's a hooker.'

'He told me I was the most beautiful girl he'd ever seen and he loved me.'

Poor Sally. She was going on and on, obviously still in shock, so I fetched her another drink.

'How much is 2000 baht anyway?' she asked.

About $80, I told her.

'He even wanted to go back to my hotel.' She reflected for a bit. 'Owen, do you think he's even straight?'

'Of course he's not fucking straight, Sally. He couldn't care less where he put it in, and I dread to think where he might have stuck it in you. His sexuality is the Thai baht; that's what he's in love with.'

'But I was in my Jimmy Choos.' Her mortification was complete.

KISS AND TELL WITH KATY PERRY

I first met Katy Perry in 2008 when she was promoting her 'I Kissed a Girl' single but got to know her the following year in a much more personal way on a Bangkok to London flight. She had been on her first romantic getaway with Russell Brand in Phuket. At that stage, no one knew about their relationship and none of the crew knew that they were going to be on board until they came down the aerobridge into first class for the 1 am flight. They were seated in the back row of first class and I was quite shocked to see them behaving quite amorously together.

They were very casually dressed: Katy in a black and white leopard-skin print dress with black leggings and Russell in his usual grunge look of a T-shirt and loose black pants. They were easy passengers; they had something to eat and went to bed.

After my break I was standing around reading the flight attendant's bible – *OK!* magazine – and Katy came up and I asked if I could get her anything. She said she was a bit bored and there was nothing on the in-flight entertainment she wanted to watch. The magazine I was reading happened to have a picture of her in it so I showed it to her and then she asked what magazine it was and we started chatting. I invited her to sit on the jump seat next to me.

'Now, darl, what's going on here?' I could see that she was immediately apprehensive, thinking I was going to ask her questions about Russell.

'I've just been reading that you made $45 million singing a song saying you kissed a girl and you liked it; well, I kissed a girl and I *didn't* like it and I'm cooking you breakfast . . . so what the hell's going on? There's something wrong with this picture.' It wasn't actually a question but Katy started laughing uncontrollably – I'm funny but not that funny.

She told me that particular song wasn't her original first choice but it was the one that had taken off internationally. These days, downloads were the way recording artists could make money faster than through traditional album sales, which had a long lead-time for royalties and returning money to the record companies.

She was well aware that people would remember her by the implication of the words, 'I Kissed a Girl' but she said she was a proud supporter of gay rights and didn't mind.

She talked a bit about her family and how they originally disapproved of her lifestyle and music choices as they were deeply religious but she wanted to be her own person and she was really happy. She didn't want to talk about the other celebrity girls she knew in the Hollywood set (trust me, I asked) although she did tell me her best friend was Rihanna (whom I said I admired and loved). She said the music business was incredibly interconnected and the best policy was not to talk about anyone as they were all just one degree of separation away from each other. While it might seem like a massive industry to the outside world, it was actually a small and incestuous business; everyone knew where everyone else was on the chequer board. 'Most people are connected in some way, which is why many of them get opportunities they don't deserve.'

We started talking about various money-making ideas; I said I just wanted the money, not the fame. She said she knew a really easy way I could make money. All ears I asked how, thinking she was going to impart some inside information.

'Magazine covers! You can make a lot of money appearing on magazine covers. Sometimes you don't even have to do an interview.'

'Yes, darling, I'm ready for Anna Wintour but is she ready for me – all 110 kilos of me?'

She laughed; she was still very innocent, not the experienced performer she is now – and quite unaware of how funny her suggestion was.

Russell woke up and came out. He talked about a movie he was doing. He was completely the opposite to his TV alter ego; he was charming and educated and I was quite surprised. When I enquired about his holiday in Thailand, he spoke intelligently of the geography and culture. He was a vegan and keen on spirituality and came across as having a very kind and gentle disposition. I could tell Russell was smitten by Katy and quite protective of her but not in awe. He seemed to be genuinely interested in whatever I said and when I made little jokes he laughed – even at the ones slightly at Katy's expense.

Interestingly, while we were chatting he said he was 'in' on the whole joke of celebrity. If you were known for being successful at something, you just worked at perfecting whatever it was. It occurred to me that it was a bit silly that his public image was to act the goose when in reality he was so much more, although I didn't tell him that; I just said, 'If you're onto a good thing, stick with it.'

I asked Katy how long she was going to be in the UK.

'Oh no, I'm not going to the UK – I'm going to London, England.'

And you're worth $50 million, I thought. I looked at Russell and he smiled at me.

We were landing at 6 am and I told them it was time for me to start cooking their eggs. One of the other crew came up and said he'd do the breakfast.

'No, I'm doing breakfast. Katy's mine,' I said.

'But you've had her all night,' he complained.

I turned to Katy: 'You choose; do you want to be served by the straights or the gays?'

'Always the gays,' she said sweetly, looking at me.

I asked if I could have my photo taken with them both; Katy said she had no problem with this just so long as I was discreet. I promised not to go off selling them to the magazines and we had some photos taken together.

Several days later Katy and Russell's relationship became public and everyone wanted photos of them. I thought I could have sold those photos after all; but at least I'd had some private time with them and was happy to respect Katy's wish not to sell them. Though their secret getaway to Thailand did not stay a secret, I kept my end of the deal.

WHOOPS! THINGS GO WRONG

Bangkok is a place where you can be drinking high-end cocktails on the rooftop bar of some gorgeous hotel overlooking the city, with an orchestra playing, or you can be down and dirty in Patpong and riding around in tuk-tuks. To be honest, I hated tuk-tuks, mainly because I hated the heat and preferred air-conditioned transport.

One night, after clubbing with several other crew, my friends Edward and Belinda decided they'd had enough and were heading back to the hotel. They jumped into a tuk-tuk and the rest of us piled into a taxi and followed them. Edward and Belinda were quite inebriated and were hanging out of the tuk-tuk as it wove in and out of traffic and screamed around corners on two wheels. Surely someone was going to come a cropper, I thought, covering my eyes.

The tuk-tuk disappeared into the courtyard of the Queens Park Hotel and when I stepped into the foyer, I wondered where the pair had gone. Laughter rang through the foyer, and I thought that one of the people behind the desk said something about my 'friends getting married'.

What? That couldn't be right! It turned out that Edward and Belinda had stumbled across someone's wedding reception and 'announced' that they too had just got married. The Thai party was all decked out in ceremonial clothes and Edward and Belinda were standing next to them holding hands and declaring their love for each other; Edward is actually gay.

Edward spotted me standing at the entrance and said, 'Come on in, Owen; free drinks.' For the next several hours we all laughed and danced around, saying '*khob khun ka*' and '*sawasdee ka*' (hello and thank you). We had literally crashed someone's wedding.

Khao San Road is where the backpackers go for their dreadlocks, tattoos and a dose of hepatitis. It smells and wasn't my scene, but it's the place to go if you want something copied. Anything can be copied in Bangkok. You can even get a fake doctor's degree; in fact I knew someone who got hold of one and went for a job interview and it didn't raise an eyebrow. The copy shops will open a display book marked 'Australia' and it will hold things such as an Australian passport and the driver's licence for every state.

Qantas crew would get their security pass with their identification on it copied because most places we went we could get discounts or 'industry rate' by showing our cards. The pass was extremely valuable; you could swipe it to access doors from the tarmac into the airports all around the world or to get you onto the aircraft at the boarding gate. If you lost it, you couldn't fly; that could be awkward to explain to the company. We would leave our original in the hotel and take the fake one out on the town. That way, if you got pissed and lost your wallet, it wouldn't matter. Unfortunately a couple of guys I knew forgot to exchange the fake ones for the real ones, and when they tried to get onto the plane, one of the managers noticed that there was no code on the back. That sort of thing was enough to have you dismissed.

You have to know the rules in Thailand. Essentially, if you get into trouble, you pay. If your driver gets pulled over for going too fast, the first question he will ask the police is 'How much?' And whatever it is, you have to pay it: no other questions asked.

On one of the trips out of the London base with a young British crew on board, three of the girls had a big night out in Bangkok. They were having a great time, drinking cocktails and dancing on tables. Like pretty much every place in Thailand, this bar prominently displayed a picture of the King; Thais are fanatically reverential about the King. This picture was the background of a clock, which the girls accidentally knocked down and broke. When the owner of the bar told the girls they needed to give her 500 baht, one of them said, 'Fuck off.'

'Royal family, royal family,' the bar owner cried.

'If you want to see a royal family, go to Britain – that's a real royal family.'

To the girls, this was just a bit of fun, but the bar owner didn't see it that way and called the police. The 500 baht suddenly shot up to 5000 baht. Still the girls didn't take it seriously; the Thai cops looked too young to be real cops. Next thing, they're in the lock-up for the night. Two of the girls sobered up, did a deal and paid up. The other one continued to argue and she was formally arrested and ended up with a six-month gaol sentence. Qantas provided her with legal help but wasn't happy.

A few times when I was in Bangkok I visited this girl; she spent her time obsessively concocting radical ways to escape, which not only put her life in danger but that of anyone else who might be prepared to help. In the end, her parents mortgaged their house to get her out of gaol and repay Qantas for her legal assistance. Naturally, she lost her job and was never allowed to set foot in Thailand again.

Once back in the UK, she rang me up and asked if she could have her job back.

'I don't think so,' I said. It wasn't my decision anyway but I knew she'd have about as much chance as I had of becoming a royal – in either country.

It goes to show that even in a fabulous city like Bangkok, things can go awry very quickly if you don't follow the rules.

A lot of us tried to do back-to-back trips; that is, into Bangkok Monday, back to London Thursday and fly out to Bangkok again Friday. If I did three long-haul flights in a row, I could have twelve days or more at home in Brussels, which was bliss.

In 2005, I was on my last of three in a row and heading for Bangkok, working on the upper deck when I noticed that my right leg was sore. I told the CSM about it and she said she'd write it up 'just in case'. When I went upstairs to do breakfast service I mentioned it to Mitch, another good friend of mine, who was working on the same flight. I said I couldn't walk properly. He said not to worry, and to look forward to having a beer on the bus on the way into town.

However, by the time we arrived in Bangkok, I didn't feel like a beer, which for me was most unusual. When we checked in at the hotel and everyone wanted to do the usual – the pharmacy, the dinner, the club – I bowed out and went to my room to lie down. At first I couldn't get my shoe off my foot because it was so swollen, then my trouser leg was so tight I ended up ripping the pants in my effort to get them off. Increasingly worried, I put on a pair of loose-fitting shorts and rang the CSM.

She came to my room, took one look and phoned the ambulance and the Qantas medical link. I was taken to a private hospital at the end of Sukhumvit, an expat area of the city; once there, it was established that my blood pressure was 260 over 140. The doctors were horrified and rushed me through various departments, all the while trying to keep me calm. It was a rather surreal situation and it was as if I was in some medical TV drama being encouraged to stay alive by breathing: 'Take deep breaths, Owen; breathe, breathe.' No one seemed to know what was wrong with me and consequently I was shuffled about for X-rays, ECGs and scans. All of that was awful as I was tired and in a lot of pain; I had a bad headache and felt sick.

Adding to the surreal atmosphere, with the exception of the doctors, no one in this enormous hospital that looked like a five-star hotel spoke English. When eventually fellow crew started arriving at the hospital to see me, still no one seemed to know what was going on.

The room I was in was as big as a luxury hotel room and one of the crew asked for a bed to be made up so she could sleep alongside me, which was lovely of her. Qantas hadn't notified my family that I was in a hospital in Bangkok, and my flatmate, Cameron, in Belgium had no idea where I was.

Finally I received a high-level delegation. Amid much bowing – in Thailand, respect is shown by the depth of the bow; the nurses were practically flat out on the floor when a doctor walked in – I was informed that I had a deep vein thrombosis (DVT) in each leg but that the one in my right leg was bigger than the one in the left. This was a topic I knew almost nothing about; the risk of DVT was something passengers are cautioned about, but never crew. Pilots were trained to be aware because they were sitting down for long periods, but as flight attendants were supposed to be up walking around for hours at a time, why would they be at risk of DVT?

The doctors prescribed oral blood thinners, with instructions to be careful shaving and so on, because if I cut myself I could bleed to death! They told me I would be in hospital for a few weeks.

Living in that hospital was like living in a gigantic mall. It had a Starbucks and restaurants: instead of hospital food, I could ring up and order from among various cuisines.

When the Qantas crew were in town, they came bearing gifts of flowers and magazines. It was so nice to see them; each also brought me treats from the flight. Honestly, by the end of my stay I had so many amenity kits and Qantas pyjamas, I was giving them to the nurses. I entertained everyone from my bed, still hooked up to various drips; the crew liked to set things up as if we were having one of our hotel-room parties. My visitors all felt so at home in the luxurious surroundings; after pouring herself a glass of wine, one friend automatically started to light up a cigarette. I had to remind her that it was a hospital.

In actual fact, my situation was quite dangerous. When I rang the flight attendants' union in Australia, they were about as handy as an ashtray on a motorcycle. As I was

'London-based', they tried to wash their hands of me, even though I was a paid-up member and stuck in Bangkok with a DVT. Silly me; I'd thought that the welfare of individual members was something unions went into bat for. My suggestion that it might be a good idea to get me transferred back to Australia appeared to fall on deaf ears.

Knocking on Qantas's door did nothing good for my high blood pressure; according to the company rules, I had to be returned to my base, which was London (or for me, Brussels). I pointed out that I would be transferring back to Sydney in about six months anyway; wouldn't it be safer to fly me direct to Sydney rather than fly all the way back to London, from where I had to continue on to Brussels.

After nearly a month, Qantas flew me back to London as a passenger then across to Belgium, where I had to see a Belgium doctor to continue to have my treatment monitored. If you have a DVT, you're not supposed to fly for three months and flying as a passenger was more dangerous than flying as a flight attendant because you're sitting down.

One day I received a phone call from the second in charge at the London base, who by then had woken up to the fact that my treatment in Brussels was quite expensive. By chance, I had a group of friends with me so I did the shush sign to them and put her on loudspeaker.

'Hi Owen, it's Donna,' she began, sounding patronising and managerial. 'We want to help you. We'd like to try and get you home so you can have the treatment you want in Australia.'

She said this as if Qantas was doing me a favour. Of course I was aware that they wanted to get me home so Medicare could pay for my treatment; they knew I couldn't make a Worker's Compensation claim in Australia – only in the UK.

Her suggestion was for me to return to Australia in short hops – say Belgium to Dubai to Singapore to Sydney – to break up the flying time into smaller stretches.

'Donna, it's the altitude going up and down that's the problem; no doctor is going to approve me flying when I'm still taking blood thinners and my blood is being constantly monitored.'

For the sake of thoroughness, I asked the doctor anyway and he said not to be ridiculous. I rang Donna back and explained to her that I had to wait until the doctors were convinced the blood clot had gone. And I would need three months of conclusive results to say I didn't have a predisposition for it and that the problem wouldn't return.

Donna rang again some while later.

'We have come up with an excellent idea. What about we get you on a cruise ship? You get on a ship at Ostend and cruise down through Asia to Sydney.'

'How many months would that take?' I was floored by the lunacy. 'How are you going to have my blood monitored during this trip – have a helicopter fly over to take my blood tests off every week? How are you going to make sure the clot hasn't moved into another part of my body?'

'Wouldn't they be able to do that on the boat?'

I said she should think the cruise idea through properly.

'So you don't think it's is a good idea then?'

'Donna, it's not about what I think. I'm not a doctor.' By then, my friends were collapsed on the floor laughing. This was a Qantas no-brainer – take a bloody cruise and relax.

Needless to say, the cruise never happened. After another couple of months, I was cleared to fly back to Sydney.

I didn't fly to Bangkok again for another year. It wasn't my choice, it was simply the way the cookie crumbled. Bangkok had been a no-holds-barred party spread over about a year and a half. Sadly, the party had come to an abrupt halt.

AUSTRALIA

WELCOME HOME

My return to Australia in the wake of my DVT adventure in 2006 coincided with the end of my London posting. A swag of pound hounds came back to Australia expecting to keep our business and first-class positions and fly out of Sydney; after all, that's what we'd signed up for before we went to London. Oh, dear no; we were shoved to the bottom of the barrel and, to add insult to injury, we even had to fly back in economy; this was because we were leaving the London base and returning to the 'Australian rules'. Welcome home, crew.

Things got worse: the news came through that we were being posted to Melbourne because there were too many crew based in Sydney. At this we ganged up and said 'no', reminding management what they had promised when we went off to London to 'help the company out'. When we took the matter to the union, the response was far from encouraging: they pointed to the clause in our contract that said we had to be available for 'operational requirements', a fancy way of saying that the company can use you to fly anywhere, regardless of where your base is.

A few of the crew dug their heels in and refused outright to live in Melbourne; they would stay in Sydney and commute to Melbourne for their work trips. Nothing, they said, would make them change their tune.

Flying out of Melbourne was only ever going to be horrendous; the roster offered a limited variety of trips – a four-day LA flight, three-day flights to Hong Kong and Singapore, and three variations on Perth–return: 7 am and back by 7 pm, 11 am and back at 11 pm and the infamous 'red-eye': 6 pm departure and 6 am arrival. In addition, the Melbourne airport may as well have been in another state, thanks to its distance from the city – just another poke in an already red eye.

Then came the release of our first roster out of Melbourne. All of us were given more than a dozen Perth–returns, many of which were the diabolical 'red-eye special'; the only special thing about the red-eye was that the passengers slept for some of the flight! Anyway, commuting from Sydney for these flights was pretty much out of the question. Of the better flights on offer, the LA ones were nearly always given to the senior crew – the ones with twenty-plus years of flying; those with fifteen to twenty years were allocated the Hong Kong flights and those with ten to fifteen years scored Singapore. As for the rest of us, ho hum! No matter which way we looked at it, we were about to be mixing it with the Ozzies.

It sounds disloyal to say this but I found Australians demanding travellers. The Australian travelling public asked a lot of questions about the Qantas loyalty scheme – wanting to know, for instance, how many points they needed to get to New York or whatever destination was uppermost in their mind at that moment. Surprisingly, giving out this information was not something we'd been trained in. Because Australians fly a lot, they generally know the travel product they've purchased and are keen to get all their entitlements – maybe even cadge a few extras. Flying Qantas is expensive and everyone wanted value for their money. The Aussies would be hanging out for the free drinks or the chance of a second meal, even if it was only a biscuit.

One way or another, the call bell got quite a workout:

'My hand luggage is two rows down . . . no, I don't want anything from it.'

'Have you got some special treats for my kids?'

'I'm feeling sick. Can I have something for that?'

And oodles of requests for more alcohol.

Typically, Australians will try to order two or three drinks in one go, but after you explain that the airline has a strict 'one drink at a time' policy, generally they don't make a fuss. Perhaps they don't argue out of fear of their drinking being cut off completely. I found that you'd return to the Aussie passenger's seat with the drink order, then no longer than a minute or two later the bell at their seat would ding again. I'd make my way from the galley back to their seat and the person beside them would have decided they would now like a drink. After returning with their drink, they would smile and, yep, two minutes would go by and then, ding. The person in seat A would now want something. I assume it's because of the relaxed Aussie culture; then again it could also have been thoughtlessness or sheer stupidity.

Ask any flight attendant and they will tell you this drip-feeding of requests is unbelievably annoying. After a while, if I was called to take a drink order, I'd ask the people in the surrounding seats – even extending across the aisle – if they wanted anything. It was far better to get a large order all at once than to schlep up and down, getting one drink at a time. Welcome to the red eye!

QUEEN KYLIE

Royalty alert. I was rostered on a flight out of Melbourne to Singapore in December 2007, and there sitting in 2E was the former pop princess, now iconic 'queen' herself, Kylie Minogue. She was travelling back to the UK with her then new beau, Spanish model Andrés Velencoso.

It was not the first time I'd flown with Kylie. On a previous occasion, her partner was sitting between her and me, and Kylie and I were talking. Admittedly I was a little distracted; in an OMG moment, I accidentally spilled wine all over his table. It was pretty full on and I was all set for her to complain but instead she laughed. It was weird because he was speaking broken English to her; she was sort of translating to me and I was just staring. Obviously, I'd succumbed to the Kylie effect. After all, she was no ordinary mortal but a one-name person, alongside Oprah, Madonna, Whitney, Britney, Mariah and Beyoncé. But for all her superstar status, she was completely down to earth and natural. She was quiet and kind.

This occasion had a special meaning because 'our queen' had been unwell with the breast cancer business; and there she was, tiny speck of a thing, looking gorgeous with her dishy new love.

I knew in advance I would be looking after her on board; while waiting in the first-class lounge before boarding she had enquired who would be working in first. Well, that would be me! Word spread like wildfire and suddenly I was being bombarded with requests from the rest of the crew.

'It's Kylie, it's Kylie; can you get me an autograph?'

'No worries,' I said, then grabbed a pile of *OK!* and *Who* magazines and flicked through to find anything on her. Being Christmas editions, they were full of Kylie retrospectives: lots of flashbacks as well as post-cancer shots; photos of Kylie and sister Dannii, captioned with stupid comparisons of the two of them; even photos dating back to her days as Charlene in the TV series *Neighbours*. Well, naturally I wasn't going to ask her to sign anything that mentioned cancer, let alone a photo of Charlene in 1980s wedding garb marrying Jason Donovan's character, Scott.

Finally I found an advertisement for her signature perfume, Darling. Once everyone was settled in, and when the right moment came along, I handed it to her with a pen and asked if she'd sign it for my friend's eight-year-old daughter, Millie. She said of course, and then she looked closely at the glossy advertisement.

'Oh, I haven't seen this one – can I keep it?' she asked.

'Very hands on, are you? I see,' I said, and we both laughed.

Determined not to pass up the opportunity, I then went running around all the other galleys like a blue-arsed fly, trying to find another copy of that edition. But it was fruitless, so I ended giving up and returning to Kylie.

'Darl,' I said, 'you couldn't call the fragrance company, I don't suppose? I'm sure they'll send you one.'

'Oh, don't worry, honey, I've got one here,' she said, plucking a magazine from her extensive pile of reading material.

I bobbed a sort of curtsey and was about to walk away when she asked me what in-flight entertainment I recommended.

Being a loyal royal, I replied, 'I like *The Best of Kylie in Concert.*'

Being the queen, she gave a royal giggle.

WHAT IS IT ABOUT BEING AIRBORNE?

Passengers just go doolally the moment they step off the aerobridge. Over the years, I've often tried to fathom why. It's true that by the time they board, passengers have already been through quite a lot. With international flying, there is that element of finality: you wave goodbye to your friend or family, which can be emotional. And then there are a lot of steps to complete; flying is such a formal process compared to, say, catching a bus or boat. Documents must be in order, belongings may be searched, all of which can be quite intimidating.

After the passengers have checked in and gone through passport control, they usually have plenty of time to get nervous about other travellers and the flight itself, for those who are that way inclined. International flying plays into everyone's suspicions and fears. Most Australians have watched 'Bangkok Hilton', the television mini-series about a fictitious Aussie girl, played by Nicole Kidman, who ends up in gaol after someone plants drugs on her. And of course there's Schapelle Corby, who made headlines around the world after she tried unsuccessfully to convince Indonesian authorities that she had no idea how her boogie board bag came to be full of marijuana; she spent the next nine years in Bali's Kerobokan Prison.

As if passengers haven't been put through enough when they board, they still have to find their seat. After lugging all their cabin luggage down the aisle, expectantly looking at the seat numbers, they find their spot and stop dead, seemingly oblivious to the queue of people behind them; they stare glumly at the seat and back to the seat number on their boarding pass, as if to say, 'Is this what I get for $2000? Didn't Qantas promise a luxurious first-class experience for economy passengers? And that's all the leg room I get?' They store their luggage along with their manners in the overhead lockers, pushing and shoving other people's baggage aside; that'll teach them for taking too much room with their oversize cabin bags. What makes passengers bring with them so much carry-on luggage? They rarely use it.

In the scramble to array those possessions within reach, the fierce competition for space in the overhead lockers can give way to mania. Trouble of a different sort brews when long lines of fellow passengers form in the aisles while fusspots arrange their stuff . . . and there's take-off still to come.

Let's be brutally honest: getting in a plane and heading off up into the clouds has an element of danger. We flight attendants are very aware of ever-present threats. Once the flight is underway, there is a certain feeling of imprisonment – at least on a ship you can move around a fair bit and be entertained. On a plane, looking out the window provides no distraction, and finding themselves without contact to the outside world via phone or internet seems to send a lot of people batty.

One way or another, loads of passengers simply go bloody nuts!

GO WEST, YOUNG FLIGHT ATTENDANT!

Passengers on the five-hour flights to Perth tended to be holiday-makers and the fly-in fly-out, aka FIFO, workers of the mining regions of Western Australia; the return flights were full of cashed-up mine workers heading back home, many of them getting pissed, putting their hands up women's skirts and generally making nuisances of themselves on the way. So often, we ran out of beer; in fact, of any sort of alcohol on the Perth–Melbourne flight. The availability of free booze after the sobriety of the mines made most of those FIFO people act like kiddies in a candy shop.

I was sick of serving Australians after one Perth–return, let alone fifteen in a row. They'd pile on board in Perth, with their conspicuously loud Aussie accents: backpackers returning from Bali – the great unwashed in thongs and with nits in their hair. They'd drop their rubbish on the floor so freely that we often gave up bothering to collect it. It was like fighting the force of nature.

'G'day, mate. Gotta Fourex?'

Only a few years earlier, when I was flying domestically, Perth had seemed like a big country town. Now there were so many flights to Perth: amazing. I used to look out the aircraft door at the near-empty airport and think, 'What the hell is going on over here?' Finally, I overnighted in Perth; we stayed in King Street, in the city central. To my total surprise, across the road from the hotel were big-name glitzy fashion shops, such as Armani and Chanel, and beautiful little cafés. Wow! That was new. When I asked the concierge where it had all come from, he said 'mining money'. Our planes were catering to the big boom of the west.

On one Perth to Melbourne flight, I was serving some rather rowdy women and one of them started telling me about her plans for her four weeks off. She told me she worked in the canteen at the mines in Karatha, at the remote Top End of Western Australia, and earned up to AU$1700 per week. There really was gold in our west!

But I remember thinking it took a certain type of person to work in those places – I would never be able to stand the heat or isolation, even for the big money. They were a fun, feisty bunch of women, even if they did ride that call bell all the way to Melbourne. And mine workers may have had pockets full of cash but that didn't change their taste buds – Fourex beer and bourbon were the staples on those flights.

Although what we were doing was considered 'domestic flying', we were operating with long-haul crew on a long-haul aircraft. Compared to the Gold Coast, Brisbane, Sydney or Hobart one-day return flights, we were servicing double the number of passengers of the smaller short-haul aircraft. In those days, the aircraft was an older version of the 747-300, renowned for its breakdowns; we almost always took an over-night bag in case we found ourselves stuck in Perth.

Crew would call in sick left, right and centre, and that very important word 'seniority' reared its head often. Everyone found it extremely trying doing such boring flying, and typically the economy galley was the least favoured position. There were quite a few of us relegated, post London, to the lower end of the seniority ladder; crew would call in sick or desperately try to swap flights if they were positioned at the bottom because they knew they would have to do the economy galley.

Morale among the Melbourne-based ex-London crew was low. Industrial action was bubbling away in the background, and until it was resolved, thanks to a seniority freeze, there was no upward progression on offer for us and as such we were destined to stay in the same work positions on the same mind-numbing routes for the foreseeable future. Was anything likely to change?

Even though we continued to signal our unhappiness to both the union and management, neither showed the slightest interest in whether or not we were happy with our flying destinations or work positions. What concerned the people who controlled our destiny was that their low levels of sick leave and high levels of disciplinary actions looked good to the manager above them.

WEIGHTY ISSUES

I experienced a lot of stress about weight gain. A few years after I started flying, especially post London, controlling my weight became a personal battle. After I'd been working in first class for a couple of years, the battle was tougher than ever. Working up the front is quite different to working down the back in economy. In economy there are only a couple of crew to look after 300 people, all dinging for another drink; those crew are run off their feet, while everyone in first class is already asleep. After that there's nothing to do except stand around galley-gossiping, reading magazines or eating off the first-class cheese board. Plus there was all the temptation on offer at those fabulous destinations. In the year before I was posted to London, I'd already flown there so often I'd well and truly had the 'Heathrow injection': that's an in-joke about the weight that goes on as soon as you land – stodgy British food helps warm the cockles in the freezing cold.

To be specific, I put on more than 30 kilograms over the years. My weight never affected my work performance, and while I didn't believe my colleagues were too worried, the airline industry is very bitchy. A colleague may flash you their brand new pearly white 'LA smile', courtesy of Bangkok dentistry (because most crew cannot afford LA cosmetic surgery), and shortly after they'll stab you right in the back with their blunt, economy knife.

I did worry about what others thought and tried a myriad of diets, but without success. I remember watching Oprah Winfrey one day and she made a remark that resonated with me. She said she would look in shop windows and see her reflection and think, 'Who's that big fat black woman standing behind me?'

A flight attendant put a photograph on Facebook of the two of us taken when we were in Los Angeles. A former flight attendant saw it and posted the comment, 'Oh, you're there with the big penguin.' That was pretty rude coming from someone who'd left Qantas after a very public indiscretion involving sex with a pilot on board. Later, she did apologise, saying she only meant it as a joke. A fat joke.

The next person to bring up my weight was a nasty CSM called Jonny Hale; we were on a San Francisco flight; Jonny was the kind of guy who'd have been good-looking in the 1970s but thirty years later he was just an old and bitter bitch. I knew he had issues with me but I didn't see what was coming when he button-holed me in the galley.

'Owen, I just want to have a chat with you. I'm a bit concerned about your weight; do you think you should slim down? Grooming is such an important issue.' All this was said in an extremely patronising way.

'Do you have medical qualifications, Jonny, or are you a dietician?' I asked. Even though I was still reasonably junior, I was trying to maintain some dignity under such crushing remarks.

'No, but my friend works for Jenny Craig,' he said, and handed me some Jenny Craig pamphlets. 'You need to lose at least 30 kilos before you start to look acceptable.'

Oh. My. God! I was battling with my weight privately but no one had confronted me with it so starkly.

As if that wasn't bad enough, he went on to talk about my teeth and while it was probably too late to do anything about them, perhaps I could get them whitened. And had I thought about a spray tan? He made me feel like I was some candidate in a beauty contest being pulled aside and told I wasn't pretty enough. I mean, what did he want me to do, have my ribs removed?

Jonny's remarks so insulted me that I spoke to Michelle, my ground manager, about it when I got back to Sydney; she's the one who'd told me to 'take one for the team' after a passenger punched me in the face, so I wasn't completely surprised when she backed Jonny, telling me I did need to do something about my weight and it had probably caused my DVT. Yes, another medical expert masquerading as a cabin crew manager.

I had struggled with my weight for a long time and I was done with diets, but perhaps there was another option? My aunt had undergone gastric banding surgery and lost a lot of weight so I wondered if it might be suitable for me. I Googled it, and on the basis of what I read, and the experience of a family member who had had the procedure and lost a lot of weight, I entered discussions with some surgeons. At a colo-rectal clinic I met people who had lost 60 and 70 kilos and felt fabulous. After a bit more research I finally made a decision to have it done. I lost 20 kilos in about six weeks! A gastric band diet is basically soup or water. Anything more solid I threw up.

Gastric banding made flying very difficult; once while working in business and just three hours into a long-haul flight, I ate a tiny piece of cheese. Shortly afterwards I was in the toilet throwing up; when I came out of the toilet the CSM was waiting.

'Owen, have you been throwing up?'

'Yes, but I'm not sick . . .'

'I'll have to take you out of service immediately,' he said, cutting me off. The OH&S regulations are very strictly enforced on flights. Vomiting and diarrhoea among crew are two big no nos with food handling – if there is any chance that you may have something that can be passed to passengers, you can't work.

When I tried to explain about gastric banding he wouldn't listen; I'd been vomiting and that was that. I concluded that it was better not to eat at all while working.

Even though I only told a few people about the gastric banding, not surprisingly, the word whirled around Qantas like a tornado. People would be coming up to me asking if I had 'that thing' inside me. Once another crew member, Lucy, commented that she and some others had been talking and thought I'd be really funny on the TV reality show *The Biggest Loser*. That was not an idea that I thought was funny.

The 'thing' was not easy to live with; it caused havoc with my life – I often felt I was choking and I had constant reflux. After about twelve months I had the band released. Having gastric banding surgery was the worst $5000 I'd ever spent.

On a flight home from Bangkok one day, I felt like I was under siege, with passengers approaching the galley and asking for drinks and their jackets to be hung; there didn't appear to be any female flight attendants around. Desperate for some helping hands, I dashed to the upperdeck and couldn't find any of them anywhere. Next I phoned the flight deck and they weren't there either. Finally one emerged from the toilet. She was a shade of orange and shaking. The girls had been buying diet pills over the counter in Bangkok. It was probably pure speed; they could barely go five minutes without pooping. It had its funny side; that was another unsuccessful way of trying to combat the Heathrow injection. Between spray tans and shitting, they looked like they were characters out of *The Simpsons*. Don't laugh though, one married a pilot.

HERE COME THE GEN YS

After a little over a year of flying out of Melbourne, my spirit was broken. The small base mentality was not a lot of fun, but it was the monotonous flying that had taken the bigger toll.

In 2008, we heard the news we had all been waiting for. Transfers and seniority could start moving again as long as we voted as a collective in the Enterprise Bargain Agreement for that year. In the new agreement, the company and the union had agreed to employ new young flight attendants on a second-grade contract with less money and more hours than those of us on the old contract. This sounded like a no-brainer to me. As if I cared whether new crew got paid the same or less than us – just get me back to Sydney!

The idea was that any new crew would come into the seniority system below those of us on the old contract and would be allotted the leftover 'scrap flying' and the worst work positions. Scrap flying refers to the flights that are rostered after all the requests are filled as closely as possible, bearing in mind that the requests at the highest seniority level are filled first.

Around about that time, I somehow wound up talking to a union official and he said, 'All of your dreams have come true, Owen.' This should have warned me to be cautious. A lot of senior crew were very sceptical about the new deal; I wasn't across all the intricacies myself. A fellow flight attendant commented to me once that ours was 'a company union' and that he'd be surprised if there wasn't a hidden agenda in there somewhere in the fine detail of the agreement.

For me there were only positives: I returned to Sydney and to my original flying patterns, doing London trips via Bangkok or Frankfurt trips and other fillers. My seniority on these trips had improved and I thought, 'Wow, this new agreement is working beautifully.' As soon as I was covering a variety of destinations and working in different positions on the aircraft, I began feeling more engaged; I was generally enjoying flying again.

The main difference was that the new-contract crew – the ones on half our wages – tended to be the twenty-somethings who 'knew' everything and had all the answers, even though they still lived at home with their parents. On one London trip scattered with this new crew, I was preparing the premium economy galley when one of them said to me, 'Oh, I think I've got a better way to do this' and, without so much as an invitation, started rearranging things; I explained that things were arranged for convenience and safety not decoration. She backed down a bit but not before she got in another remark that flaunted her Gen Y confidence:

'Well, when I'm a manager, I'll be changing things.'

'Mmm,' I thought. So this was what the company had dangled to them: come on board with lesser conditions, upset the old apple cart and get on a fast track to promotion; their low wages would increase and the company could break up the 'old crew' camaraderie. Once these pushy young things became managers, they would be micro-managing people who had worked for Qantas for more than twenty years, correcting them – and, of course, reporting every infraction to the company. Talk about snitches: the Gen Ys would even report you if you weren't wearing your tie in the required Windsor knot.

A different flight stands out in my memory: I was working with my good friend Angela. We were collecting meal trays after the tea and coffee had been served when we noticed that progress with the collection cart on the other side of the plane seemed to be very slow. Angela crossed over to see what the hold-up was. There were two young flight attendants, cart stalled in the aisle, handing out biscuits and coffee instead of collecting trays. When she enquired what they were doing, one of them said, 'Just a little bit of individual service. The airline needs a little PR.'

'The airline already has a PR team, so why don't you do your job, collect the trays and get the cart stowed before it gets thrown in turbulence?' Angela said briskly. The young things looked back at her blankly. They were concentrating on trendy brainless things; there were no thoughts about safety.

On another flight, an emergency call came through from the flight deck: in this situation, all crew are required to pick up the nearest interphone. I was up in business class and while I was listening to the interphone announcement, I happened to notice a young crew member standing in the galley reading a magazine. I mouthed to him, 'It's an emergency call.' After I hung up, I told him there were two passengers who required medical attention: they happened to be in our area.

'Boring. You get paid more than me; you deal with it,' he shot back.

That was enough for me: 'Listen, sweet cheeks, you want to know what will be boring? When we're standing in the coroner's court because one of them died. I'm sure you'll find that process long and boring. Now grow up and help.'

After a while, we 'old hands' started questioning other things about the newbies, like what happened to the 'scrap trips' they were supposed to be getting as part of their contract. One day a few of us on the old contract were signing on for a London trip and there were a whole heap of new crew standing around.

'Where are you guys off to?' someone asked one of them.

'San Fran,' Danni replied, smugly.

Far from being allocated the leftovers, it seemed to have become commonplace for the new-contract crew to get the plum trips, such as LA, San Francisco, London – all long-range ones. It was obvious; this was about cost cutting.

A few of us contacted the union and Qantas management to voice our objections; our grievances were dismissed. But our observations were right.

By chance, I had a most revealing conversation with Leigh Clifford, the Qantas chairman. It was on a London flight and he popped into the business-class galley and was standing there chatting to crew. One of the company's main goals, he said, was to reduce wage costs and long-range pay for flight attendants. He considered it ridiculous that some flight attendants were earning more than their managers on the ground.

This comment did not reflect compensation for shift work and the delays crew often experienced, a fact I pointed out to him:

'I've been on flights that have been delayed five or six hours before you get going; you're absolutely exhausted when you arrive home.'

'And you think you should get paid more for that? If you're too exhausted, you should quit,' was his brutal response.

Well, it was easy for him to say that when he was lying in his first-class bed sinking the company's finest. For free.

As 2008 and early 2009 unfolded, the real reason for the new labour contract was unveiled. It had nothing to do with helping crew engagement and variety; it was all about getting staff on board and trained for transition to the A380 aircraft.

As the giant, much-exclaimed-over A380 fleet came on, it was the new-contract crew who were transferred to it. The A380 was a separate aircraft, not covered by the enterprise bargaining agreement. It must have been designed to be crewed by the new cheaper labour. The first few A380s to come on stream serviced the LA route – of course, the new-contract crew didn't get long-range pay – and Singapore. The Australian crew terminated in Singapore and the London to Singapore crew flew back to London; slowly but surely the London flying I loved became a thing of the past.

The old crew had been right all along – they could see what was coming. When the union and the company band together to tell you they have the best deal for you, inevitably there's an underlying agenda.

With London gone as a destination, where would I go next, I wondered. I glanced at the roster of a flight attendant with roughly the same seniority as me and noticed an 'old friend' – Perth.

CHINA

MILE-HIGH NOODLES

Chinese passengers, it must be said, are very demanding. I started flying to Shanghai before I flew to Beijing regularly. Shanghai and Beijing were similar flights – fifteen hours direct from Sydney on a small A330 airbus that carries 335 passengers. The difference is that crew only stay overnight or forty-eight hours in Shanghai and two to three days in Beijing. Shame it wasn't the other way round as Shanghai was the more popular of the two cities. But I was quite happy to work the China route regardless: a thirty-hour duty over three days was a quick way to get the maximum time off and hours up. If you did eight three-day Shanghai trips in a row, you could notch up twenty-four days' work and thirty-two days off in one roster (or, to put it another way, you'd work two days for four days off). It was even quicker than the LA trip.

Shanghai was a lot more Western than Beijing; it offered a colourful night-life, amazing restaurants and good cheap shopping. In fact it was known as the knock-off capital of the world. Fortunately, customs officers in Sydney didn't seem fazed by the fake Jimmy Choo shoes or Cartier watches coming back in crew bags; they were too busy pulling out an array of mysterious and bizarre things from the luggage of the Chinese passengers! I once saw customs officers totally stumped as they gazed into the open bag of a tiny little bespectacled woman who looked the picture of innocence. The bag was crammed with at least 20 kilograms of packaged raw meat; it looked as if she had dismembered something.

'Look, it's the Chinese Hannibal Lecter!' a flight attendant quipped. I laughed along with him – it was a funny sight, even if a little disturbing.

For obvious reasons, Qantas rostered a lot of Chinese speakers on the China flights – often they'd bid for the trips because they had family in Shanghai or Beijing. China flights were hard flying and nearly always full; the Chinese spat on the floor, coughed all over you without covering their mouths and smoked in the toilets. Because they smoke everywhere in China, they took no notice of the no smoking rules on planes. You could request that they please not smoke all you liked; the classic fob-off was 'No English'. Mind you, the English of those same passengers was remarkably good when they wanted something. Passengers were mostly made up of tour groups, students or ex-pats going home to visit family, or business people.

There is no horizontal crew rest on an A330, just a curtained-off area where crew sit during their rest period. The use of the word 'rest' on a China flight is a misnomer. Even when you were resting, the Chinese passengers would pull back the curtains – you'd look up to see a face saying, 'Excuse me, can you . . .'

The worst crew position to draw on China flights – but the biggest entertainment value for the rest of us – was doing the duty free. In economy, we would set up the duty-free carts at the back of the plane like a stall and the passengers would form a line and file past; well, they were supposed to file . . . The Chinese love a bargain, and everyone would be calling out, 'Duty free, duty free; I want to see that,' loudly telling you what they wanted, crowding around and pushing forward, trying to touch everything – even climbing on the carts. You had to be really on the ball to keep track of everything and it usually fell to the Asian crew because they were skilled at crowd control in Mandarin.

On one particular flight, a Chinese crew member had given instructions to a poor little junior Gen-Y flight attendant on how to set up the cart and what he should do, but when the onslaught of loud demands came thick and fast, he burst into tears and disappeared. Eventually, we found him in the crew rest, crying. Of course, he had to have a drink of water and go back to work; it was not like he could just go home. We poached another Chinese flight attendant from the front of the plane to take over duty-free for him and he was given other duties.

China flights had a de facto 'second service' after the first service was cleared away: cup noodles. Chinese travellers inevitably wanted noodles, noodles and more noodles. Crew had to be prepared for the noodle onslaught; we had them stock-piled in the galley. Desperate not to miss out, passengers would practically fall over themselves trying to grab a cup of noodles from the galley. It was like trying to cram a hundred people in a broom closet – highly risky, with all that boiling hot water sloshing around.

On one flight, a man was leaning over the aisle waving chopsticks and calling me: ''Scuse me, 'scuse me, 'scuse me,' as I was passing him to deliver a drink further up the aisle;

I thought I'd deal with him on my way back, but as I tried to step away from him, he flicked me with a hot chopstick, which got caught under my watch strap, burning my wrist. I wanted to smack him but the professional in me kicked in and instead I said, politely, 'Can I get you something?'

'More noodles, I want more noodles.'

I brought him some beef noodles.

'No like. I want chicken noodles.'

'Sorry, no chicken noodles. You want these noodles or no noodles?'

'I want these noodles.'

SHANGHAI, SPICE GIRLS AND BEIJING BABES

In China, everything can be bought. In a country of over a billion people that has relatively recently cottoned on to the lifestyles of people in the rest of the developed world, money has become more important than ever. One night, a group of us went to a club and I noticed how flamboyantly the Lamborghinis were parked and how many Patek Philippe watches were being flashed around. Inside, the club was abuzz with wealth. The bottles at the table and the amount of table space showed how important you were. Naturally, I wanted to be at the table with the in crowd so I found the pretty girl from the group and we started to chat. I'm not sure if the drinks were strong or spiked with ethanol or perhaps I was badly jetlagged but I was convinced that this stunning-looking girl was Zhang Ziyi, the lead in *Memoirs of a Geisha*. We hadn't been talking long when her boyfriend turned up: in many ports, foreigners are feared above any other guy, but he was lovely. She said something to him in Mandarin and they laughed, and then he invited me to join them at their table. Gotcha. Never fails for the gays: get the pretty girl on side and the rest takes care of itself; it's a natural order.

For a while, we watched the others at the table playing a Chinese board game. They told me they were film producers so I pitched an idea: I could break into the Chinese market with Ziyi as a sweetener. They said they loved it. Wow, with a few more drinks, the bigger the star she became, and so did I. Next, I told the DJ to turn up the music and showed them how we danced on tables in the Western world. Cameras flashed and so I played it up even more. Ziyi danced and I was a hero. At around half past an ambulance, I was blind drunk. They gave me their card and dropped me back to my hotel.

At breakfast, probably still pissed, I recounted the story of my star-studded night out to my friend Natalie, who was gobsmacked. She convinced me that the Chinese ultra-rich have their playtime well away from the eyes of anyone not in their elite circle. When I checked the card, it read, 'You've been punked – Ziyi'. My career in the Chinese film industry, and the millions I'd visualised myself earning, evaporated before my eyes.

Later, I happened to be in the neighbourhood so I popped into the bar and had a natter with an English-speaking security guard. After checking a few details with him, I discovered that the pretty girl was an actress but not Ziyi. She and her 'film producer' friends had all enjoyed a joke at my expense.

On a later Beijing trip, the crew and I headed to a jam-packed club and found ourselves talking in the queue with people from all kinds of interesting places, like rural China,

Taipei, Uzbekistan, Kazakhstan and Moscow. Already that day, we'd done plenty of patient queuing: we'd lined up at the Imperial Palace and the silk market and various other places, and we were a bit over it.

When I spoke to the security guy, saying we were a band and asking if he'd accept a donation to hurry us inside, he said the only way to jump queue was to go onstage. To me, that didn't seem difficult, and the others agreed to step up to the challenge. So up we went. The club threw on a Spice Girls song and we hit it. Heaps of clubbers took out their phones and were recording us and dancing along. You'd never seen a club more packed. People were buying us drinks and we were stars. Later on that night, I 'fessed up that we weren't musicians, just flight attendants.

There we were: China 1, Owen 1.

COFFEE, TEA OR ME?

Flight attendants were not encouraged to 'fraternise' with the passengers but naturally they did, especially in business and first class. We were supposed to uphold some professional code; giving out personal details and disclosing where we stayed was seen as a security issue – if the kangaroo court could lay that charge against you, then you could find yourself in big trouble. Of course this was a complete about-face from the 1970s posters of smiling mini-skirted airline hostesses more suggestive of Playboy bunnies servicing the well-mannered and well-dressed passengers. Oh, how times have changed.

Nevertheless today's female flight attendants still went fishing. They would parade through the cabin and bend down smiling with a sexy 'Hhhi' to the chosen ones, married or single, although their eligibility increased if they were single. It was quickly established who was the BOB (the real Best on Board).

In places like China, we would run into expatriates who were there following their dreams. When you met those people socially, they were usually more than willing to shout you a drink, to share what they had. I guess when you are living abroad it can be hard to let loose. That's where we came in. Crew always headed to the bars – the expensive ones, where the calibre of the guys was better. Typically, the guys there were straight though. As far as gay expat men were concerned, the petite Asian guys had the game sewn up. But a gay bar is a gay bar, and you always had the consolation of listening to Kylie.

One of my friends, Michelle, who was working out of the London base was having an affair with a married man in Australia she had met on a flight; he was head of a major company and had a wife and family stashed in a mansion in one of the best suburbs in Sydney; when he wasn't on a legitimate business trip he would sometimes pretend he was and catch the same flights Michelle was working on so they could have a couple of rip-roaring shagging nights together in Singapore or London and then she'd go off to her London life and he'd go back to the wife. Situations like this were actually very common.

Often the crew would be staying at the same five-star hotels as the businessmen on the flights. One flight attendant I worked with was notorious for boasting about her 'rewards' from the previous night's activities – a Givenchy bag here, a piece of nice jewellery there – until someone dobbed her in, probably out of jealousy. Nevertheless she had the last laugh; she married a rich guy and now travels the world as a first-class passenger with all the perks of a trophy wife.

It was not uncommon for girls to fight over the more eligible men. A good friend of mine, Analiese, was working with me in first class one day and seated in the front row of business class just on the other side of the curtain that separated first from business was the lovely Australian CEO of a very big international IT company. He was obviously smitten by Analiese, who was gorgeous enough to be a model, and there was lots of happy chat and serious flirting going on.

The supervisor on the flight, Pru, came marching into first class, took one look at the man we were talking to, motioned me into the galley and asked what was going on. I explained quietly that we were giving him special attention because he was going to put his business with Qantas; that stopped her short – the only comment she could make after that was, 'Very good, Owen. A pat on the back.'

Analiese came out to the galley holding the gentleman's card and whispered excitedly that he wanted to take her out.

'No flirting with the passengers, Analiese,' Pru said, whipping the card out of Analiese's hand. 'You could get into a lot of trouble for that.' And she walked off.

I told Analiese not to worry; I'd get his number on the sly for her.

As the passenger left the flight he approached me and said he wasn't sure what was going on but Pru had returned his card to him with her own number on the back! Talk about cheeky. I took it and gave it back to Analiese.

And yes, there was some occasional sex action in the toilets, although people did try to be discreet; it was usually when there were only two of you working. Having sex with a passenger on board broke every rule in the book health- and safety-wise and was very risky. But thanks to the Ralph Fiennes saga, the bar had been set. Every second would-be actor to come on board probably fantasised about a toilet frenzy with a flight attendant, and there are some colleagues I know who took up the challenge. They would make their advances subtle, but to know a man is to know he will be horny. In first and business, if the stars aligned they would entice the Ralph Fiennes wannabe to the galley. From there the girls would ply them with alcohol – but not too much, if you know what I mean. If things developed, the next step could well be to the toilet. Most of the time you would only find out much later on but, yes, it happened, and more often than not the guys were repeat offenders. Miranda Kerr recently came out as a member of the mile-high club. Perhaps it's more widespread then you might think?

Mile-high sex between flight attendants and passengers or between passengers happened more often in business; it was occasional in first simply because there were fewer passengers. Economy passengers can be sexy but rarely are they marriage material – that's a bit like choosing between French champagne and sparkling wine – so not worth the risk. A lot of young couples travelling in economy would have a go; they were usually found trying it on at the toilets at the back of economy. But it was harder to get away with it in economy because the toilets were smaller and there were more people lining up to use them legitimately. There was also more crew working in economy and so more chances of getting caught.

Getting caught was always a risk, especially for crew; the Qantas flight attendant who had sex with Ralph Fiennes in the first-class toilet got caught and got the sack! There was also an infamous incident in 2011 when a pilot flying as passenger was caught in a first-class suite with a female passenger. Apparently he didn't get the sack, although 'the inappropriate incident' was widely reported.

Although there was a certain amount of flirting and fun between passengers and crew, the more you did the job, the worse the passengers looked. For me personally, after a long flight, the last thing I wanted was to shag anyone. My idea of a happy ending was a long Radox bath, a mud mask, blinds down and a sleeping pill.

HISTORIC BEIJING

My first flight to Beijing was in 2009, and I spent five days there. Although I knew it was the less popular of the two Chinese destinations, I was keen to experience it. I was working in economy. The rest of the crew there were junior to me, so I found myself acting as a sort of a parental figure to them. Non-Chinese junior crew often did not cope well with the China flights; the culture was vastly different and they found some of the behaviour weird.

Beijing is a magnificent destination for historical sites and three of the crew and I were keen to do a trip to The Great Wall of China; I'd seen all the posters and glossy brochures but I had a really skewed idea of what it might look like. Aidan had given me a bit of its history because his grandparents were from Mongolia, but even so, in my mind it was a big wall that surrounded the city – a bit like Dubrovnik (funny when I think about it now). Someone had given me the name of a tour guide and I'd arranged for him to pick us up next morning at 6 am.

It was winter and we were rugged up in beanies and gloves waiting for him at what we considered an ungodly hour. A very nice limo turned up and we set off. It was a two-hour drive to get there and none of us was prepared for the sheer size and magnificence of it. You have to climb about a thousand steps and all the way up, and while walking along the top, you're offered coffee, Coke, soup and snacks by stooped vendors huddled over small stoves. So much about the day was unexpected.

The wall was covered in snow and we couldn't resist throwing snowballs at each other. It was actually quite icy and slippery; I slid around like a hippo on ice. It is so corroded and broken in parts, it would be hard to walk on it even in the best of weather. Although we were extra careful not to fall and injure ourselves, we came back bruised and sore. Naturally, being the disobedient little crew that we were, we had not told Qantas where we were going and OH&S would probably not have been happy about an excursion on which we may have been injured.

Back at our hotel, I decided to have a foot massage: my feet were sore from all the walking I'd done on the Great Wall expedition. The crew hotel was a magnificent place opposite the famous Lotus Complex where the opening ceremony for the Beijing Olympics was held in 2004. Next door, I found what I thought was a suitable place. There were a number of women sitting around waiting for customers. I told the woman in charge that I wanted a foot massage.

'Which girl you want?'

'Oh, whatever.' I wasn't fussed; it was only feet.

'You must pick.'

I wanted someone strong. 'Which one's got brothers?' I asked, addressing the room loudly. Finally, the manager selected a small mountain of a woman, who escorted me to a back room. The room contained a day bed covered with an ugly floral bedspread; this was overlaid with what looked like a human-sized doily in the shape of a giant panty-liner.

The woman instructed me to roll my trousers up and lie down on the bed; she reappeared with a giant bucket full of mud, although I couldn't see what the bucket contained due to my reclining position. Next thing, she picks up a foot and plunges it into the bucket. The mud was boiling hot.

'Fuck,' I yelled. 'What are you doing? I need to stand on these feet tomorrow!'

'No, no, no,' she said. 'Relaaaaax feet.' I couldn't pull my feet out; they were stuck in this boiling mud. Then she starts moving her hands further and further up my leg. Her hands seemed suddenly a long way from my feet. When her head was about twenty centimetres from my crotch, she looked up at me.

'You got wife?' she asked, slyly.

Then I twigged – more money for 'extra service'.

'Yes. I got wife. Very happily married, thank you. Back to the feet *now*.' It was something I would not have found unusual in Thailand or the Philippines but I had never pictured sexuality as part of the Chinese experience. Later, at the hotel, I mentioned what had happened to one of the Chinese crew and told her it was a bit of a shock.

'Why?'

'Well, it's not something I expected to find next to a five-star hotel!'

'Why not?' My colleague was a puzzled that I was shocked. 'Do you know how many businessmen stay at this hotel?'

Ah. How entrepreneurial! Well, I didn't give the poor woman her 'extra' but she did relax my feet.

Over the Beijing trip, we did several tours around the city. I was struck by the number of bicycles – millions of them – and I couldn't imagine how anyone could tell which was theirs from a huge parking lot. There were apparently no road rules; cars came from every which way at intersections and it was complete chaos. I asked the guide how drivers knew who to give way to. He told me there was no such thing as a 'give way' rule. It was a case of 'Whoever get there first,' he said.

The pollution was very bad in Beijing; it hung in the air. The streets were crowded but I didn't notice the noise all that much and for some reason it wasn't as claustrophobic as India. China was a developing giant but I never saw any wealth displayed in a flashy way like it was in India.

Beijing was a trip that all flight attendants wanted to do – once. Usually, they'd tick it off the list of destinations and never bid for it again. I went twice. Beijing was one of the international destinations Qantas axed in 2009. The glory days of the international flight attendant were a thing of the past. Economic rationalism had seen to that. Restructure by restructure, the long-haul flights were disappearing from the roster.

MUMBAI

I'M A VEGETABLE

Mumbai used to be a very unpopular destination for flight attendants. There were usually four types of Indian passenger on the Sydney–Mumbai route: in economy you'd get the smelly and demanding holiday-makers and the returning subcontractors; in business class you'd see the wealthy Australian-Indians or the colonial elite homeward bound.

I first flew to India in 2007 after I returned from my London posting and, as I had reverted to being lower in seniority, I was mostly working in economy. In economy, crew were confronted by a range of challenges that made the India route less appealing. As soon as passengers boarded you were bombarded with the aromas of the world and people calling out, 'I'm a vegetable, I'm a vegetable.'

Yes, I know you are; that's fine. Sit down please.

Being a 'vegetable' meant they were vegetarians – that is until they saw something their neighbour was having they liked better and then it was, 'I'll have the chicken', 'the lamb', 'the fish' but of course, as the cow is a sacred animal, never 'the beef'.

There was a bewildering number of vegetarian diets that had to be catered for: root vegetable, Asian vegetarian, gluten-free vegetarian and plain old vegetarian – and these were on top of the standard meal variations, which included things like diabetic, gluten-free, lactose-free, all fruit, low-fat, low-salt, low-calorie, children's and Muslim. The number of special-requirement meals on the list made India a bloody nightmare for the galley operator.

The galley operator's job is to pull out all the racks, cook the meals and put them in the carts. Out of 250 economy passengers, there might be 100 special meals. All the special meals had to go out first and be delivered individually; it was a huge headache for the poor galley crew, especially if people had moved seats after boarding. Qantas eventually woke up to the idea that rather than making 100 special meals, it would be easier to offer two selections, chicken and vegetarian. But it didn't rule out all the special vegetarian meals.

After the special meals went out, the regular meals were served; by the time the regular meals had gone out, the special meals were ready for second drinks. As you dashed about over the aircraft, it seemed as though every second or third passenger grabbed you to get your attention. They'd latch on to you everywhere they could – from the apron to your tie. What stands out most in my mind about working on those Indian flights is that you had to be ready for the guests to tell you all about themselves.

To a great many Indians, drinking whisky is a sign of wealth. Consequently, we'd reach Mumbai without a drop of the stuff left. Of course, there are no issues quite like this in business class where class-bred Indians are unfailingly polite and don't drink like there's no tomorrow.

In economy, the caste system, or centuries-old system

of cultural hierarchy, frequently raised its head. Many's the time I witnessed new-money Indians – who speak in a mixed Indian–English dialect or who have religious affiliations slightly outside the norm – ordering about individuals whom they considered to be of a more lowly status. Take, for example, the flight out of Mumbai on New Year's Day in 2008; halfway through boarding, there was a huge amount of commotion, with all sorts of people getting up and changing seats and moving luggage about in the overhead lockers. At the centre of it all, bossing all and sundry around them, were two pretty Bollywood-style young women.

'Excuse me, what's going on?' I asked them.

They were, said one of them quite rudely, 'very tired' and needed to be able stretch out and be comfortable; the others were of a lower status and had to make room for them.

'Excuse me, darling,' I said, 'I'm actually higher up the chain than any of you today as I work here and you won't be moving anyone around. If you need to be horizontal, give me your credit card and I'll send someone out to the service desk to see if we can move you up to business class.'

In case you think I was being officious, passengers need to be seated in allocated seats for the weighting of the plane for take-off.

In the meantime, the people moving for the girls were nodding subserviently: 'No problem. No problem.' To be honest, that sort of moving about was a frequent occurrence on those flights; it played havoc with the special meals seating. Getting the right special meal to the right passenger was often a nightmare.

On my first ever flight to India, I was still fairly junior, even though I'd spent two years flying in a more senior capacity from the London base. But I knew little about what happened on the India route. A young woman in economy kept pressing the cabin assistance button and asking me for a drink of Coke (the real stuff). I'd no sooner delivered the can when – ding – the bell would go again; each time the Coke was for yet another relative – the young woman seemed to be surrounded by family members.

As they watched me trot backwards and forwards, the rest of the crew said nothing. After about seven trips, I turned around and announced to all those seated nearby my button-ringing passenger, 'Right; is there anyone else here who wants a Coke and I'll bring out a crate!' Then I marched back to the galley.

'Talk about asking for Type 2 diabetes,' I huffed to my colleagues. They started laughing.

'Open the can,' one of them told me.

'Why?'

'Just open the can and give it to her.'

So next time I answered the 'ding', I handed her the opened can. She looked at me sideways but the Coke requests stopped. What I didn't know was that she had been stockpiling cans in her hand luggage. At the time, the Coke brand was extremely hard to obtain in India. The country has its own cola drinks, but Indians loved to be able to show off the real Coke brand – being able to display cans of a popular American product at home signalled wealth enough for international travel. Likewise some passengers were so thrilled to get hold of a Qantas pen, you'd think you were giving them a bloody Rolex.

Some things you'd assume are culturally universal are not; now and again I was totally floored by certain behaviours that haven't been covered in the Qantas training. Don't ask me why, but many gay men have a particular sense of smell and can pick up when a woman is having her 'monthly time'; on one such occasion, the young woman in question was sitting near the economy galley, and my suspicions were confirmed when I saw that she had blood all over her sari.

I asked one of the female crew members if she could deal with it but she happened to be pregnant and declined the job; she said she'd spew all over the woman. So I fetched a pad from the supplies box we carry for such situations and discreetly handed it to the young woman. Instead of heading for the toilet, she stood up and put it in a bag in the overhead locker, as if it was a prize to be saved. She seemed unfazed that everyone around her could see the state of her sari and that she was exuding a certain smell. I drew the situation to the attention of the other flight attendants, all of whom were as bewildered as me by what we were witnessing. At the end of the flight, the seat cushion had to be removed and destroyed.

IF WE'RE DYING, WE'RE DOING IT QUIETLY

Lightning and turbulence can provoke hysterical reactions.

'Oh, my God; are we going to die? I'm going to a wedding.'

'Well, if we're going to die, love, you won't be at the wedding and I won't be here to comfort you.'

When lightning strikes, cabin lights go out temporarily and ever since 9/11 people have been alert to every little blip. The rosary beads would come out and everyone was Oh, my God-ing and asking if I could send messages to their children. *Well, no – if the plane's going down, I'm going down with you.*

In those OMG moments, the last thing a passenger wants is a flight attendant jumping up and down saying, 'Oh, my God.' Experienced crew knew that when we were flying in turbulent areas, if we sat it out in our crew seats calmly talking to each other, this would reassure passengers. So it was a bit disconcerting to look across and see one of the junior crew mouthing, 'Oh, my God, are we going to die?'

'No. But if we are, we're going to die quietly,' I always mouthed back.

Another nightmare for flight attendants is parents travelling with young children. Everyone is warned about turbulence – that's why the captain made the announcement and turned the seat-belt sign on. So parents would put their seat belts on and leave the toddler standing up in the bassinette with its head just 10 centimetres from the roof of the plane or crawling around on the floor. I've seen a baby that wasn't locked into a harness or secured with a parent's seat belt literally fly across the cabin.

To add insult to injury, parents get offended when you asked them to secure their child as a precaution against turbulence. Picture a child being calm and goo-gooing and waving its rattle in the air: to a flight attendant this is dangerous; to the parent it's a few minutes of peace. They haven't witnessed babies in emergency situations catapulted like rockets into overhead lockers and even toilets.

The most common thing that gets a passenger's feathers up is asking them to please open their blind. While it may have been annoying to them, it was worse for me having to request it – there was no way I wanted light streaming in waking the darlings up. The blinds have to be up for take-off and landing because it's important to be able to look out the windows and see if there's fire. Try telling a stroppy passenger that it's a safety issue and they'll argue with you.

'Why is it a safety issue?'

Next thing, they'll pull the blind down again. But when you tell them the safety issue involves fire, they're suddenly alert.

'Am I going to die?' they will ask.

People sitting for hours squashed up in economy get tired and uncomfortable. Consequently, a minor irritation can escalate into a full-scale war, with passengers smacking the person in front of them or behind them because they thought the occupant of that seat had more leg room than they did. The flight attendant can become the boxing adjudicator. Sometimes I'd have to physically separate people because they'd just lost their minds.

'The person in front of me has got more room. He keeps pushing back his seat.'

'Yes, well your seat goes back as well and you're allowed to recline too.'

'I can't eat my pear now because he's reclined his seat.'

'Why don't you recline your seat too.' *Why don't you stand up and eat your bloody pear?*

An absolute nightmare is dealing with the failure of someone's in-flight entertainment; inevitably they would want to move seats, and nine times out of ten this would be impossible. It was far worse if the plane's complete system went down; then the whole plane would be complaining and ding, ding, ding, they're all calling you. It was quite astonishing the number of people who deliberately sabotaged their in-flight entertainment (we were privy to this thanks to a panel in the galley). If their entertainment system wasn't working, they insisted on being upgraded to business.

No, dear, you won't get an upgrade but I'll give you a duty-free voucher and you can entertain yourself in the dark.

There are always people on board with health issues. And the more seriously sick they are, the less likely they are to complain; they just slump over in their seat. Moderately unwell passengers will tell you about their ailments because they expect you to administer their medications for them. Admittedly, it's always a good idea to inform a flight attendant if you are diabetic because crew can keep an eye out for problems. Regardless of the circumstances, medications can't be stored in galley refrigerators or the on-board ice-boxes because if they leak into ice that is subsequently used in someone else's drink, that person could end up becoming ill. But there is always a solution. After you've explained the situation in a reasonable way, passengers look at you in disbelief:

'If I don't have my insulin, I could die.'

'I'm not stopping you from having your insulin but we can't keep in the ice-box.'

'But I want you to keep it chilled for me.'

'Okay, here's a sick bag full of ice.'

If the travelling public weren't asking me to chill things, they were asking me to heat up their baby's milk to a particular degree – as if I would know what it was.

EAT, PAY, LEAVE

To start with, I hated going to India but in the end I absolutely loved it; for one thing, flight attendants by nature like to do 'easy flying' – basically, the fewer the passengers the better as the service is over nice and fast. Well, the two most important phrases for a flight attendant are 'seniority' and 'crew rest'! On the Singapore–Mumbai sector there was only one meal service, whereas on the Singapore to Sydney flight, which is almost the same distance, there were two meal services. The other attraction was the hotels; the Qantas rule of thumb being the poorer the destination, the better the hotels and conversely, the richer the destination, the cheaper the hotels (see chapter on London).

The hotels Qantas used in India were five-star opulent; marble everywhere, huge water features, twenty-foot high ceilings, massive check-in desks, stunning pools and attentive staff bringing you refresher towels and cooling drinks. When I first started flying to Mumbai, Qantas crew stayed at The Grand Hyatt, which sits on four hectares of beautifully mani-cured grounds in Santacruz near the Bandra business district, about nine kilometres from the international airport.

The Grand Hyatt was quite decadent; there was even an attendant to take your little swim bag down to the pool. It had a wonderful champagne buffet on Sundays with all you could eat and drink between 11 am and 4 pm for the equivalent of about AU$30. Needless to say, the whole crew emerged from the buffet pissed and would either party on at the pool or in another crew member's room – often it would be a junior female flight attendant and a pilot hosting.

The China Doll Bar at The Hyatt was one of Mumbai's hotspots and a lot of crew got into trouble there. It was fre-quented by Bollywood stars and wealthy Indians. Our flight landed at midnight and once we'd checked in we'd head for the bar to have a good session before it closed at 4 am because there was nothing much to do the next day unless you wanted to shop or tour Mumbai, which of course was a whole other experience.

Upon entry, we were given a special crew currency credit card which could be swiped every time we ordered drinks and we'd settle up at the end of the night in cash or by charging it to our room, or quite commonly to someone else's. Wine was either not very good or very expensive and so it was best to drink bottled beer; if you drank cocktails and it contained ice made from tap water, you could end up with Mumbai belly. Of course we always asked if the ice was made from filtered water and of course the answer was always 'yes'; nevertheless people still got sick. The problem was the more you drank, the less careful you were.

I came unstuck on one of my first nights at the China Doll Bar; while it was a great bar, it was also very dark. Pissed and peckish, I spied an array of food platters with interesting looking delicacies sitting on the bar and, assuming they were tasting plates for general consumption, handed them around to everyone I knew. I turned around to a tap on the shoulder.

'Excuse me,' an Indian man said politely, 'that's our dinner you are handing around.' Oops!

I paid the price when I practically shat through the eye of a needle for the next two days. I have no idea if anyone else I offered the food to fell sick or even if that particular food was responsible; but it was a lesson in being careful.

When not socialising in the bar, most of the crew would get together around the pool. The pool bar was under a tropical-looking hut where we could sit sunning ourselves for hours. Generally the crew on the India trips were quite junior so we were all of the same seniority. It was too expensive to order drinks at the bar and we were not allowed to take alcohol to the pool but we could take bottles of soft drink or water so we'd toss-up who would go to the off-licence to buy the drinks. I usually lost.

To get to the off-licence I had to go out the entrance of the hotel and onto the street, past the cows and the three-legged dogs while trying not to make eye contact with the people offering me live chickens; any glimmer of interest and the head would be off and you'd have the headless chook in a bag in your hands in less than thirty seconds.

The off-licence was at the back of the hotel and it doubled as a pharmacy. This came in quite handy as it was a place where we could also stock up on the pills for our little pharmaceutical bags. I'd buy a bottle of vodka for about AU$10 and a few bottles of mixers, take them back to my hotel room where after tipping out some of the mixer drinks and topping up the bottles with vodka, I'd return to the pool with the doctored mixers. As the day wore on and the crew started drunkenly snogging each other, it surely must have been obvious to hotel staff that we were on something stronger than whatever soft drinks we were ordering from the bar.

Hotels all over the world were always tendering for an airline's crew business and the Westin Garden City must have put a bloody good bid to Qantas because it became the crew hotel in 2010. It was even more luxurious than The Grand Hyatt; I didn't think that was possible. After navigating chaotic traffic, streets full of beggars and lean-to shanties, the hotel approach was a palm-fringed road. What a contrast; it was a bit like arriving on Gilligan's Island.

The multistorey hotel had rooms the size of a house with great views over the city's only national park. Not that

I ever spent much time in the room; mostly I lazed around the infinity pool chatting with the other crew. I'd go there for breakfast with newspapers and magazines and stay there for hours; waiters would bring me drinks and someone would massage my feet as if I was a wealthy guest, not just a lowly flight attendant.

Apart from paid-for accommodation we got a daily allowance of about AU$200 for food and drinks to cover breakfast, lunch and dinner and two snacks, either using room service or the à la carte restaurant, calculated on the company's OH&S regulations on what it would cost to live at the hotel. The flight attendants' union negotiated another twenty-five per cent discount off meals, the bar and room service, which Qantas was not happy about. But crew rarely ate at the hotels anyway, most preferring to go out and buy cheap curries or groceries so they could eat in their rooms and save their allowance.

No one can take Indian currency out of India – if you are a visitor you have to spend it there or change to another currency; but the exchange rates were a rip-off so we'd smuggle the money out in our underwear or secret pockets and pray we didn't get a random body check. Once we got to Singapore we'd head for the money changer under the crew hotel, the Stamford Swiss, where we got the best rate in the world. A flight attendant could make money this way and if really prudent, could come home with another AU$800 cash on top of their salary. In this way a lot of flight attendants managed to buy mansions in the best suburbs in Sydney and Melbourne and drive around in Mercedes and BMWs.

Of course a lot of flight attendants did shop; you could get leather jackets and clothes made in twenty-four hours; crew would drop their bags at the hotel and head off into the night to get measured up so they could pick up the finished garment before flying out again. There were all sorts of exotic things one could buy but I rarely shopped; the only thing of note I ever bought was a beautiful silk scarf sprinkled with elephants (with raised trunks, which is good luck) that I still wear.

The Westin was literally across the road from a big shopping centre which had a very upmarket supermarket and a food court with the major international fast food outlets like McDonald's and KFC. India is not a place where you want to get adventurous about food so when we had hangovers we'd head over in the morning because fast food outlet menus are pretty much standard all over the world and at least you knew what you were getting.

I like hot, spicy food; a KFC Zinger burger in Australia is hot and spicy and I always asked for extra chilli sauce. The first time I ordered it in Mumbai, I asked for extra chilli sauce – something I never did again; it was so hot I raced out into the food court and vomited, crying out for 'Water, water' then remembering 'Don't drink the water' and calling for Coke.

Back at the hotel I lay in my room for hours with the air-conditioner on full blast, staring at the ceiling, waiting for the heat to leave my lips. I lathered my lips with paw paw cream but I still had welts popping up all over my lips and mouth; the blisters on my lips took days to heal.

Once the crews cottoned on that the hotels in Mumbai were not like crew hotels we stayed at in other destinations, such as the ghastly Holiday Inns, they thought it was maybe worth putting up with the passengers for five hours to get there. Many got into the whole spiritual guru thing; India had become a popular destination after Elizabeth Gilbert's

2006 bestselling memoir *Eat, Pray, Love* with plane loads of enthusiastic Americans and other Westerners looking for the same mystic experience. It became even more feverish after the Julia Roberts movie came out in 2010.

But the last laugh was actually on us. Once, when we were checking out, one of the crew, an Australian-Indian from Mumbai, started laughing at something that the receptionist said to her in Hindi. I asked her what she was laughing about. She explained that while the locals were happy to serve the influx of tourists on the *Eat, Pray, Love* trail stuffing themselves with food and living like royalty, they were happier still when we paid up and pissed off – eat, pay, leave.

TIPS FOR INFREQUENT FLYERS

People are pretty savvy travellers these days. Especially now that you can buy tickets online, travellers have usually trawled through the internet, compared tickets, read all kinds of travel advice and come on board fully informed about what they're entitled to. Still, there are a few basics that could be helpful next time you fly.

Your seat – decide whether you want an aisle or a window. Most people either like one or the other. A window seat will let you lean against the fuselage to sleep, and the aisle lets you stretch and get out more freely. However, you never want to be on an aisle across the middle, as that is where the families get put and you will be sitting with the fidgeting and screaming kids. Also no one wants to be in the middle, especially if you're travelling alone and you're likely to end up stuck sitting upright and uncomfortable. If possible, look at the seating diagram of the plane online and come up with a good reason why you need a certain seat. Then try to ring someone up pre-flight and book that seat. Chances are they'll give you what you want as they won't want you complaining; it should be all sorted when you go to check in.

Stowing baggage – only bring what you need; pack a light jumper, as planes get cold, and a magazine and some water. If your bag is small enough, put it under the seat in front of you. That way you can access it quickly. If space in the overhead lockers is tight your bag could be stowed wherever it can fit, which sort of defeats the purpose of needing it on board.

Do . . . bring some extra snacks. Also come on board with a plan about when you want to sleep and when you want to watch movies.

Don't . . . drink alcohol before the flight and don't drink lots on board. It really dehydrates you and it's a rule of three to one: one drink in the air is equivalent to three on the ground. And don't get the flight attendant off side. They are your best chance of being properly looked after and comfortable on your flight.

Sit back, relax, and enjoy your flight.

OMG, IT'S A BOMB!

In November 2008, I was staying at the Hyatt in Mumbai when the magnificent downtown Taj and Oberoi hotels and the renowned tourist haunt Leopold's Café were bombed. I had taken my very dear friend Jenny along on this trip; she worked in finance, and as the industry was going through the global financial crisis she was having a tough time.

'Come to Mumbai with me,' I urged. 'It will be so relaxing. We can do the spas, laze around the pool and go up to the Taj Hotel for cocktails.'

The loads were low and I was able to put her on my staff travel and upgrade her to business. We flew the direct route to Mumbai and Jenny was relaxed and ready to continue that way. I remember how impressed she was with the room at the Hyatt: 'Wow, wow, wow,' she exclaimed as she surveyed the king-sized beds in the room the size of a billiard hall, and the bathroom with its three-metre long tub.

We'd showered and were getting ready to go down to the bar for drinks when the phone rang. Of course I didn't answer it – there was no way I wanted to be called out if someone was sick, especially as I was about to go exploring with Jenny. Everyone had a mobile by then, and if you wanted to stay in touch with someone you'd text them. No, I wasn't answering the phone.

Next minute there's a knock on the door and one of the hotel managers stood there with a several other unsmiling staff and said Qantas was trying to get in touch with me and I must answer the phone. I told him I was sorry but we were tired and were going to bed.

'Please, sir, you must answer phone. There has been a big event.'

The phone was by then ringing non-stop in the background and I started to think someone must have died. I picked up the phone; it was Carl, a cabin-crew manager in Sydney. 'You haven't been answering your phone. Are you in your room?'

Obviously I was. 'Carl, I'm trying to sleep.'

'Do you know where Kate and Natasha are?' he asked.

These were two other flight attendants; on arrival they had headed off to get measured up for some jackets. I had no idea exactly where they'd gone but told Carl they'd gone to shop.

He adopted an odd tone and said this was not a time for games. He demanded to know where all the crew were, as if I was the crew coordinator, and then asked:

'Have you been watching TV?'

'No, Carl. As I told you, I've been trying to sleep. What's going on?'

'Don't be alarmed but you are to stay in your room; don't order room service; don't open the door to anyone. There have been terrorist bombings at two hotels in Mumbai and staff have been involved.'

Jenny and I turned on the TV to see footage of our hotel – surrounded by police and security guards with guns! Did that mean our hotel was one of the hotels targeted? Don't be alarmed, Carl had said!

Jenny's stress-free sojourn appeared to have just gone up in smoke. Well, we decided the best thing to do was to break out the mini bar; we proceeded to drink our way through the crisis, glued to the TV. Sleep wasn't an option because Qantas kept calling every thirty minutes to make sure we were still there. Yes, we were – with various bottles of tranquilisers and a mini bar! Not that we mentioned that to Qantas.

Night turned into day and we were still stuck in the room, wondering what was going on. Kate and Natasha had turned up but none of us was any the wiser; the Qantas manager in Mumbai actually lived in the hotel, but no one was telling us anything. Our only information was coming from the news channels on TV. The beautiful old Taj Mahal Palace Hotel, where I'd planned to take Jenny for drinks, was on fire. The other hotel attacked was the Oberoi Trident. Both hotels were located on the other side of the city and were frequented by foreign business people and rich tourists. Hotel guests were being shot and it appeared that the terrorists were looking for Americans and Brits. Being Australian was not comforting.

Pissed and starving, finally we decided to risk ordering room service. If we were going down, we decided were going down eating! Everyone's a hero until it's time to open the door. When the knock came, Jenny bolted for the bathroom and locked herself in. I gingerly opened the door a crack and saw a waiter with a tray of food, flanked by two security guards with guns. Confronted with guns, my life literally flashed in front of my eyes and I screamed. The waiter reassured me he had just food and passed me the tray. No shots were fired, and we ate like there was no tomorrow.

A bit later we were instructed to meet the rest of the flight and cabin crew in the lobby. From there the dozen of us were escorted through a rabbit warren of meeting rooms under the hotel for a briefing with the local Qantas manager and a special security consultant. We were informed that the death toll was more than 100 and the terrorists, believed to be from some Pakistani organisation, had also bombed a hospital, a Jewish centre and the popular tourist spot Leopold's Café as well as the railway station.

What concerned me most was Jenny – she was my responsibility, not Qantas's – and although I'd heard a lot of 'Qantas Family' crap about looking after crew, little of that rhetoric had been about anyone else. Yes, I was assured, they were looking after crew and 'of course' they would look after Jenny too. The security consultant, an Australian who had been in Thailand advising the government after the Bangkok riots, had been flown in to brief us on the evacuation plan. There were no Qantas flights coming in or out as the airport was considered a high danger zone.

We were told we could eat in the restaurant but were not to go outside the hotel under any circumstances. The hotel was in complete lockdown because it was not known if it was also a target. Being in India tends to put you on 'alert mode' anyway; now we were on the highest alert possible.

After the meeting, Jenny, me and some of the crew retreated to the pool bar. Over the next five days, I spent about two weeks' wages there, on the mini bar and in the restaurant. During this time, fearing this might be our last hurrah, we discovered a lot about each other; one of the pilots even came out as being gay and we all had a half-celebration, half-memorial until we ran out of money.

Thinking you might be going to die does have a dramatic effect. For instance, no one wants to take secrets to the grave; the idea really does crack into a thousand pieces. So out came all this stuff: Jenny confessed that she had shagged the head of Qantas security and they had been having secret flirting. Women know how to use their eyes, there's no doubt about it. Maybe that's why some men don't trust women, even in a burka.

It was hardly a relaxing time and we were on edge. Once and once only, in our room we dared open the curtains a little bit – to find some kid sitting on a fence looking straight across at us; we quickly pulled the curtains closed. All of us stayed tuned to the hotel channel, which showed what was going on outside the front entrance, to see if anyone was getting shot. We wore a track to the mini bar; there's nothing like a Tanqueray or two to take the edge off.

In the end, we were told that Qantas was bringing in a special flight to evacuate us to Singapore. At the appointed hour, we boarded the bus quickly and quietly. Airline crews are good hostage targets and it was a pretty tense trip to the airport, with the curtains drawn and a guard sitting at the back of the bus armed with a machine gun.

Mumbai's airport was chaotic at the best of times. Now it was a thousand times worse, with planes flying out all over the place. Naturally, Qantas had not sent in an empty plane to collect us; it was loaded with Indian passengers wanting to get home and, because everyone else wanted to get out, Qantas being Qantas also sold seats outbound. We milled about among the chaos, half-tanked and not convinced we would even get a seat. When all the crew were eventually issued economy seats up the back near the galley, the pilots complained that according to their award, they were not allowed to 'passenger' in anything less than business class. Poor Jenny hadn't even been assigned a seat. After some shuffling and a lot of heavy-handed pressure from the pilots, they were moved up and a seat was found for Jenny.

The plane had been double-catered out of Singapore as it wasn't able to take on catering in Mumbai. No cleaners had been allowed on board so the plane was filthy. There's not much else to do on a dirty plane, packed to capacity, but to down the drinks, which the crew threw at us during the five-hour flight to Singapore. When we got to Sydney, the media was out in force to greet us. It was surreal – like being in a movie and we'd arrived for the premiere. Camera lights flashed, there were people everywhere and after it was all over, we were on our own to digest what we'd just lived through.

ANY CHANCE OF AN UPGRADE?

During boarding is when you suss out passengers. For one, they are standing, so you can tell whether they are friendly, dismissive, painful, intoxicated or fine. It's also the passengers' opportunity to buttonhole members of the crew. You'll hear all about their 'special circumstances', whether they be relationship problems, illness or impending death of a loved one – whatever they think will get them the best seat or, even better, an upgrade. But flight attendants are nothing if not practical: straightaway we can recognise if someone's likely to string it out and be a handful. The ones with real problems tend to be quiet and get sloshed and that's when these things come out.

It's surprisingly easy to signal to other crew – even complex messages like 'another death' or 'needs an upgrade because her husband left her'.

Once in a while, when someone's trying to have a lend of you, there's an opportunity for a bit of fun. One day, a well-known person made a big deal of showing me her ticket and telling me it was incorrect.

'I was told I would have a first-class seat,' she claimed.

I said, 'No. Looks like your ticket and seat match up.'

After trying a little flirting and pouting, finally this woman came to the point: 'Well, is first full?'

With glee, I turned and replied, 'No, it's not.'

'Well,' she said, 'couldn't I be moved?'

'Sure. Give me your credit card and I'll whip up to customer service and see if they can process it.'

Somewhat sulkily, she took her seat.

Before I had the experience to grasp the intricacies of first class, I found those passengers tricky too. Individuals would sit up and have the service and then go to 'talk to their friend' and swap seats. The friend would then settle in and want to start a full service too. Obviously there wasn't enough food for this to go on and so when people wanted to swap seats to let their friend 'rest', we would say, 'You must decide who is sitting in here once and for all; you can't swap back.' You must remember, these passengers generally fly a lot so they are up for the game as much as anyone and are happy to push the boundaries.

If someone is a real handful, the crew will put their heads together in the galley to figure out a way to handle them.

GOODBYE, INDIA

I took Cameron, the friend I'd shared the Brussels house with, on a trip to India. It was somewhere he wouldn't normally go, and I told him the crew was great and he'd better come before The Westin discovered our scams and kicked us out. Eventually, the good hotels were bound to get sick of dealing with airline crew and we'd get the boot.

It can be quite exhausting taking a friend with you when you're working; they're resting up in business class, and on arrival at the hotel they immediately want to go out and do something while you're tired and want to lie down. But even before that comes up, first you have to get to the hotel; and just getting out of the airport itself in Mumbai is challenging. As soon as you get through customs, there are hundreds of people grabbing and pulling at you. The poverty-stricken masses come into the airport from the surrounding shanty towns, which sprang up around the tip that used to take all the food and rubbish from the aircraft; it's now cut off by a huge barbed wire fence at the end of the runway.

Beggars beg; everyone is trying to sell you something; and once people surround you, someone will slip their hands into your pockets before you know what's happening. When I first encountered this, it made me feel claustrophobic and from then on I was careful not to keep anything in my pockets. Everything was in my bag and, with one eye over my shoulder and the other on my luggage, I'd race at speed for the crew bus while dodging fifty money-changers all calling out that they'd give me the best deal.

Not only did I worry about getting robbed, I also worried about getting sick. Everywhere you went you'd be confronted by the sight of little kids with jaundiced eyes, weeping sores and skin irritations. Falling ill in India and needing to stay for treatment was a scary prospect for airline crew: it didn't matter how sick you were, your visa was issued for a limited time. Ours was usually for three days, and getting it extended was difficult; you would have to make your way downtown to the consulate, which was a nightmare if you had Mumbai belly. Even if you were really sick, it was still better to get into your uniform, get on the plane and sit in the crew rest until you got to Singapore, where you could stay and recover as long as you liked.

Even though I'd primed Cameron on the art of running for the crew bus, nothing could have prepared him for the impact of the odours as we drove off – the overpowering smells of burning rubbish, diesel and raw sewage. Any flight attendant who didn't know she was pregnant would soon find out in Mumbai as the smells would immediately make her nauseous.

Once on the bus, the ten cabin crew and two pilots would crack open the beers we'd brought from the plane. Normally, we'd bring two each, and open one on the way to the hotel. This was now against company policy – the rules had been tightened – but Mumbai was one of those places crew could turn a blind eye and be social. Out the windows of the bus you were confronted with a seething mass of people and everywhere possible, there was some sort of makeshift dwelling; any space for lying down was occupied by someone. Cameron was looking a bit discomfited but when we pulled up outside the opulent Westin Hotel, the look on his face changed to one of complete disbelief.

In the morning we went down to breakfast, where you could order anything you wanted to eat; we sat in the dining room enjoying views of mists slowly rolling in over beautiful trees. Afterwards I called up my usual taxi driver so I could show Cameron the sights. First, the driver said, we had to go via the Spice Markets, where his uncle had a stall, and this necessitated detours at various places where other relatives had shops.

I was fine with that; I thought the Spice Markets would be a great place to shock Cameron with the contrast between the opulence of the hotel and the poverty of the streets. They were an assault on the senses – every imaginable spice and colour and smell was arrayed there. Barefoot people squatted on the ground, mangy dogs sniffed around, bird cages sat on top of fish tanks; the heat was sweltering and flies stuck to everything. I'd told Cameron to video everywhere we went so he could show people back in Australia; I also wanted evidence in case anything went wrong (for Qantas).

I made Cameron go into the meat market, where blood dripped from hanging carcases; personally, I couldn't go in – the smell from the outside was enough for me. Everywhere we went was amazing in some way. Cameron was wearing sneakers and I was wearing shorts and thongs; at one stage I looked down and realised I was actually standing in an open sewer drain; nearby, a loose electrical cord was swinging and letting off sparks.

Afterwards we visited the usual tourist spots: The Taj Hotel, the Taj Mahal, The Oberoi Hotel, the waterfront, the Gateway of India, where the ships docked. Add to that list what is reputedly the most expensive house in the world – 'Antillia', in southern Mumbai, one of the best parts of the city. This privately owned residence stands twenty-seven storeys high, with water views and 600 full-time staff; it looks like an unspeakably vulgar five-star hotel.

Later we went to Jhujhu Beach, where you can see the most spectacular magical sunsets over the Indian Ocean. As it's home to some up-and-coming Bollywood actors, we tried to spot a few strolling along the walkway. Some of the finest restaurants in Mumbai are located along the beach and at one of them you can get the best chicken masala in the world. In the distance we could see a giant ferris wheel. Highlighting the difference between India and Australia, it had no safety harnesses or belts to stop people – mostly children went on it – from falling out. Workers routinely climb around on forty-storey construction sites without harnesses or helmets. Life appeared to have little currency here; when a major construction collapsed, burying many workers, the construction company simply abandoned the site and moved next door to start building again within a day or so.

On the night before we left, we were out drinking with some of the other crew. We were having jugs of vodka with ice; the more you drink, the less careful you are. That ice! What was I thinking? Then again, maybe it was something I touched; they say that ninety per cent of English pound notes have traces of cocaine on them – well, I bet ninety per cent of Indian rupees have traces of E-coli. On the flight back to Singapore I started to feel sick but managed to get there okay.

Normally, I would have stayed on in Singapore and rested for a couple of days but because I had Cameron with me, I decided to carry on to Brisbane. Halfway through the meal service on the flight to Brisbane, I thought, 'Oh, my God, I'm going to throw up.' I bolted, but the economy toilets were occupied so I raced to business class, where I sat uncontrollably shitting while also throwing up in the basin.

The CSM kept knocking on the door, asking if I was all right. There was nothing she could do; there was no point in putting an oxygen mask on me because I couldn't stop spewing. Soon I was so dehydrated I was practically hallucinating. When we were about to land, a fellow crew member had to take over my duty and man my door; I emerged from the toilet at the last possible minute and sat on the crew jump seat squeezing my bum cheeks together and holding a sick bag.

Weak and dehydrated, I struggled off the plane. Luckily, the pilot had radioed ahead that I was very ill so while the rest of the crew were transiting on to Sydney and taking Cameron with them, one of the Brisbane-based managers met me at the airport in a crew bus and took me straight to hospital. There I stayed for ten days after being diagnosed with giardiasis, a parasitic infection caused by unsafe water, contaminated food or personal contact.

None of that put me off India and I pretty much had an India trip every roster. The only time it wasn't easy to get an India trip was during the cricket season, when the crew dynamic would change from ten years seniority to thirty-five years; all the straight male flight attendants would go up to watch the cricket. Crew of that seniority tended to like long-haul trips, such as the US, where the passengers were easy, the shopping good and the food recognisable. Normally, they wouldn't choose India; cricket made the difference.

Of crew who were drawn to India, many got all spiritual and bought places there. For all the missing limbs and begging children, you never saw child sex exploitation like you did in Manila and Bangkok. And while there was a generic feeling of unsafeness, I never felt physically threatened like I had in other places. Put it this way: I felt I might get robbed but wouldn't have my throat slit or been thrown in the back of truck and sold into sex slavery! It was the chaos and claustrophobia caused by the clamouring masses that was discomfiting; but I never saw being swept up in the swirling crowds as a safety threat.

So I kept bidding for India. Then came the day where one moment I had another India trip on my roster and then suddenly, when I checked, it had disappeared. When I asked why, I was told we were not flying there anymore. Qantas had started shutting down routes that weren't always full, and India was one. There it was: eat, pay, leave! Goodbye, India.

INDONESIA

JAKARTA – TRAFFIC JAM CENTRAL

Jakarta, much like Manila, was a relaxing filler trip, except Indonesia didn't attract the leering old men that the Philippines did: working on a flight full of sex tourists was never an enjoyable experience. Even though the Philippines was stunning, the cosmetic procedures were cheap and good and the Sofitel was hands down the nicest crew accommodation I ever experienced, nothing made up for the sleaze that I saw going on before my own eyes. By contrast, Jakarta wasn't worth many duty hours but it was easy flying and the passengers were varied and interesting. A lot of diplomats, politicians, federal police and expatriates flew Sydney to Jakarta.

After landing, you walked through the erratic older-style airport; the stinking heat combined with overwhelming body odour from passengers arriving from everywhere plus hawking money changers all reminded me of arriving in Mumbai.

Jakarta probably had the second-best crew hotel in the whole Qantas network, the regal Mulia Hotel Jakarta. It had a beautiful Bahamas blue pool that crew loved to lie around and the most divine Chinese and seafood buffets. The problem was getting there.

I hadn't had a Jakarta flight on my roster for some time and I'd forgotten how seriously Muslim the place was. Consequently, I was a little taken aback when I walked out of the airport and spotted a mass of burkas and beards – for a second I thought I'd gone with the A380 crew instead of the A330 and landed in Dubai.

Next it was a case of here come the traffic jams; after navigating our way to the crew bus, it then took a minimum of two hours to get to the hotel, moving about 100 metres every ten minutes. The CSM was well prepared; he came on the bus with a carton of local beers and boy, did we need them. This CSM was such a regular he knew everyone – from the Jakarta-based airport staff to the hotel clerks – and all by name; he spoke some Indonesian as well. The flights always had a crew member who spoke the local language, which invariably came in handy.

Thankfully the flight had been uneventful, which meant the crew was relaxed, and we needed to be. The one good thing about being stuck in traffic was that it gave us a chance to put our heads together and plan our stay. When the CSM was in Jakarta, he did volunteer work with an orphanage some distance out of the city and would try and convince the crew to go with him to help. Although I supported what he was doing and the idea of helping appealed to me, I'd previously had a bad experience visiting an orphanage.

All over the world I had visited orphanages to see where I could help out and donate – Thailand, India, Kenya and Africa; I was particularly affected by the one I visited in Mombasa in Kenya. My mum came with me on an African trip and we visited an AIDS orphanage with a translator. The people who ran the orphanages would often 'show off' the children like they were trained performers; if you felt particular empathy for one child, they reasoned, you were more likely to give the manager money. When we arrived at this place, they brought all the little kids out and stood them in a line and (through the translator) gave us a run-down of each child. It was awful.

I gave the manager an AU$200 donation towards running the orphanage; we understood this would be used for food and medicines. This man said something in Bantu and gave me a look of disgust. I asked the translator what was wrong and he said that the manager called us 'cheap'. That really offended me. Expectations that Westerners would make big donations had become standard after the Hollywood brigade swept through. I could see an open market across the road.

'Well, not everyone is Angelina Jolie or Madonna; if we're too cheap I'll take the money and buy a whole lot of supplies you need and I bet I have loads of change from $200.'

He took a swig of his whisky and grunted but didn't return the money.

However, at the same orphanage I saw a little girl wearing a bright yellow dress, with big eyes and a smile that could light up Times Square. In spite of her surroundings, she was so cheerful and looked like she could have achieved anything in this world that had been so cruel to her. How badly I wanted to take her with me and give her a better life! But of course it's not that simple. As Mum said, even if I could help, how could I raise her when I was flying around the world? Turning my back on that little girl and walking out of the orphanage haunts me to this day. No, sorry, but I would not be paying a visit to the Jakarta orphanage, though I did make a donation.

Although Jakarta had the biggest Australian embassy in the world and there was a very large Australian presence,

I didn't find the city relaxing; I was always extremely wary. Of course, the same could be said for many destinations but I felt it quite strongly there. Everywhere I looked, there seemed to be millions of Indonesians looking back at me strangely. The people didn't seem overly helpful or friendly either, perhaps because I was a Westerner in a country with the biggest Muslim population in the world.

On one trip, I was out with crew drinking after dinner and we were walking around the cobbled and broken streets and suddenly we ended up in a dark and mangy area where there were few people. We asked a group of Muslim women how to get back to the main part of the city but they would not talk to us. We walked and walked and although I didn't feel physically threatened, I was relieved when we turned the corner and suddenly we were back in city melee and found the hotel.

Another time, I had an interesting experience at a food court. After a relaxing massage, I was about to have something to eat and I headed for a long table where some women were seated. They all looked at me strangely as I sat down, then without uttering a word, they all stood up and left. A friend who worked for Emirates told me that it didn't matter whether it was Jakarta or Saudi Arabia, Muslim women would not sit with non-Muslim men. This was a bit disconcerting as it wasn't behaviour I was used to but it was all part of the life of an international flight attendant.

I only went to Jakarta a few times and treated it as a nice 'holiday trip' where I stayed at a beautiful hotel for a couple of days. I have to say that's where the attraction of the city began and ended. After a couple of trips, I rarely left the hotel.

CALMING SCREAMING BABIES

Many people's enduring memory of flying involves upset babies. Like all flight attendants, I've had my fair share of ear-splitting experiences. When you take your work position, you will know whether you are going to be around the area with bassinettes; if you are, that can be a real pain. It means that your section is more likely to be woken up and therefore your passengers will be wanting more from you: ding, ding, ding. The other downside is that mothers who are travelling with more than one child usually expect you to be their in-flight nanny.

More often than not, you will get some frantic parent bursting into the galley saying they need to go to the toilet and simply pass you their bundle of joy. You are left holding the baby, so to speak.

Parents of infants often have special requests too; typically it's 'Can I have my baby's milk heated lukewarm, to say 60 degrees?' Spoiler alert here: hello, all we ever do is run it under warm water and hope for the best.

Screaming babies, I must be honest, are a flight attendant's worst nightmare. Rarely do you need to ask a mum if she's okay; it'll be written all over her face when she is in a state of helplessness. You can offer to try and nurse the baby, but the harsh reality is that a plane makes them vulnerable – their little lungs have to deal with the condensed air, and their teeth and ears – with those immature eustachian tubes – often play up. A lot of mums travel with Phenergan, which is a little helper for infants. What often worked best for me was distracting them the old-fashioned way, with a pencil and paper.

```
```

BALI HIGH

My feelings about Jakarta were totally unlike my feelings about the very spiritual and gorgeous holiday destination of Bali. Although it's a province of Indonesia, it might as well be a completely different country. Well, the Balinese are eighty-five per cent Hindu, and the rest of Indonesia is about eighty-seven per cent Muslim, so the contrast in customs was bound to be noticeable. Over the years I got the impression that the Muslim Indonesians felt superior to the Hindu Balinese because the Balinese accepted the Western lifestyle and lived off tourism.

Bali attracted a completely different market; Qantas flew Bali and return out of Australia before it became a Jetstar service. Although I went to Bali many times on holiday, I never did a work trip there myself. From other colleagues, I knew that the flights were full of loud, boozing holidaying Aussies and the poor crew basically walked to Bali and back and would step of the plane stinking of beer, B.O. and spew.

POOLSIDE FASHIONS

Jakarta is the only place I have seen the 'burkini' – fashion swimwear brought to Western attention by TV cooking goddess Nigella Lawson: she was snapped wearing one on an Australian beach in 2011 – not because she's Muslim but because she wanted to keep the sun off her impeccable porcelain skin. I was sitting beside the hotel pool, having a beer and reading the paper and I noticed something slightly strange in the pool. At first I thought it must be a burns victim in a pressure suit. On looking more closely, I realised that there were four or five women either swimming or lying by the pool wearing what looked like black space suits.

When I ordered my next drink, I asked the waiter what was going on and he told me that it was a religious thing; the burkini allowed the women to swim while remaining covered up. Well, I had to get a photo and I pulled out my camera, but I was quickly told that it wasn't permitted.

The Mulia Hotel was a popular venue for weddings and on numerous occasions while staying there I saw Muslim women in the foyer coming and going to these affairs. Gradually, I realised that while they may have looked like they were wearing the same gear, there were subtle differences denoting wealth or individuality. Some had gems and stones sewn around their burkas which reflected in the light; some even had burkas designed by famous Western designers.

Over the course of my career, I was exposed to all kinds of cultural differences. Some were easier to deal with than others. It was amazing how you learnt to adapt and just get on with your job.

GUILTY OR NOT . . .

As our A330 was winging its way to Jakarta one time, I was chatting with the crew in the galley and we got talking with some nice, friendly men who were standing nearby; they said they were Australian Federal Police (AFP) heading to Jakarta on business. Naturally enough, the conversation soon turned to the convicted Australian drug smuggler Schapelle Corby, who was serving a twenty-year gaol sentence in Bali. Personally, I had always believed Schapelle was innocent. It seemed unbelievable to me that anyone would try to get away with carrying in *four kilograms* of marijuana: the smell of it alone would have been enough to attract attention. I could smell someone smoking pot a mile away, and the whiff coming off such a huge amount would have been extremely pungent! Theories about how it could have got in the bag were rife at the time, including that a baggage handler or someone else put it there in transit to Bali. To me, Schapelle didn't look like a girl who would do something like that.

One of the AFP guys turned to me and said, 'She is as guilty as hell, mate.'

He explained that she had been under surveillance for some time and that she was 'in it up to her eyeballs'. They said that for some time the Indonesian authorities had also been watching Schapelle as she came and went from Bali.

My natural reaction was to question why she wasn't stopped in Sydney before she flew out. They didn't seem to want to talk about that but they were adamant that Schapelle was no innocent angel, no matter how sweet she looked.

Obviously there was a lot more to it than the light-hearted natter we had in the galley. To this day, however, I am not convinced.

SOUTH AFRICA

JO'BURG, THE POOR MAN'S LA

Johannesburg used to be known among flight attendants as the 'poor man's LA'. To get there, it was a hard flight *and* hard flying; the first expression reflects that it was a long day flight (fifteen hours) out of Sydney, leaving early morning; the latter refers to the demanding nature of the passengers. On the South Africa flights, they were either smelly backpackers or haughty colonial South Africans. It was also a high-alert destination and for most of my career had the highest incidence of sick leave among crew. Johannesburg was one of the most dangerous cities in the world, with appalling crime rates, violence and rape. Plus the rand was practically worthless. Voilà, all the elements of hideousness.

I hadn't had much to do with South Africans before I started flying so wasn't too familiar with the culture. I was in for a quick lesson! I did a few Sydney–Johannesburg flights before I got posted to London and they were a wake-up call. On my first flight to South Africa, I was working as 'assist' in business class and I heard a finger clicking, clicking.

'Boy, git me an Appletise.'

'Pardon?' I'd never heard of this apparently popular commercial drink in South Africa and I'd never been addressed as 'boy' before.

'What's an Appletise?' I asked one of the crew.

'Apple juice and soda water,' she shot back.

The same man continued to order me to 'git me' this and 'git me' that. Back in the galley I said to one of the other crew, 'Can you believe this guy?'

'Oh, of course, it's your first South Africa. You'll get used to it – they're very demanding and rude. Why do you think the crew sick leave is so high on these flights?' Being veterans of South Africa flying they were desensitised to the superior attitude of the white minority.

Later, when I'd done more South African trips, I broadened my view and came to recognise the people as kind and hospitable. Also, I realised that the demanding way many of them acted was a reflection of the way they'd grown up: with servants at their beck and call, they'd developed an ingrained sense of entitlement. It didn't matter whether they were in economy or first class, it was the same. They complained about everything and expected to be treated like royalty. Most of the trip you were running around answering finger-clicking and constant loud calls spoken in harsh South African accents: 'Excuse me. Boy! Git me, git me . . . You, you!' We may have been in subservient positions as flight attendants but we weren't servants and they didn't know how to deal with us. Some of my responses even surprised me with their rudeness!

I could say, 'Excuse me, I'm not your slave. Apartheid finished some years ago,' and ignore the demand. And they'd look at me in bewildered astonishment. Accuse a South African of being racist and they'd invariably say, 'I'm not racist.' They would be absolutely flabbergasted and so indignant, and go on about how South Africa had just become the whipping boy for everything that goes on in the rest of the world.

As the number of black South Africans increased, flight attendants found ourselves dealing more often with 'preferential seating' issues. When people discovered they were sitting next to a black person, they'd often refuse to sit there and insist on being moved.

On one flight, a woman refused point blank to sit next to a black guy. When we reported it to the CSM, down the aisle he came; we sensed that the woman was about to be firmly put in her place.

'Sir, will you come with me and bring your bags,' the CSM asked the man, who must have thought he was in trouble.

'Thank you,' the woman said, satisfied she'd got her way.

'That's okay,' the CSM said. 'You enjoy your flight in economy. I'm taking this gentleman up the front.'

Now some readers might think that this is not a true story but that is exactly what happened.

And on the topic of bizarre tweets and texts, there was one doing the rounds about the marketing executive who is supposed to have said, 'I'm going to South Africa, hope I don't get AIDS. Just kidding, I'm white.' As crazy as it sounds, we flight attendants have seen plenty of travellers with those astoundingly stupid notions.

Although the attitudes of the passengers and the tensions they created may have been superficially funny, they were nevertheless unnerving at times. On another occasion I was working in the galley in premium economy; on a 747, this section has its own cabin and galley, hence I could usually avoid interacting with the masses. Because no one could go on a break until everyone was finished, I went down to economy to help out. Someone was calling out, 'Boy, boy.'

'Yes, sir.'

'What sort of wine do you have?'

'Red or white.'

'What style of white and what style of red?'

'There's only one type of each and I'm not sure – maybe a chardonnay and a shiraz.'

'Oh, well that's not acceptable; I want you to go to business class and git me a—'

Interrupting him mid-sentence, I said I was sorry but I was in the middle of collection; I could give him a bottle of whatever we had for now and try to find what he wanted later.

Next minute, the manager summoned me into the galley and said he'd had a complaint about me. He was going to have to write a report on me, and that I should have just said 'Yes, sir; yes, sir,' and given him a bottle of whatever we had there and then – the theory being that the passenger wouldn't know the difference between a chardonnay and a sauvignon blanc, and once they had the bottle they would stop complaining.

I never quite grasped the logic of this theory.

The manager showed me what he had written in the report: 'Owen is totally fantastic in premium cabins but struggles to identify with the economy passengers.'

'I totally agree with you,' I said. 'I'm going back to premium. Goodbye.'

When Sally and I flew together, we worked things as much as we could in our favour. Once, we were rostered on the same flight to South Africa, both of us working in premium economy! Yay, we thought: we were going to have an excellent flight. The two of us started the trip by pulling down the blinds, thinking let's make this dark and get the passengers settled in. We raced through the service and turned off the lights to make the cabin pitch black; if we got the passengers off to sleep, they'd ask for less. After lights out, we heard a kerfuffle down the aisle and, 'Git me, git me . . . no, no, git me . . .' Holding our torches, Sally and I approached the commotion. A little old man stood up and reached into the overhead locker, lifted out a cane and proceeded to hit the young black South African man sitting next to him.

'What's going on, sir?'

'He won't do as he's told,' the man spat angrily. 'He's my um, um, assistant.' He finally found the right occupation.

'I'm sorry, sir, I don't care what he is. You cannot assault him on this flight. If you don't stop, we will have to handcuff you, and you will have to sit in the crew rest until we land.'

'No, no; he understands.' The old guy lowered his cane and addressed the young man. 'You understand, don't you?'

'I'm sorry, I'm sorry,' the young man was muttering quietly.

'Excuse me, sir,' I said to the man with the cane, 'it doesn't matter if he understands or not. Do *you* understand? I don't care if you purchased him at the Tunisian markets, you can't hit him on this plane.'

The elderly bloke sat back down but was clearly unhappy that he wasn't allowed to whack his assistant with a stick. Sally and I returned to the galley, where we just rolled our eyes at each other. What could you say?

It was not uncommon for white men to travel with black assistants; apparently they had become popular in a certain market. Often the assistants were well endowed. So when a guy introduced his black travelling companion as his assistant, it was a roundabout way of saying he was his squeeze.

After Sally and I checked into the Sandton Sun Hotel, we went down at about 5 pm for drinks with the rest of the crew. The pilot was meeting up with a couple of local women he knew and we decided to all go out together. There were armed guards everywhere around the hotel and someone knew someone who could buy some cocaine from the armed guards. There was a lot of alcohol involved that night; we partied hard and a few of us ended up back in my room still going. The first night turned into the second! At about 6 am, I said I was taking a Xanax and going to bed.

Next thing I knew, something was buzzing in my ear and I struggled to wake; it was my mobile.

'Owen, are you coming?' It was Sally.

'Coming where?'

'Home. Everyone's downstairs in the foyer waiting for you.'

'What?'

'Aren't you ready?'

'Darl, please get one of the other girls and come up to my room now.'

While I was in the shower, still blind drunk, one of them ironed my shirt and the other packed my bag. Sally was still pissed too. So the pair of us did *drunk*, *hungover* and *recovery* all on the flight home and it was not one of our favourite flights together.

Johannesburg was fraught with danger and a place where we knew we had to be on our toes. In our security training, we'd heard stories about crew who'd been robbed and there were cases where female crew had been raped. Caution was a major byword. A tour of Johannesburg woke me up to the incredible poverty; my abiding impression was of the fences of gated communities – there to keep the rich safe from the poor.

When I visited Johannesburg's poverty-stricken south-western township, better known as Soweto, scene of the famous 1976 student uprising, I felt like I was connecting with living history. I'd grown up learning about Nelson Mandela, and I had followed the fall of apartheid via the TV news. It was quite mind-blowing being in this place, but the sense of danger was still very real.

A good friend of mine, Sammie-Kay, badly wanted to go to South Africa so she could fulfil her dream of going on a safari. I offered to take her with me on my staff travel, jokingly telling her that anyone I took away normally got more than they bargained for. Excitedly, she did all kinds of research, and we arranged to go on a full-day safari the day after we arrived and then do some local tours the day after that. She had a fabulous flight in business class, watching me work.

The first night in Jo'burg, we had drinks with the other crew in the basement bar of the hotel, then went off to bed, leaving some of the guys in the bar watching the cricket on TV. In the morning Sammie-Kay and I were having breakfast with two of the crew before our safari.

Jason, one of the flight attendants we'd been having drink with the night before, limped into the breakfast hall, his face and hands covered with bloody cuts and grazes; he was wearing the same clothes we'd last seen him in except that now they were dirty and dishevelled, and he had no shoes on. Looking almost comatose, Jason propped himself up in the doorway. A couple of us went up to him and asked if he was all right. Angrily, he pushed us and said to get off him. Somehow, we got him to sit down at the table and I raced out and phoned the CSM and the captain.

Much drama ensued. Within minutes, the captain, crew and hotel staff surrounded Jason, all desperately wanting to know what was going on; when I'd told Sammie-Kay she'd get more than she bargained for on a trip with me, this wasn't what I had in mind. All we could glean at that stage was that Jason had been robbed, raped and dumped at the side of the road. A couple of security guards had found him and managed to get out of him where he was staying and then dropped him off.

Immediately, he was taken to hospital, where he had to undergo treatment for his many injuries and be subjected to tests for STIs, especially HIV.

Sammie-Kaye and I went off on our safari in Kruger National Park and had a fantastic time in spite of the morning's drama. It was amazing to see the animals in their natural habitat. One of the highlights was the feast set up for our group in a few huts in the park; we ate this sumptuous food in the vicinity of an array of wild animals and considering we only had the protection of a guide with a stick and a small rifle, we wondered if we might be on the animals' menu. Nonetheless, I was to later risk going back again; I took my mother and sister on that trip – just for the taste of that scrumptious buffet.

Later that day, we returned to the hotel to confront the thumping reality of what had happened to Jason. Gradually, more of the story had come out. It transpired that after we'd gone up to bed, two local black hookers approached Jason in the bar, chatted him up and drugged him. The women got him up to his room, from where somehow they managed to get a couple of man friends past security, so they were also in Jason's room. These men took him off drinking somewhere while the girls stayed and did his room over, taking all his money and laptop. Jason couldn't say where he was taken, beaten up and raped, but he was left for dead in the middle of Soweto. He was lucky to be alive.

Jason ended up suicidal, screaming and inconsolable in his room. All his furious wife wanted to know was what he had been doing with prostitutes, and Qantas management wasn't helpful, blaming him for putting himself in a position of danger; rumours went around that later they tried to get rid of him. It was a big deal with Qantas at the time and made us all realise that anyone was fair game. It was an experience that really opened my eyes about the danger of some places we flew to and how complacent some of us had become, including me.

Shortly before the departure of our plane for home, Sammie-Kay and I had one final drama: Sammie-Kay almost didn't make it onto the flight, thanks to high winds. There are tightly enforced weight restrictions to counter such strong winds during take-off, and as I crossed over through passport control to start my work duty, Sammie-Kay was held back and told she had to wait for approval to get on the plane.

'Please don't leave me behind,' she screamed after me. 'Not after what we've been through.'

I called back that I would sort it out and I did – with the help of the CSM, ground staff and the captain. At the last minute she got a boarding pass and ran onto the plane, where I was waiting for her with a large scotch.

STAYING IN THE RED

'Excuse me. Do you know the score at the game in Subiaco?'

'No, I don't. Sorry.'

'Do you think you could see what the score is or what quarter they're into?'

'We are on our way to the States and I doubt if an Australian football score will be on the news there but I'll talk to the pilot and see if he can find out.'

Heaven forbid if I got caught up responding to someone else's demand and didn't call the pilot for the score immediately. The sports nut would accost me as I passed to remind me they were still waiting but, 'You needn't worry about it now – the game will most probably be over.'

Of course being the good flight attendant that I was, I'd always try to pacify the poor tragic; offer them a drink.

If the match was so bloody important, perhaps you should have booked tomorrow's flight.

A particularly good trick passengers often used on flight attendants was to ring the call buzzer and just as you got there they would announce, 'I'm going to vomit,' which they would then proceed to do – all over you.

Puh-lease! You didn't feel this coming on five minutes ago? You didn't think about getting up and going to the toilet?

On the flights to countries like India and China, where a large percentage of the population smoked, Asian passengers would try to get away with smoking in the toilets. A flight attendant can smell cigarette smoke a mile away on a plane. In fact, I could smell if someone happened to have rolled a joint prior to boarding. If I knocked on the toilet door and opened it, nine times out of ten the occupant would be standing on the toilet lid blowing smoke into the vent.

'I blow into chimney; it okay.'

The 'chimney' they're blowing smoke into happens to be the smoke alarm.

'No, it's not okay – get down. Santa is not coming down that chimney.'

Food is another thing that occupies the minds of passengers. They wanted me to know what their requirements were as soon as they boarded; they're vegetarian, they're allergic to seafood, they're coeliac, they're dairy intolerant. Prior to take-off, I would try to sort out all the last-minute, mind-boggling catering issues. 'I may be able to get an extra couple of special meals on board,' I'd say. Then after you'd pulled in favours and worked a miracle for them, when you handed over the special menus and the passengers had by then compared them with the normal menu, they'd say, 'You know what, I think I'll just have the chicken.' You'll have to excuse me if I sound cynical about absolutely necessary dietary requirements; too often they proved to be not so absolutely necessary after all.

Meals on planes are a really big thing. Some years ago, Qantas hired a motivation consultancy to look into the issue of food. The philosophy of this company was that people were intrinsically dumb; they followed each other like sheep but the flight attendant could make the difference. So what did you do if you were down to the last row and you knew you only had chicken meals left and white wines and someone asked for the beef dish and a red wine? According to the consultant, if the flight attendant was in the happy-clappy red zone (what Qantas referred to as 'being in the red') they could turn the passenger's 'wants' around by suggesting something like this:

'I think you'd really like the chicken; how about the chicken and complement that with a beautiful chardonnay from the Barossa Valley?' Put it in front of them and they wouldn't know the difference because you'd been so nice to them.

Who's more batty here – me or the passenger?

The passenger looks straight back at you and says, 'I wanted the beef with a red wine.'

Cynically, I wonder if this was one of those light-bulb moments from some manager who got the great idea from a whiz-kid they'd gone to university with who now runs a marketing consultancy and then won a nice fat contract to put it into action. The crew know it's all nonsense and none of it will work in the air, no matter how convincing it might seem when you're in a training room on the ground.

Best just to say, 'Sorry, we've run out of the beef and the red, but we'll start with you at breakfast.' Plain and simple and they're happy. After the consultancy's ridiculousness, being 'in the red' became an in-house joke among crew. No chicken left? 'Are you in the red, darl?'

One of the programs I did believe in was the UNICEF one that Qantas is involved with; it's a simple program that raises money for poorer nations. I would walk through the cabin with the UNICEF bag asking for donations.

'Any spare change?' I proffer the bag.

Out comes a pile of stock-piled rubbish for the UNICEF bag.

'No,' I would say, 'coins – loose change to help people.'

'No, no, not helping.'

Enough said. Interestingly but perhaps not surprisingly, most of the donations did not come from the pointy end of the plane. It seems that those with the most always give the least. Such is life.

SOUTH AMERICA

SLEEPLESS IN BUENOS AIRES

Until 2012, Qantas flew to Buenos Aires in Argentina, its hub for South America; from there two partners in the OneWorld Alliance, American Airlines and LAN Argentina, would carry passengers to other destinations in South America. It's a massive continent and it was a blur of energy; it seemed that there were planes from all over the place servicing it. It was a very long and demanding flight but the passengers were not generally considered difficult. Having said that, Buenos Aires to Sydney was the only flight I ever did where I came to my wit's end; more about that later.

My first Sydney to Buenos Aires flight coincided with the annual Rio Carnival in Brazil so the plane was filled to the brim with party-mode passengers who were on-flying to Rio de Janeiro. They wanted to drink and eat all the way. And all the way was day flying – because of the time zone, you leave in the morning and fifteen hours later you arrive in the morning of the same day.

Back then, the Buenos Aires flight had a full bar service, even in economy. South Americans love to live life to the full – it was a case of 'more, more, more' – and they drank and ate everything on the plane. We had just finished serving the four-hour bar and lunch service and I heard ding, ding. I approached the little guy to see what he wanted.

'We will have four beers, two Bloody Marys, one wine and a whisky and when is the next meal?'

'Pardon?'

'When's the next meal?'

'In about ten hours.' I couldn't believe it. Apparently, neither could he.

'Ten hours?' he questioned, puzzled. 'We like to eat something more in a bit.'

'Shit,' I thought, 'this isn't a restaurant.' And believe me, he wasn't the only one expecting more of everything.

All passengers received a Q Bag, which included water, fruit and a muesli bar and we had nuts and some snacks in the galley.

The flight was hard enough to get through, but if I was looking forward to sleep upon arrival, I was to be monumentally disappointed. Because I'd not experienced this high altitude before South America, I didn't anticipate how much being at high altitude would affect me. It was harder to breathe when walking around and more difficult to sleep.

Even though the hotel was the gorgeous InterContinental, when we booked in and I retired for a snooze, I found I could not get to sleep all day – plus there were no English-speaking TV channels, such as BBC World or CNN, to distract me. Luckily, I did find some tennis to watch. At about 7 pm, I met the rest of the crew for drinks, after which we went out for dinner. When the meal was finished, it was already midnight. Our next stop was a gay club called Bar America. It was a place where a lot of flight attendants from other airlines hung out too – sure enough, we met crew from Air Canada, British Airways and American Airlines; party, party, party.

Among the many things I'd been told about South America was that I was destined to get robbed. And I probably looked wealthy as I'd dressed up a bit to go to the night club and was wearing jeans and a striped cowboy shirt with pockets on the front. My wallet and cards were safely locked away in the hotel; all I had on me was money and my room key, which I put in the shirt pockets. Apparently the local patrons were so nifty that you could be talking to someone while they were lifting your wallet from your back pocket and you'd have no idea.

The entry fee of fifty pesos entitled you to as much free beer, wine or spirits as you wanted; the place was very dimly lit and at one end of the bar there was even a 'dark room', where all sorts of things went on and off; people either emerged without their undies or without their wallets.

I met a handsome young guy who wanted to tell me his life story. After a couple of margaritas, I was all ears. He was turning on the charm and when I asked about having another cocktail (because they weren't included in the free drinks), he said I could have all the cocktails I wanted. I thought, 'Beauty, bring on the margaritas!' and I became the runner to get cocktails for the rest of the crew as well; they were downing tequila shots all night so were pretty messy by the morning.

In the meantime, this guy was doing a number on me; he was telling me he was a student and lived a long way away, and maybe he could come and stay in my hotel room. I relayed his request to the others and they warned me that if I wanted to wake up in a bath without my kidneys, then go ahead.

At five in the morning, we all staggered out to make our way back to the hotel.

'Where are you going?' my 'student' friend called after me. Despite all of those free cocktails, I wanted to hang on to my kidneys and didn't take him with me. Later I found out that the hotel had been having a real problem with these 'guests': crew were forever getting robbed – money, laptops, watches. Everyone now had to sign in with their ID – without ID you couldn't get into the hotel.

Of the twelve of us who had gone to Bar America, I was the only one who didn't get robbed. Next day, everyone was sitting around the pool comparing robberies – watches, wallets. I told them I had nothing stolen, not even my kidneys!

Despite having got about two hours' sleep through the day, I still couldn't sleep properly that night; the following day was the flight home and everyone was coming back from Rio. They're wearing sombreros and someone has a guitar and playing music and it's 'Hey, ciao, ciao, amigo, can we have five beers and two wines?' And we haven't even taken off yet.

It was fun for about the first hour and then it was not fun. I was working in economy with five other crew servicing 315 people. There were little parties going on all over the plane; the music didn't stop, nor did the relentless demands.

'Hey, amigo, you got some more food?'

'Hey, my friend, can we have three beers here?'

'Hey, let's get the castanets down.'

Even when I sat down on the crew seats to close my eyes for a minute, it would be, 'Hey! Amigo, you got some more wine?'

At the end of the flight we had emptied every single cart on the plane of food and drink; there was nothing whatsoever left to feed or water anyone in first, business or economy. For forty-eight hours straight, I'd had virtually no sleep and was so fatigued I was hallucinating. The return flight was also daylight all the way, so when I got off the plane at about six o'clock that evening, I had literally been walking for fifteen hours; my feet were swollen, and exhaustion reduced me to tears. By then I was so excruciatingly tired I couldn't actually sleep, even with sleeping tablets. I had to call in sick for my next flight as it took me a week to get over that one.

As I got more experienced with that flight, I noticed that coming back from Buenos Aires there were often a lot of medical emergencies because people were coming home from holidays with injuries and illnesses. Dehydration was common as well as chest and respiratory problems, along with cuts and bruises, from trekking. Two hours into the flight on my second Buenos Aires trip a woman told me that she wasn't well; she'd had salmonella poisoning in the last few days and she was extremely dehydrated. She was running such a high fever we had to cool her down with ice packs and call for a doctor to come forward; we then had to rig up a makeshift drip from supplies in our medical cupboard. During all this I was somewhere between a flight attendant, nurse and coun-sellor. She seemed to get much worse before she got better and at one stage I was thinking I might have to call for some rosary beads and take on the role of priest as well.

Buenos Aires is the capital of Argentina and a top tour-ist destination in South America, with lots of things to do. Often, attractions seemed to be open at weird times so I got into the habit of always checking at the front desk of the hotel to make sure it was open when I wanted to go.

Although Buenos Aires was a high-alert destination, you

could easily forget its potential dangers because the hotels were so beautiful and we were in a wealthy area. Take a wrong turn, however, and you'd see gangs hanging around and guys with knives. Once, I went out to get some food and I felt so unsafe that I waved down a taxi to take me two blocks.

However, as exciting as it might have been, I only did a handful of trips. A lot of the Spanish-speaking crew were originally from Argentina and consequently were used to it. Many other crew seemed to cope with the flight and conditions better than me – many traditionally did the LA flights and mixed it with the South American flights.

A SLIP IN MY BRILLIANT CAREER

All flight attendants have to submit to ongoing training, known as EPs. Any flight attendant will tell you, it's the thing they fear above all else. Whereas most airlines do it once a year, Qantas does it every six months so they can boast about their good safety record. If you fail, you can't fly and if you fail a test twice, you're sacked. The pass mark is eighty per cent at Qantas so the pressure is always on.

So there I was at the Qantas training facility in Sydney on a freezing winter's day – 8 August 2011 – a day that would change my life forever. At 7 am things were kicked off with a practical drill showing people what to do in an emergency. Later in the day we did something called crew resource management, when pilots and flight attendants sit around for about two hours having sleep-inducing discussions about what we can learn from accidents and how to minimise risky situations.

Then we did land-based emergency exercises in the 747 simulator, which is inside a big building with no windows or natural light. The simulator is pitch black inside to mimic a crash situation – evacuation might have to take place in the dark. As I emerged into the brightly lit building, with my eyes still adjusting, and made my way down the stairs, I had trouble getting my footing, and I slipped and fell heavily. A couple of people asked if I was all right; although I was shaken, I thought I'd just twisted my ankle.

By then, there was only one set of exercises left to complete, which was on the 767 simulator and involved throwing exit windows outwards. I didn't want to come back again for the sake of that one last exercise, so I limped in and explained to the instructor what had happened. I would be fine, I said; I'd just ice it when I got home. The next day I was rostered on a flight to India that I really wanted to do.

Like everyone else, the instructor had had a long day and was keen to get out of there. She was happy to sign me off as having passed, joking that 'in a real emergency' there would be 'a few injuries'.

When I left the Qantas centre, my legs and back were starting to feel extremely sore. Someone asked if I'd be all right to go to India and I replied that I hoped so.

Most of the time I lived in Melbourne, where I'd bought an apartment, but when working out of Sydney, I stayed with my friend Cameron. I dragged myself in the door at Cameron's, hardly able to walk. Both of us concluded that I might have actually fractured my leg. Cameron helped me into the shower then popped across the road to the gym; half an hour later, he came back to find that I'd crawled out of the shower and now lay paralysed on the bed. He called an ambulance and I was taken to Sydney's St Vincent's Hospital, where a series of tests revealed that I had broken my spine in the fall.

Qantas had to approve employee compensation for an operation on my back so the first thing I had to do was notify my manager. In what turned out to be the first in a depressingly long list of disappointing behaviour on the part of the company – a neglect of its duty of care to an employee – my manager berated me for not reporting the injury at the time it happened; in fact it was the trainer's responsibility and I did report it. None too subtly, he added, 'You don't want to put this as worker's compensation, do you?' What he meant was, 'I don't want to be involved in this.'

Qantas is a self-insurer, that is, it runs its own worker's compensation insurance scheme. WorkCover was set up by the New South Wales Government to provide limited support for injured workers in that State. Qantas cannot deny WorkCover claims but it can deny or accept workers' compensation under the WorkCover guidelines. I didn't want to take worker's compensation because Qantas monitors the managers and the managers' job is to try and convince anyone with an injury to use their own sick leave rather than claim worker's compensation because sick leave is an expense a business expects to incur. I didn't want to use my sick leave because it didn't cover a workplace injury.

Cutting the bureaucratic red tape took so long the surgeons decided not to wait as the situation was dangerous. I had a micro-dissection to stabilise my lower spine, giving me movement in my left leg but my right leg still wouldn't function. I then started the long process of rehabilitation.

After an agonising time in hospital and at a rehabilitation centre opposite the hospital, where I had to learn to walk again, I eventually flew back to Melbourne. Once home, I continued the intensive physiotherapy to help me walk without dragging my leg.

To cope with the pain associated with the physiotherapy, I was on serious medication – Oxytocin and Endone, Panadeine Forte and sleeping tablets – quite a cocktail of strong and dangerously addictive drugs. Whatever little 'helpers' I had got over the counter from pharmacies in Asia did nothing to prepare my system for a mix of this magnitude. This stuff was an instant smack in the face; in fact the effects of these drugs have been likened to heroin and are allegedly harder to come off.

In Melbourne no one was managing my pain medication and I was on my own for weeks with none of Qantas's promised home care or nursing assistance. I got a lawyer to help me deal with my spiralling battle with my employer to get help for an injury I'd sustained while working. In the meantime, I was becoming increasingly reliant on my pain-killers.

Naturally I couldn't drive while taking the medication and so I had to catch taxis to the physiotherapy sessions to help me get my leg to function again; Qantas refused to pay taxi fares to my physiotherapist. But what apparently got up the Qantas nose was the cost of the rehabilitation gym program and the physio's fees, not to mention the high cost of medical treatment and medications. I was told I had become a 'big expense to the team'; one of the managers informed me that Qantas wasn't a charity.

'I realise that, but this is not a charity issue. If a plane has broken down, what do you think the engineers do?'

'Well, fix it.'

'So what happens when a crew member is injured?'

'We try our best to fix it within the law. The law, incidentally, does not provide for taxis but does provide for someone to drive you at the rate of 55 cents a kilometre.'

'When was petrol 55 cents a litre?'

She told me I was being very difficult and flying straight into the radar; in other words, attracting the attention of the ground team, who would soon begin to harass me.

Because Qantas underwrites its own injury insurance it was, I suspect, trying to cut my money supply off early in what it thought might be a long and expensive exercise. To mitigate expense from the many cabin crew injuries over the years, Qantas has tried to shake the injured apples from the tree early. Qantas obviously takes advice from its own medical and physiotherapy team and knew my case would be protracted – expensive operations involving medical specialists, physios, occupational therapists and psychologists with the end result being I would not be able to fly again.

To get through my strong physiotherapy exercises I had to increase the medication to cope with the pain. One day after a physio session, I came home zonked out and drowsy and put a pan on the stove to cook some fish; I woke up to the sound of the fire alarm screeching loudly. My house was on fire. I looked around to see flames licking at the ceiling; the smoke was stifling. I had no idea what to do but I grabbed a blanket and headed for the front door, which was by then very hot.

I managed to escape and sat outside, dazed, listening to the sirens – the fire brigade, ambulance and police cars all came. Firemen put out the fire and the police interviewed me and my neighbours and the ambulance checked me out and left. I rang one of my Qantas managers and told her I didn't know what was going on but I'd burnt my house down. She put me on hold and I was transferred to another, more senior, manager. This manager informed me in no uncertain terms of what must have been on management's mind.

'Don't think you can pin this on us, Owen.'

Actually, I was feeling very alone and all I wanted was a friendly voice and perhaps an offer of a hotel room for a few nights from my wonderful 'Qantas Family'. No. Suddenly I was the enemy. I had heard that once you became a cost to Qantas, you were out of the warm kangaroo pouch and into the cold, but it was a shock when it happened to me.

I became another staff number. I was unable to fly and get paid for my flying hours and as my base pay barely covered my mortgage I was struggling financially; the very un-merry merry-go-round started and I couldn't seem to get off it. There were obstructions at every turn. Qantas workers' compensation was one. Cabin crew management was another.

Cabin crew managers were like chickens on a rotisserie – turned over regularly. The manager at the time, let's call her Ellen, suggested it was best that I take the redundancy package they were offering in a drive to reduce the workforce. She told me I had become a cost to the company and was letting the 'team' down. Unbeknown to me she went to the human resources department to get a voluntary redundancy payout figure for me. Ellen presented me with the amount Qantas thought would get me out; this was ridiculous because I wanted to work.

'Ellen, I want to work; I'm supposed to be rehabilitated and returned to work, not pushed out,' I told her.

What followed was a few heated conversations with cabin crew management and after legal advice, I declined the redundancy. At that moment I knew it was no longer a question of would the kangaroo tail strike me, me but when it would strike.

Ellen suggested, later backed up by the base manager in Sydney, that I work on the ground until I could fly again. No one could tell me how I was going to do that when I couldn't drive while on the pain medication and Qantas wasn't prepared to pay for taxis to get me to work. Every time I asked how I could overcome a barrier, they shuffled the responsibility backwards and forwards between the divisions.

Part of the rehabilitation process was to return me to the work I was trained for; I wanted to get back to flying and angled for some 'ease in' short distance flights but Qantas saw this as problematic. It would depend on my seniority as to what flights I could get. So, most unhelpfully, the first flight they gave me was Dallas – the longest flight known to man. This was followed by New York then Santiago, two other very long-haul destinations.

I had a meeting with Caroline, the head of cabin crew in Sydney, to see if I could get back to short-range flying; I got another lesson in seniority. No, she couldn't help me as she was bound by the restrictions in the seniority system. So I asked if I could I please return to work in business or first class to minimise the impact on my back. No. Every suggestion I threw at her, Caroline simply said no.

Okay; so Muhammad having come to the mountain, I asked her what she suggested.

'Why not go on the A380?' she said sarcastically.

The A380 referred to a new contract for crew hired from 2008 onwards; it was a separate section of our enterprise bargaining agreement (EBA), with less pay and worse conditions.

Going on the A380 would have had me flying long range and doing an extra 50 hours per roster. I visualised myself telling her not too politely where to get off and then I thanked her but politely declined and asked that we get back to sorting out the problem under my current working agreement. (NB: By 2012 the company had reached its goal to minimise long-range pay – all new-contract Qantas crew were employed on the A380.)

Later, my new ground manager – let's call this one Lynne – said she would help with the occasional flying pattern. This meant that if my normal roster came up with a Frankfurt trip, followed by Africa then Santiago, at her discretion she could replace one of those long trips with a shorter one, such as Manila or Jakarta. In the 'kangaroo world' this was called 'case-by-case management'; why could we possibly need a union? Being discretionary made it very unfair but there was no use complaining that someone else was getting a fairer deal because Lynne would say it was a case-by-case decision. It was made quite clear that either I was fit enough to fly, like any other flight attendant, or I was not.

That was it; basically, they couldn't help me at all. I had to shape up or ship out.

THE WAY WE WERE . . . AND THE WAY WE BECAME

Things have changed in the airline industry. Years ago, you used to see the old dinosaur flight attendants, the matrons of the air. They liked to do things the right way, and they were particular. No raised voices, no crude language and no time for magazines. Their logic was, if there is time for that, there is time for another water run or cabin check. Similarly, in those days you had the old-school respectful passengers who really dressed up in a suit or their Sunday best to fly. They respected it as the industry it was, and although they looked sweet, I used to think, gosh that must be uncomfortable. Especially on long flights.

Many of the changes I've seen, though, have been driven by strategy. When I first started flying international, Qantas flew to a lot of destinations across the USA, Europe, Asia, Africa, Antarctica and South America and it was a job I was really proud of. Being seen in a Qantas uniform was special; you'd put your shoulders back and walk tall. People would smile at us when we passed them in the street. Qantas was making money and things were on the up. But the days of easy profit disappeared, and destination after destination went by the wayside too. No stone was left unturned in the quest to turn a profit, and slowly but surely, the spotlight came on crew; we became a cost, an expense, rather than the friendly and indispensable face of a proud company.

In the early days, the culture was as clean-cut and transparent as the rule book the matrons of the air followed to the letter. Because a lot of management and ground crew had worked for Qantas when it was a government-owned airline, the crew was a unionised and experienced team; there was generally a high level of mutual respect in evidence.

The first real inkling of change came in 2004, with the opening of the London base. Even though the company applied pressure on me to 'get on board', once I made the move, I was happy to be there: I was an international flight attendant enjoying the contract conditions from the airline's

Government-owned days, which were to last until 2008. However, it was an open secret that the London move coincided with a new agenda: to change the workforce culture. The London base leader sent out a memo telling us that we were 'family' and were there working for a common goal. Passenger satisfaction became the be all and end all; where safety of the passengers had been our primary concern, it quietly slipped down the rankings. He instituted 'Excel' badges; no longer were we a team but a bunch of ambitious individuals. Everyone's goal became to self-promote and get noticed so they could earn a badge. You didn't have to be Einstein to realise that a bottle of French champagne could smoothe the path towards a glowing passenger feedback form. Quickly, negative comments on feedback forms became a thing of the past; it's so easy to stow things in strange places on descent.

A guy I was working with on one flight loved only one thing greater than Qantas and that was a mirror. He was blond and bouncy and generally annoying. Without a word of a lie, I'm telling you he described himself to me as 'The blond, Australian Mario Lopez' – referring to the handsome TV host and actor.

I said, 'So nothing at all like the Latino, American-based Lopez then?'

He laughed. 'You're sooooo cute!'

I went on my break and when I came back, Mario was talking with the CSM. He told me he'd made me some green tea and would I like to 'freshen up' before he left?

'No, Mario,' I replied.

'Owen, I've stacked the glasses on top of the fridge so they are easy to grab when we do our cabin patrols.'

The CSM pipes up:

'See, Owen, isn't it beautiful and so tidy – do keep it like Mario left it.'

There was only one way to undo the do-gooders – get them on a safety issue. I asked the CSM to pass me the service manual. When he asked why, I pointed out to him the section that said glasses stacked and not secured anywhere at that height were a massive safety risk – regardless of how many candy cones and teddy bear stamps he had in his report book. Once I'd pointed out that the glasses would fly off and smash in turbulence, the CSM had to immediately agree.

The emerging reporting and dobbing culture caused so much uncertainty among crew that everyone started to cover themselves by shining a negative light on others. I served as a union rep in 2005 and 2006 and literally found myself appearing at discipline hearings pre- and post-flight. On one pre-flight occasion, I represented a close friend who had revealed to a colleague in the course of an informal chat that he was receiving some medical treatment. Immediately he'd been stood down: on the basis of that tiny disclosure in the course of a private conversation, he had been classified as a 'safety issue'. It was a low blow, and I tried everything to help my friend, even appealing to the better nature of the base manager.

'But we are a family. When someone in the family mucks up, we help them and show them the way.'

By then I saw the whole 'we are a family' mantra as pure bullshit. And in this instance, they showed my friend the way to the door; the guy was sacked.

After the hearing, I dashed straight to a briefing at Heathrow and then boarded the aircraft for a London–Bangkok flight. Both my plane and the Qantas flight to Singapore had taxied out onto the runway when they were called back to bay. Why? A crew member had left their crew bag at the counter where crew bags are cross-checked; after 9/11, this was a total no no. The interphone went, and everyone was asked if they had signed the baggage manifest. Then it clicked: in my rush to represent my friend, I hadn't picked up the bag; yes, the offending bag was mine. That was quickly fixed and we taxied out again and soon were on our merry way.

Of course, when I got back to London, a ground manager phoned to inform me I was charged with purposely delaying an aircraft and causing the company 'economic loss'; there were a whole heap of other minor infractions.

I rang the other union delegate at the London base; we met with base management and pointed out that I'd been appearing at disciplinary hearings in my capacity as a union official and flying on the same day. Strictly speaking, it was illegal to have me doing multiple duties within a day. Within fifteen minutes I was acquitted, but I was subjected to a dressing down about my poor 'attitude' and unwillingness to embrace being part of 'the family'. Strict devotion to this mythical family struck me as unhealthy.

Many colleagues must have agreed with me on this point as after I came back from London I saw that crew dissatisfaction and morale had become worse as conditions further eroded; Qantas was voted in an online forum and in a major financial newspaper as having the most disengaged workforce nationally and one of the worst internationally. This disengagement had not been helped in 2008 when the Qantas board tried to sell the company to a now non-existent US company; this action was partly stymied thanks to the number of shares that crew, pilots and other employees owned. It was clear to us workers that management was about to screw the 'roo for all it was worth and the beautiful brand we had all loved so much was not in safe hands.

Like employees in any big organisation, Qantas staff do their fair share of training and company courses. In most companies this is a fairly benign activity, but at Qantas, in-house training became more cult-like the longer I was there. They even had a centre for it in Sydney; it was known as The Centre for Service Excellence and Training, and while it looked like a harmless big brick building on the outside, what went on inside was similar to a micro-chipping robotics factory.

When I came back to work in 2012 after my back injury, I had to attend the one-day 'Customer Service Excellence Course' before I could return to flying. That was on top of two days of recurrent emergency procedures training – in another big building with no natural light. Trust me, three days of Qantas preaching was a lot to take. I went along, resigned to putting up with a bit of the usual company psycho-babble; how unprepared I was.

A mix of crew and staff from other Qantas departments were doing 'excellence' that day. All of us arrived at the training facility by bus and were taken into a darkened auditorium, where we sat in seats, waiting. Suddenly, out of the darkness came blaring motivational music so loud that we were all looking around at each other – WTF! As the music faded, a woman facilitator appeared on stage and welcomed us. First, she explained, she wanted to bust the myths which had grown up around the good media publicity that Virgin Australia, Qantas's major competitor in the Australasian market, was getting and the bad publicity that Qantas had attracted.

For what seemed like hours, the woman proceeded to 'correct' rumours and misreported facts and figures and explain why the international division was haemorrhaging. This led into other points: the necessity to reconfigure aircrafts and amenities on board, and why we should be proud of the airline. Her Qantas knowledge was profound and she spat out facts and figures like an overloaded coin-fed poker machine paying out.

We heard about Qantas's generosity to its passengers with extra leg and seat spacing and the ratio of toilets to passengers, and how wonderful it was that passengers could now answer a phone app questionnaire fresh off the flight, giving their impressions of the flight. Next she covered how the company's budget offshoot, Jetstar, had not caused losses in the Qantas International division.

She reiterated that we were all there together and if we ever came across another flight attendant who was not operating at their best, and didn't address the problem with them or report it to management, we too had let the brand down.

'The negative situation you turn a blind eye to makes you as guilty as if you had done it yourself.'

Wow!

Then she changed tack. We were, she told us, about to be taught useful ways to never say 'no' and only use positives in any crew or passenger experience. We would learn the principles of 'staying in the red' as distinct from being in the negative black and we would round out the day with practical and theoretical examinations to determine our level of 'excellence'. Anything less than eighty per cent was a fail and we would need to be retrained.

Eventually, the guru turned her attention to us and asked for questions. The questions of the A380 crew focused on the company's decision to relocate two toilets to an area so close to the galley that crew had to fight their way through the queued-up passengers just to do their galley duties. Their concern was that a cost-cutting measure had made their work in the galley not only more difficult but also unsafe: sooner or later, someone's foot was going to get crushed by a passing cart.

The facilitator was so prepared she was rapping out her answer within a nanosecond of hearing the question. According to her, the relocation of the toilets had created more economy and business seating, and far from compromising convenience safety, was in fact 'industry leading and architecturally brilliant'. For too long, she continued, 'we have been too generous and this has cost the airline.'

Too generous! Have you ever seen an economy passenger limp their way off a London or LA flight?

When the sensitive topic of Jetstar arose, the line she peddled about how it was paying back Qantas the start-up funding *and* was still able to be profitable lost her the attention of most of the audience, who by then were laughing and talking. It was time for a break.

Things became more animated when we moved on to the new service initiatives. There were queries about the focus on 'staying in the red' and always being positive. Could our individual excellent customer service really turn a passenger around from wanting, say, a white wine that you had just run out of to happily accepting a red wine?

'It seems like you are relying on passengers being stupid and compliant,' a flight attendant near me responded.

She was shot down: 'No, it's about you providing the type of service that can guide them to an alternative.'

A couple of colleagues came in late to the lunch; they'd been kept behind and given a 'talking to' about asking negative questions. Their managers, they were advised, would be informed they were not toeing the line. Word of this spread. No one wanted to get into trouble or to have to redo this boring session so there was a lot of nodding and smiling throughout the afternoon.

At the end of the day we had to sit an exam in which we were expected to be positive and serious. One question was stumping a couple of us so we put up our hands to ask for help. One of the cloned trainers looked at the question and spoke to another trainer who, at the time, was having a heated discussion with another crew member. Sparks were flying off this woman and she came over and told us not to ask such silly questions and to take the exam seriously; we were not being 'positive or in the red'. Shortly after this I saw her looking completely deflated, like a lifeless blow-up doll, sitting with her hands over her very red face.

Ralph, who was sitting next to me said, 'That's what happens when she's not been in the sun all day.'

'What do you mean?'

'Well, she's obviously been micro-chipped and she's solar powered. When she doesn't get sun, her battery runs flat and she deflates.'

I thought it was very funny and had a ring of truth. The robot trainers were peddling crap to an army of flight attendants – crap they were expected to live by. When the trainers encountered a question that wasn't data on the microchip, they looked physically as if they were short-circuiting.

I got a 100 per cent pass on service excellence and I was able to fly again.

Crews on the 747, who were usually older and more senior, seemed to get the whole micro-chipping joke. If you came across someone standing in the galley seemingly deep in thought, you'd gently ask, 'Are you in the red?' At first, we called training days 'micro-chipping days' but then switched to 'rebooting the hard drive' when the company changed its mind about a previous edict, swearing right was now left or what was once was black was now red; they had to upload this new information onto the chip. Of course it was the crew who had to go and test this indoctrinated rubbish on the unsuspecting flying public.

When I returned to flying, I noticed that I was getting a performance review on every flight. Crew told me they'd heard I was a headache for the company, and on flights the managers told me I was being watched. To me, this constituted harassment; I'd had an injury and extended time off work. Surely I was entitled to a grace period to become familiar with the new aircraft configuration and generally get back into the work flow.

It all seemed ludicrous. Anyone could make a report on any colleague, regardless of their seniority; when even reading non-company issued material such as a magazine was an offence – and we were urged to be responsible and report any slip-ups – then we might as well have been living in the former East Germany.

At first I took it as a bit of a laugh; that is until a senior crew manager advised me to be careful. Management had its disciples, and if I ever questioned anything from now on I could be in big trouble. On further quizzing, she told me a lot of crew were being subjected to 'clause 11s' (investigations that could lead to being sacked); someone had even had a

clause 11 for asking for another hotel room when she arrived
after a long flight to find her hotel room was not yet made
up. The manager on her flight had overheard her asking hotel
staff and reported her; she was told she had no right to ask
for anything.

I began to see a cult mentality everywhere as all sorts of
weird management buzz words and work practices sprang up.
For instance, once when I stopped to talk to a manager, this
is how the conversation went:

'How are you, Owen?' he asked.

'Good thanks.'

'Great positive first response,' he answered, fixing me with
indoctrinated eyes.

What on earth was that corporate jargon supposed to mean?
Two words popped into my mind: 'Prozac' and 'nation'. It
seemed like the robots were everywhere and it was disturbing.

On the excellence training day, we had been asked to help
out 'the family' wherever we could and I wrote to Peta, the
international executive manager with an idea that could have
brought in about AU$15 million extra revenue a year: it was
for in-flight shopping, as distinct from duty-free. I'd observed
that other airlines were doing this successfully and was positive that it could work on flights to holiday destinations like
Perth, Townsville, Cairns, Hayman Island and so on.

I did not get a response. When I saw Peta at Qantas headquarters sometime later, I queried her about it. Peta said she
wasn't interested in my idea and added that besides, I probably wouldn't be around too long anyway. Oh, and by the
way how was my back?

There was not much 'engagement' in that little exchange.

Subtle suggestions that I take voluntary redundancy had

been coming my way for a while; this, however, was about as subtle as a punch in the face.

NO ENGLISH IN SANTIAGO

In March 2012 Qantas stopped flying to Buenos Aires and moved its South American hub to Santiago in Chile; I didn't care too much because I knew I wouldn't be bidding for any more South American trips – any long haul for me would be London and Frankfurt. Then in mid-2012 Qantas announced an alliance with Emirates, which meant its London flights would now be transiting through Dubai instead of Singapore and passengers to London and other European destinations would be shared between the two. Qantas crew flying up from Australia would terminate at Dubai, and Dubai to London would be served by London-based crew on the A380 – so goodbye London and Frankfurt.

All this was happening while I was recovering from my spinal injury and trying to get back to flying. Then, coinciding with my return to work in 2012, I got a lot of Santiago trips. Santiago came by default as it wasn't popular; flight attendants have a special 'trip swap' page on the internet which lists all the trips people want to swap or give away and Buenos Aires, Santiago and South Africa were the hard flying destinations that everyone tried to ditch.

This was how Qantas was looking after me following the trauma of my back operation, my addiction to strong pain medication and subsequently setting fire to my house: allocating me the most junior, least popular long-haul flights. Did they want me to sustain further injury or give up quietly and take the redundancy?

During the crew briefing before my first Santiago trip, the CSM announced that 'Owen was coming back from serious injury' and that everyone should be mindful of each other and be careful not to injure ourselves. I knew what to expect from the flight as it was around about the same hours and similar passengers to the Buenos Aires flight and I thought it would probably be a nightmare.

It was also day flying all the way, leaving Sydney mid-morning and arriving 9.30 am the same day local time. As expected it was hard flying and the crew somehow seemed different post-surgery but I couldn't quite put my finger on what it was. Then as we came out of the clouds prior to landing I looked out the window and my tired spirits lifted; below was the most stunning mountain scenery – I thought we had arrived in the Swiss Alps.

Crew stayed at the InterContinental – another gorgeous hotel. Crew who had been before me advised me to go straight to the supermarket and get my supplies so as not to run up the room service bill eating goodies before falling into the South American jetlag coma. It was also a cheap way of getting some champagne for a post-flight debrief. After my surgery I knew well and truly how to medicate myself to sleep but getting up was sometimes the problem. I did my little shop, knocked myself out then woke up in time for drinks and dinner with the crew, then I went back to the hotel and fell asleep at about 9 pm. At about 2 am, I woke and couldn't go back to sleep so went up to the crew room, where I found the rest of the crew were already congregated. It was something we had to accept – sometimes you were awake when everyone else was asleep.

It was on this Santiago trip that I met a senior flight attendant, Bianca, who had been flying for about thirty years. The two of us became firm friends. On that first night, when a few of us went to a popular bar and then on to Da Bunker, another nightclub, Bianca took a genuine interest in my back injury. Refreshingly, she didn't have stars in her eyes about the 'wonderful' way Qantas treated its crew; she understood exactly where I was coming from because she'd had her own issues with Qantas and had seen how they dealt harshly with others.

Ironically enough, that night we had dinner with a crew member who banged on about how fantastic the company was and how he was the luckiest person in the world. We both looked at him and asked, 'Have you ever had an injury?'

He said he hadn't and he didn't even take sick leave.

'Well, let's hope it stays that way for you,' I told him.

He did admit that he had heard terrible stories about workplace injuries but had never met anyone who'd had a serious injury. Now he'd met one but it was too late. He had swallowed the company pill.

Everyone told me Santiago was a shithole and no one spoke English – they were right about the English but there were many good things, such as the brilliant skiing (not that I was in any position to ski with my back), and everything was cheap, the food was good, the bars great, the wineries enticing and the mountains beautiful. I ended up really liking Santiago and Bianca, and the two of us ended up doing several trips together.

Santiago had only one crew coming in and one going out at any one time and was one of those destinations that turned out to be a great partying place and a lot of fun – provided you didn't need much English having it. And one in which what happened away, stayed away. It was also a port where pilots and cabin crew generally mixed together.

The same night I became friends with Bianca was also the night I got robbed; I was a little more relaxed than I was in Buenos Aires and let my guard down. While Bianca was off getting more drinks, I was standing chatting to two guys in a group and by the time she came back they'd whisked my Bvlgari watch from my wrist and wallet from my back pocket; it happened in about two seconds – I didn't feel it and no one saw it. The first I realised was when Bianca and I went to get into a taxi and I had an OMG moment when I thought I'd dropped my wallet somewhere. I was told to forget any idea of ever seeing watch and wallet again – they were long gone.

It was a happening night because I also met a Lan Chile pilot called Juan; I thought Juan was quite an exotic name until I discovered every second person in Chile is called Juan – it's the Latin equivalent to John and I met about nine that night! Juan and I hit it off and started a bit of a relationship, and every time I went to Santiago we'd meet up.

I also became friendly with Luka, the check-in clerk at the hotel, who was the only one who spoke good English – well, any English really. He was a real heart-throb and the female crew loved him. He asked me if I could help him 'get the girls' by inviting him to have drinks with them and he would help me get the guys.

'No problems, mate,' I said.

Luka became my interpreter and date-maker; I had to use his help with my relationship with Juan. Even though Juan could speak a little English, he couldn't read it. I would still send him text messages to tell him when I was arriving; then I would ask

Luka to call Juan on the hotel phone and make the meeting arrangements in Spanish, which he would then relay to me.

I never really knew what Juan's story was; his limited English didn't help. When I was in town he would stay at the hotel with me. He pulled the wool over my eyes with, 'Not married; I live at home with my parents; it's my job to look after them until I get married.' For some reason, I didn't stop to really query why he had no problem spouting pious Catholic bullshit while in bed with me, his cross bouncing on his well-built Latino chest and the Virgin Mary watching from the wall.

Suddenly I received a lot of female voice messages in Spanish on my mobile; I thought it was someone trying to sell me something and deleted them. When they kept coming, I asked a Spanish-speaking crew member to listen and tell me what they were about. She listened, eyes widening.

'Oh, my God, Owen; are you sleeping with somebody's husband?'

'What?' I said, aghast.

She kept on listening. 'That Juan guy is married. That's his wife. She's really crazy; she's going to kill you. She's going to come down to the InterContinental with a knife!'

Obviously, the wife had gone into his phone. Imagine her face when she worked out what the text messages I sent said – stuff like, 'Hi Juan darling. I'm in Santiago. Let's meet.'

In actual fact, I'd been having an affair with a married man without knowing it. So it wasn't only the girls who got conned with that sort of crap; it happened to gays too.

Whichever way you looked at it, the game was up with Juan and we went our separate ways.

My leg was still playing up badly, especially after long flights like Santiago so to get it working again I'd walk. One day I walked down town to a statue of the Virgin Mary. I decided to get a taxi back. The first taxi I hailed and said, 'InterContinental Hotel please' – no English; second taxi – 'No English . . . Oh, okay, 20,000 pesos'; third taxi, 'No English.' Bloody hell, the InterContinental Hotel was a landmark. Finally, I saw a travel bureau but as I drew near they pulled down the Closed for Lunch sign. Eventually I approached a group of young people who between them spoke enough English to help me get a taxi but they warned me I would get ripped off. That was just the price I had to pay to get back.

Later back at the hotel I was telling Luka about my taxi experience and asked him why so few people in Santiago spoke English. Luka explained that between 1965 and 1989, when Chile had been under communist rule, no English was taught and so only people who had lived and studied abroad had learnt to speak it.

This bit of information was very helpful as it meant that the people most likely to speak English would be young. From then on I always looked for the youngsters when I was out and about and needed help.

Also, I told Luka that with his excellent English, he could get any tourism job and name his price.

When I started flying again after my injury, I had a totally different perspective about my health and I was extremely cautious. I knew I had to be very careful; I was having cortisone injections into my spine every couple of months, taking prophylactic antibiotics and analgesia for pain.

On one flight I was working in the economy galley – horrendous – and the first day after we arrived I felt fine and went out to dinner with the crew; the second day I felt tired and a little bit sweaty but put it down to the antibiotics. I went out to dinner as usual and had a glass of wine but, feeling weird, went straight to bed. Somehow I got up in the night and went downstairs, where I was observed talking to one of the statues in the foyer. I have no recollection of this conversation but next morning staff reported it to the CSM; no one had offered to help me as they just thought I must have been pissed. The flight left in the early afternoon and next thing I knew the CSM was knocking on my door.

'Owen. Are you coming on this flight?'

If I answered, I wasn't making any sense. Downstairs people were discussing my midnight ramblings with the statue and it suddenly dawned on them perhaps there was something wrong with me. The manager came back and knocked again.

'Owen, are you all right?'

'Someone's here in my room . . .' My temperature was so high I was hallucinating.

The crew had no choice but to continue on and fly home, leaving me there with a fever and an English problem. I contacted the hotel staff to get help. This in itself was a game: one would pass the message to the other and so on until someone called and spoke to me in broken English. Being a relatively new destination, the hotel did not know who the local Qantas doctor was (Qantas has a designated doctor in every port) and I had to ask the hotel manager to call Qantas in Australia for the doctor's number in Santiago. Once I got the number, I phoned and he was away on holidays but his doctor's receptionist told me I should go to the hospital.

Without the doctor in Santiago being available to contact Medlink, the American-based company that provides worldwide medical assistance to Qantas crew – who could have organised my transport to hospital – Qantas had to fax the hotel some medical forms from Australia; everyone at the Santiago end had little English and I was delirious and had no Spanish. The hotel staff eventually put me in a taxi, urgently telling the driver:

'¡*Llevelo al hospital, llevelo al hospital!*'

At the hospital, sweating and feverish, I sat in a queue for an hour before I was put in an isolated room – they probably thought I was contagious. The nurses all spoke to me in Spanish.

'No Spanish, no Spanish,' I said.

'No English, no English,' they said, and gabbled on among themselves. They put a saline drip up and I assume they ordered tests and started me on some antibiotics. Another hour went by.

An English-speaking doctor finally turned up. After I explained about my back, she rolled me over and examined me. She told me I had a staph infection in the wound area of my back; its severity was most likely caused by my compromised immune system. For the next twenty-four hours they drip-fed me stronger antibiotics, which dropped down my temperature slightly, after which I was sent back to the hotel. And there I remained for a week, lying in my room, trying to get well enough to fly home.

Qantas did not inform my mother that I had been left behind in Santiago very ill. She had no idea until I rang her from the hotel.

Under normal circumstances, when crew become unwell in a third-world country, the company would make every effort to fly them home immediately; in my case, however, I was too sick. Several crews came and went while I was recuperating. Some of them popped in and brought me water or juice but I was just so sick that I slept most of the time.

Finally, I was able to passenger home on a flat bed in the newly configured business class, although it was even a battle to get that. The CSM on the flight was a bitch and would have had me sitting up in economy had I not put up a fight. She was the matron type, with a clipboard and a pen, and sternly told me, 'Well, if you can have a glass of wine, I don't know why you needed such heavy restrictions on your flying arrangements.'

I explained that I had broken my back, which didn't interfere with my alcohol absorption.

Whenever she saw me up and talking to a crew member she would say, 'You wanted a flat bed, so go and lie in it.' Additionally, she went into considerable detail to tell me how expensive it was for crew to be sick overseas.

'Well, perhaps the company needs to re-evaluate its return-to-work program,' I suggested to her.

In that, I was being totally serious. The company used the seniority system, which determines work positions and destinations, to minimise its responsibility to injured crew like me, and if called on their practices, they blamed the seniority policies on a union agreement. But if they could simulate a crash over the Pacific in pitch black, surely they could use simulators to train the thousands of injured people every year to see how work-ready they actually were; it's one thing to pull weights in a gym but it's entirely another to move carts in a bumpy tin can surrounded by obstacles such as other crew, passengers and equipment.

'The company is a business, not a charity for servicing crew,' the CSM told me, crisply.

I looked at her and thought – please don't ever let me turn into this robotic indoctrinated bride of the company. Suddenly, the 'no English' barrier was looking more and more attractive.

EXIT

JOINING THE DOTS

After Qantas announced that it was entering a code-sharing partnership with Emirates, to commence in 2013, and would become the world's super-airline, everyone was very excited – well, not quite everyone and certainly not me. I'd coped with Jakarta and Middle Eastern passengers, but Dubai was not on my list of preferred destinations.

'Joining the Dots' was a cultural training course set up to teach us how to look after our Emirates passengers. In reality, it was a course for non-Muslims on how to deal with Muslims. One of the suggestions in the 'Resolving Customer Issues' manual was so controversial that it made the news. This is how that particular tactic for resolving issues with customers was expressed:

'Sometimes the best person to resolve an issue may not be a woman. Don't take offence, don't continue to try to sort something out, simply hand it over to a male colleague. It doesn't matter whether you are a manager or the supervisor, the fact that he is male will make a difference.'

Another helpful piece of advice included knowing which way Mecca faced and understanding that, in preparation for prayer, Muslims might want to wash themselves:

'. . . so don't be surprised if you find the bathrooms wet – just clean them down and make sure they're looking their best for the next customer.'

Additionally, we were informed that in the United Arab Emirates it was unlawful for non-married couples to share a room. There was also a reminder that homosexuality was illegal – pretty ironic considering the demographic of the Qantas workforce.

Yes, 'Joining the Dots' was a non-subtle way of instructing us – a largely gay workforce, in which women were promoted and respected – that we must change to be part of the 'new' Qantas.

But it was not to be for me. Finally, in 2013 I took redundancy. After two back operations and the trauma of what happened to me afterwards, I was officially diagnosed with post-traumatic stress disorder.

A good six months after parting from Qantas, I was once again sleeping through the night in my own bed, I was no longer talking in acronyms or living out of a suitcase on my floor. I was eating cooked meals, not reheated catering food, and I did so sitting at a table. I no longer thought that working for fifteen hours straight or being monitored for a hair out of place was routine, and I was mixing with non-'family' members. I was becoming normal again and it was liberating.

That one unremarkable incident of falling down the stairs while working for Qantas had changed my life forever. Thanks to that broken back, I could no longer do the job I once loved with the circle of friends I loved. In the years before my injury, I had begun to see the culture of the company change; in the years after my injury, I felt the full force of this change. In the end I didn't have the desire or strength to withstand the forces of management and their increasingly bizarre ways. The cosy family had no room for an injured non-believer, and I had to go.

There is an expression: 'When you have your eyes opened and innocence taken, you can never get it back.' I felt this way with regards to the 'roo. I had witnessed corporate politics and greed to excess. It was something you didn't necessarily take stock of when you flew.

One thing I believe – more strongly than ever – is that companies should not be able to self-insure. It takes away that level of impartiality.

The news that I was leaving reached people in many forms. One version that got around was that I had been sacked, another was that I had been paid to write a story by the company. The more removed it was from people who knew me, the more absurd the explanation for my departure. What I found around that time is that when you face the kangaroo court in leaving, you are able to see with clarity your friends, the corporate players and the spine of the union. It is dangerous knowledge; Qantas would never want me back, that's for sure.

In order to get my release form signed, I took all of my uniforms in my little wheelie bag and suit pack and handed them in. The carefully made-up blonde looked across the desk at me.

'Owen, working for Qantas has been such a great journey for you.'

What could she possibly know about my journey? It had begun and ended in Sydney and taken me all over the world. I had lived globally, met some fantastic characters and seen some terrible things. I had made lifelong friends and met people I never wanted to see again. I had seen great managers leave and go to competitors and our precious luxury brand end up more like a bargain-basement offering. I had seen the erosion – almost to the point of non-existence – of first class and the deterioration of certain destinations. Worst of all was the memento I carried every day – my bad back . . . What that woman had in that file would be lucky to cover two per cent of my life with Qantas.

'In closing your file,' she went on, 'I found some complimentary letters from passengers and I can see you've given tremendous service to the company.'

She smiled, waiting for my response. I said nothing.

'Working for Qantas is like being part of a family and a lot of people go through an adjustment period when they leave.'

She lost me at 'family'; my eyes started to glaze over. 'Please, just give me the release form,' I begged inwardly.

'Like any great relationship when it ends, there's a lot of hurdles and bumps along the way,' she prattled on. 'Owen, I need to ask you out of a duty of care: how do you feel?'

Looking her straight in the eye, I said, 'I feel like a certain well-known actress in recent times, running from a scary, scary religion.'

I walked out, smiled and said goodbye to the 'roo. My next chapter awaited me . . .

ACKNOWLEDGEMENTS

So many people have played a part in bringing *Confessions of a Qantas Flight Attendant* to life. Above all, I must thank my family for unconditionally supporting and believing in me, particularly my mother, Pam, and my Aunty Carolynne. Being a first-time author is like walking around a forest with a blindfold, not knowing what I might stumble over next. You helped me gain perspective and acted as my focus group, counsellors, censors, chefs, confidantes and, most importantly, friends. A special thank you to my brave mum and dad, for adopting me in times when no one else wanted an Aboriginal baby; for raising me with a thirst for reading, writing and education; for always believing I could achieve my dreams; and accepting me at my darkest times as well as when I was at my best. You encouraged my spirit, let me go into the world to discover my own path in life and kept a beacon burning to light my way back. Although Dad is watching over us now, not a day goes by I don't draw inspiration from you. Thank you, Mum.

When I started at Qantas over a decade ago, I bet they didn't realise that they were unwittingly giving me more than just a job. I have had access to so many interesting characters – some devoted and truly annoying flight attendants and some funny scoundrels; I feel like I have been a character in a show for ten years – not to mention that I have visited five continents, lived in Sydney, Melbourne, Brussels and London, and travelled extensively, and I am grateful to have had those opportunities. Through my career I have met some of my best friends as well as many celebrities along the way. I especially want to thank Katy Perry for encouraging me to follow my heart and instincts and for the wonderful chat we had over a particularly long trip. To meet celebrities of such calibre was amazing.

The latter part of my career was overshadowed by a spinal injury and I would like to warmly thank my medical team: Dr Coniella Sgroi and physiotherapist Tom Bosna in Melbourne, my wonderful neurological surgeon, Tim Steel at St Vincent's Private Hospital in Sydney, and Dr Daniella Cahill in Grafton, who became a compassionate project manager of all of the surgeons and specialists, getting me to the right people and for taking a close interest. Thanks also to my lawyers, Michael Hyland at LHD Sydney, and my entertainment lawyer, Rebecca Mason at Von Muenster Attorneys in Surry Hills, Sydney.

Thanks too to my brother, Daniel, and sister, Elizabeth, and their families, especially my nephews Tyler and Riley for providing inspiration. I love you all. Also my grandparents, Jack and Dorothy Martin, and my Uncle John, who would ask about the book and then argue with me at family lunch on Sundays. He used to commonly ask me, 'What will Qantas think?' Well, indeed.

To my dearest friends in the 'Queens Council' – Matthew,

Michael, Alan, Chris, Lee, John, Clare, Beate, Emily, Mark, Rochelle, Emma, Duane, Shaun and Scott – thank you all for your contributions to the book, a bed when I dropped by, and for the laughs, vodka and your very valued friendships. You guys have been an unbelievable support; you amazed me and kept me positive through the tough times. You are very much valued and loved; you are all much more than friends.

Confessions of a Qantas Flight Attendant was made possible by the ghost-writing contribution of Libby Harkness, who also helped facilitate the publishing deal with Random House. We finally met in Bali after two years of talking and spent a wonderful weekend getting outrageously drunk and laughing, sharing my stories. Together we wrote an amazing synopsis and were offered several deals from publishers. Libby steered me towards Random House – thank you for that, Libby.

The fabulous Alison Urquhart, an inspiring publisher, welcomed me to the Random House family with a wicked sense of humour and a bucket of wine. Ali, you brought me back to earth when I needed it; I am eternally grateful to you, even though sending me the Nigella cookbook was possibly the meanest thing you could have done; I had to go on the Optifast diet as consequence.

The two other fantastic women from Random House I want to thank are Anne Reilly and Nerrilee Weir. Anne's editing helped bring my ideas to life. She quickly got with the airline terms and acronyms and the entire inside scandal and even confided to me that she is a much more 'alert passenger' now. Remember, Anne, it's all about booking the right seat. In October 2013, before there was even a first manuscript, Nerrilee was in Frankfurt at the International Book Fair. With no book cover, text samples or photos – only verbal stories and the short synopsis – you managed to ignite the interest of ten publishing houses. What a professional. Thank you, thank you, thank you!

Finally, I want to thank a special lady: Lynn Brodsky, my PR representative extraordinaire in New York. Lynn was highly recommended (she had worked with EL James on *Fifty Shades of Grey*). I thought I had little chance of attracting her attention but she saw the possibilities, took me on and encouraged me. Her first question to me was what did I want to accomplish; I told her be I wanted to be 'New York's Graham Norton'. She hit the pavement with our vision and had people making offers almost immediately. It was so humbling and flattering. I can't thank you enough, Lynn.

In the process of achieving this dream of writing a book, a lot of naysayers have crossed my path. Those people are held back by their own fear of failure. To quote my idol, Nelson Mandela: 'To get to the mountains and see the view you must first travel through the valleys and canyons.' It is so true.

Owen Beddall

ABOUT THE AUTHOR

Owen was born in Darwin and is of Anglo–Aboriginal descent. He studied Arts/Law at the University of New South Wales before leaving to work in Hong Kong and then London. Owen worked in an Aboriginal community and at an Aboriginal college before being accepted to Qantas in 2001. The September 11 attacks resulted in an unprecedented downturn in the travel market that delayed his start but he was employed as a casual and in the domestic division before transferring to the international division in 2004. He became a first-class flight attendant and went to work in London for the opening of the new international base in 2005–06. He lived in Brussels.

Owen returned to Australia to continue his flying career post London and continued flying internationally. Owen suffered a workplace injury, breaking his back in three places. After a period of rehabilitation, he intermittently returned to flying but could no longer take the long, manual and tiring conditions of an international 'hostie'. He has since put his energy and time into writing and retired from Qantas in 2013.

Along the way Owen has travelled to over forty countries on six continents and among the countless people he has met are Princess Anne and other royalty, political and religious leaders, and celebrities including Katy Perry, Russell Brand, Kylie Minogue, Lily Allen, Cate Blanchett, Kelly Osborne, Venus Williams, Lisa Raymond, Casey Dellacqua and Caroline Wozniacki, plus bands Franz Ferdinand and Oasis.

Currently, Owen is writing, working with charity beyondblue, and still recovering from his injury. He has signed with an agency in New York and has also been taken on by the fabulous Sue Amaradivakara. He lives between Sydney and a country home in Grafton.

Loved the book?

Join thousands of other readers online at